EXTENDING THOUGHT IN YOUNG CHILDREN

Chris Athey, M Ed, was Principal Lecturer in Education at the Roehampton Institute of Higher Education (RIHE). Funded by a Leverhulme Research Fellowship, she directed the Froebel Early Education Project from 1973 to 1978. She has taught all ages of primary-school children in State and private schools. She has considerable experience of initial teacher training and INSET. She has lectured to over 10,000 professionals on her own research, including teachers in Malaysia. Publications include Humour in children related to Piaget's theory of intellectual development, in A. J. Chapman and H. C. Foot (eds.) (1977) *It's a Funny Thing Humour*, Pergamon Press, Oxford, and Parental involvement in nursery education, in R. Evans (eds.) (1981) *Early Child Development and Care*, Vol. 7, no. 4.

EXTENDING THOUGHT IN YOUNG CHILDREN

A PARENT–TEACHER PARTNERSHIP

CHRIS ATHEY

P·C·P
Paul Chapman
Publishing Ltd

Paul Chapman Publishing Ltd
A SAGE Publications Company
6 Bonhill Street
London EC2A 4PU

British Library Cataloguing-in-Publication Data

Athey, Chris
  Extending thought in young children:
  a parent teacher partnership.
  I. Title
  155.413

  ISBN 1 85396 182 5

Typeset by Burns and Smith Limited, Derby
Printed and bound by Athenæum Press Ltd, Gateshead, Tyne & Wear
G H 9 8

This book is dedicated to Molly Brearley, CBE, and Joyce Bishop, DBE, who worked together to initiate, to raise money and to guide the Froebel Early Education Project. Their public lives have been spent advancing educational ideas and policies. As teachers and as private persons, they have transformed the lives of many staff, pupils, friends and others who were lucky enough to meet them.

CONTENTS

PREFACE

This book is written for teachers, students of education and other professionals working with children under the age of 5 – as well as for interested parents. It describes, analyses and gives detailed results of a five-year 'Early Education Project' carried out at The Froebel Institute, Roehampton, London (the Froebel Institute is now a constituent college of the Roehampton Institute of Higher Education). Two groups of children were studied and tested: an experimental, multi-ethnic group from socio-economic groups four and five, and a comparison group attending a fee-paying kindergarten from socio-economic group one (see Appendix III for the funding and background of the project).

The book contains a detailed analysis and documentation of over 5,000 observations collected by professionals, parents and students from twenty children during a two-year teaching programme. Each child in the experimental group was studied daily in order to:

1. identify developments in each child's thinking;
2. describe the development of symbolic representation from early motor and perceptual behaviours; and
3. identify curriculum content assimilated to developing forms of thought.

The analyses of the observations show that systematic advances in 'forms' of thought (schemas or concepts) were made by all project children. The progressions from early 'motor' and 'perceptual' behaviours to later 'conceptual' forms of thought are documented, analysed in relation to available literature and illustrated with 124 line drawings.

Standardized tests show that the experimental group made highly significant gains in test scores that were sustained during the first two years of primary education. These findings provide support for the efficacy of early education. The methods and findings of the project are generalizable to early education in industrialized countries.

The National Curriculum requires more attention to be paid to 'continuity' between stages of education. This requires teachers of young children to be more articulate about the nature of successful learning in the early years, how this learning comes about and how professionals working with parents can facilitate such learning. This book addresses these concerns in that high quality early education is defined, described, analysed in relation to theory and illustrated.

Reasons are given for the relatively uncharted area of positive thinking in children from 2 to 5. The book argues against the deficit descriptions that prevail and provides a positive alternative. Discussion and illustrations throughout the book focus on what children, parents and teachers can do rather than what they cannot do.

The findings of the project show that early learning has its own recognizable and valid characteristics. The author makes the case that improvements in education come about when later learning is based on earlier achievements rather than when early learning is conceived simply as a preparation for a subsequent curriculum.

The Froebel study provides evidence that curriculum content offered to children is selectively assimilated by them to developing forms of thought. Project children found their own 'match' between their current cognitive concerns and aspects of environment. Several chapters show how spontaneous 'forms of thought' are 'fed' by experiences provided in home and school. The book provides empirical support for the importance of particular kinds of experiences in early education. The nature of enriched thinking is discussed and illustrated with reference to school visits and subsequent symbolic representation.

The book shows how multi-ethnic parents (mainly mothers, and from an Educational Priority Area) were able to understand the objectives of the Froebel research as well as the methods adopted for improving their children's knowledge and understanding. The book describes the role played by parents and provides examples of parental help.

The book draws on a wide range of theory for the illumination of project findings.

Chris Athey
London, 1989

ACKNOWLEDGEMENTS

Many friends and colleagues have read and constructively criticized the manuscript of this book. My special thanks go to Molly Brearley, Elizabeth Bevan-Roberts, Jenefer Joseph, Beryl McDougall and Lydia Smith for their detailed suggestions on how the manuscript could be improved. Thanks also go to my friends, Eva Lauer and Barbara Chapman, for their help with proof-reading.

During the Froebel project many friends and colleagues helped in many different ways with project children, parents and siblings who attended the project during school holidays. Special thanks are due to Mollie Davies, Leslie Forward, Nan Hodge, Ruth Scott, Peter Shaw, Pauline Vincent and Gill Williams.

Particular thanks go to the staff of the Froebel kindergarten (teachers of the Project Comparison Group) – Annette Hickling and Cynthia Lindup – who saved examples of their children's work over two years with the necessary background information. They helped in the analysis of video-recordings and many other time-consuming tasks.

Thanks also go to Carlotta Berger and Dan Levy for weeks spent on research chores; to John Matthews, who has shared ideas and has also reproduced many of the illustrations used in this book; to Margaret Palladino, who contributed examples used in the last chapter of this book; and to Marianne Lagrange, the Editorial Director of Paul Chapman Publishing, who gave much appreciated editorial help with the manuscript.

Last, but not least, thanks are due to the people most closely involved in the Froebel project: the parents, the children, the teacher and the secretary.

The years of the project were exciting, illuminating and intensely satisfying. One aspect of the project that has just been touched on in this book is the degree of cohesion possible in a multi-ethnic group when the focus is on what people have in common rather than what divides them.

This also has a bearing on staff working together. The project secretary was flexible and always helped where help was needed. She was capable of 'down-to-earth' scepticism and humour, which helped to allay teaching and research anxieties. The writer of this book, as researcher, and Tina Bruce, as teacher, shared a set of principles, understood each other conceptually and were consequently able to develop ideas from shared starting-points.

The families attended the project during mornings only, but detailed recording and creative discussion continued between researcher and teacher typically until evening. This attention to detail (unstintingly paid for by loss of free time) was an invaluable aspect of developing ideas as well as providing higher-quality communication with parents. As one of the project parents wrote recently, 'We all learned a lot from each other during those years'.

Acknowledgements for funding the Froebel projects are given in Appendix III.

NOTE ON *FORM* AND 'CONTENT'

In order to simplify reading, the *form* of schemas is printed in italics and the 'content' is enclosed in single quotes. This will assist the reader to differentiate between the spontaneous form of thought, and environmental or curriculum content which has been assimilated to that form. For instance the use of the *arc* or *semi-circle* reflects cognitive form. Objects that are assimilated to the form may be 'smile', 'eyebrows' 'bridge', 'peaked cap' 'beard', letter 'C', and so on.

PART I

1
IMPORTANT ISSUES IN EARLY EDUCATION

PRE-SCHOOL PROVISION IN BRITAIN: QUANTITY

This book is not about the 'quantity' of early education that is, or is not, available in the UK: it is mainly about 'quality' of educational interaction between teacher and child, parent and child and parent and professional. Quality of educational interaction is very difficult to describe and illustrate – much less to measure. While discussions about quantity tend to be carried out against a background of political and financial constraints, communication on high-quality education requires professional knowledge.

However, the emphasis on quality to be made in this book does not imply that the 'quantity' of pre-school services is unimportant. Although, theoretically, high-quality education can take place almost anywhere, from a common-sense point of view, quality is more likely to be facilitated in some kinds of physical situations rather than others. In the UK it is to the credit of professionals who work within institutions such as the National Children's Bureau and organizations such as OMEP, BAECE, TACTYC and VOLCUF that they persistently and indefatigably publish information on the quantity and suitability of provision available for children under 5 – together with suggestions for future development.

Available space in primary schools because of falling school roles – alongside parental pressure for 'real' school – has meant that the number of 4-year-olds in primary schools is increasing. DES figures show that almost half of maintained education for children under 5 is now taking place in primary schools (DES, 1989c). There is evidence that the teaching of 4-year-olds in many reception classes is inappropriate and that they are being taught the formal aspects of three 'R's at the expense of practical activities (Stevenson, 1987). Caroline Sharp (1988) of NFER suggests that the new 1988 Education Act will encourage more heads to admit 4-year-olds.

In a time of financial stringency there are no important reasons why young children should not be educated in available space. Location is relatively unimportant compared with the professional skills and knowledge of the teacher, an appropriate pedagogy, appropriate curriculum content and forms of organization suitable for the ages and numbers of children being taught.

Recent policies have not extended early education and care services as a response to public demand or as a potentially enhancing experience for children. Where possible, provision is being pushed from the public into the private domain (*ibid.*). However, even in a political climate where equality of opportunity is not high on the agenda, it is up to teachers to improve children through education. Teachers must believe that all children can flourish irrespective of initial IQ, of the effects of social class on entry to school and of future job opportunities. Bringing about improvement in individual learners is at the heart of teaching. The focus in this book is on how to extend cognition in young children because this is where professional advance in early education is most needed.

A recent publication on both the quantity and efficacy of existing pre-school provision comes from the Child Health and Education Study Group (CHES) based in Bristol (Osborn and Milbank, 1987). Osborn and Milbank used data from CHES, which is a longitudinal survey of all children in Britain who were born during one week in April 1970.[1] This is the first British study to show that early provision, or lack of it, is associated with later educational achievements.

The report shows that there is a large gap between estimated public demand and the supply of maintained provision in the UK. When compared with other countries in Europe, the UK is second from the bottom in the amount of nursery education provided: Belgium has 95 per cent of children in nursery education for five or six hours per day; France has 95 per cent in nursery education for up to eight or nine hours per day; and the UK has 23 per cent in nursery education, mostly for two-and-a-half hours per day (Judd, 1988).

As far as the supply of educational provision in the UK is concerned, there is not enough and the small number of children who are receiving it are not having it for long enough. The Plowden Report (Central Advisory Council for Education, 1967) estimated that places were needed for up to 90 per cent of 4-year-olds and 50 per cent of 3-year-olds. In 1972, Margaret Thatcher (as Secretary of State for Education) issued a government white paper, *Education: A Framework for Expansion* (DES, 1972), promising that, within ten years, nursery education should become available without charge within the limits of demand estimated by Plowden.

Bone (1977) carried out a social survey and concluded that 89 per cent of mothers of 3–4-year-olds and 65 per cent of mothers of children from birth to 4 desired day provision. This is a larger demand than the Plowden estimate, and Osborn and Milbank (1987) suggest that demand has probably risen since 1977. They put forward the view (*ibid.* p. 34) that close to 100 per cent of parents of 3–4-year-olds would like their child to attend a pre-school group of some kind.

In short, it can be said that the promises of the 1972 white paper have not been fulfilled, public demand has not been met and the UK is lagging behind almost all European countries.

THE EFFECTS OF PRE-SCHOOL PROVISION

The substance of this book is a report of an experiment in the early education of two groups of children from very different socio-economic backgrounds. A few facts and figures from the Osborn and Milbank (1987) study show differences in the social-class composition of children attending different types of institution. Of the most advantaged children, 79 per cent attended independent institutions such as play groups. Only 20 per cent of the most disadvantaged children attended these. In maintained nursery schools, classes or local-authority day nurseries, the reverse was the case. These contained 33 per cent of the most disadvantaged children and only 11 per cent of the most advantaged group. Of the most disadvantaged children, 46 per cent received no form of pre-school provision compared with only 10 per cent of the most advantaged group. These figures suggest that the children and their families who may need pre-school provision most are the least likely to receive it.

Osborn and Milbank found general statistical evidence that children who attend pre-school institutions achieve higher test scores at 5 and 10 years than children who have had no pre-school experience. Health visitors gave developmental and vocabulary tests to the children at the age of 5, and teachers administered a battery of tests at the age of 10. These tests covered general ability, vocabulary, reading, mathematics and language skills. 'Behaviour' scales were completed by parents at the age of 5, and testing was carried out by class teachers at the age of 10. Children who had no pre-school experience achieved the lowest mean test scores in four out of the seven tests and had the second lowest score in the other three.

Children in LEA nursery schools consistently scored higher than children who had different types of pre-school experience. They did not, however, score as highly as children who attended independent institutions (play groups). Children who attended LEA nursery schools showed cognitive and educational gains compared with non-attenders and children who attended LEA nursery classes.

Maintained nursery schools and classes have a responsibility mainly for working-class children, particularly those known to be at a social disadvantage. Children who attended home play groups had the highest mean scores in four of the seven tests and had the second highest score in the other three. Osborn and Milbank (*ibid.*) suggest that either home play groups are singularly effective in promoting children's cognitive development or, despite statistical controls, enriched home environment based on socio-economic status is of paramount importance. Children from home play groups were of above-average ability. The home play groups were small, with a child:adult ratio of 13:2 (hall play groups had a ratio of 23:4).

'By operating in a private house, the home play group was likely to have a homely atmosphere in which young children might respond more readily to the activities provided' (*ibid*. p. 216). Parental interest in the child's education was found to be positively associated with several test scores (*ibid*. p. 211).

The base lines of Osborn and Milbank's test results were established at 5, after and not before they had experienced pre-school provision. If base lines of competence had been established at the age of 3, subsequent measured achievements could be less equivocally attributed to different types of pre-school provision. The age of the children at initial testing, together with the social-class difference in types of pre-school attended, may have biased the findings on the association between types of pre-school provision and later achievements.

It is worth emphasizing two findings of the Osborn and Milbank study:

1. Socio-economic inequality remains the most powerful determinant of differences in cognitive and educational attainment in children (*ibid*. p. 214).
2. Children who had no pre-school experience scored the lowest on the tests.

The most worrying finding is that 4-year-olds in primary-school reception classes were on a par with children who had no pre-school experience. Children who attended infant reception classes from an early age did no better than children who started school after their fifth birthday. Placing 4-year-olds in reception classes does not result in measurable improvements in children's cognitive and educational achievement or behavioural characteristics. Many professionals have been worried about this situation for some time, but there is now evidence that there is something wrong: 'Recent research has shown that early entry into infant classes was not found to increase children's educational potential. This suggests that the curriculum of the under fives as practised in LEA classes and playgroups was more effective than those of infant-reception classes' (Curtis, 1987).[2]

The well-publicized findings of the American study (Lazar and Darlington, 1982), although using a smaller sample than Osborn and Milbank (N = 2,100), show that socially disadvantaged children who attended pre-school benefited in all kinds of ways as a result of the early-education programmes: there was less school failure, more likelihood of completing secondary education, more success with finding employment, and so on.

Statistical evidence can be interpreted in different ways. Although statistics do not reflect values, interpretations do. One interpretation of the British and American studies is that it is worth investing in early education in order to compensate for socio-economic inequalities. This value is not voiced as frequently now as it was in the 1960s, when hopes for the effects of early education were high. The high hopes were dashed when the Headstart programmes were first evaluated. However, later evaluations showed that the programmes had been effective after all but, rather like 'apology for error' in a newspaper, it is the erroneous banner headline that sticks in the mind.

Most research findings suggest that it would be a good thing to increase both the quality and the quantity of pre-school provision, but it is political ethics and values that determine the resources to be given to competing sectors of society.

Osborn and Milbank (1987, p. 30) express the situation as follows:

In times of financial exigency it is not surprising that local authorities have turned a blind eye to demands for the provision of all-day care for under-fives whose parents have full time occupations, and have instead favoured Kellmer Pringle's ideas on home-based care and the provision of part time nursery classes and playgroups.

A more specific conclusion of the British study is that placing under-5s into vacant places in primary-school reception classes, without further steps being taken to provide for their particular needs, is not the way to redress inequalities. Parents might think that their children are being given a head start in that they are in 'real' school but the test results do not support this. Although high-quality early learning can take place almost anywhere, it cannot take place without high-quality and appropriate teaching.

Pre-School Provision: Quality of Care

Improving the quality of pre-school provision can be tackled in many different ways. One obvious way is to improve the qualifications of the people working with young children. In the UK, many thousands of adults, most of them women, are involved in 'minding', 'caring for', 'rescuing', 'keeping healthy' and 'educating' over a million young children. Qualifications range from none, through minimal to advanced. As in other countries of similar wealth, many of these women experience low status and long hours of work (Katz, 1984). There is little doubt that untrained but experienced 'caretakers' of young children are cheaper to employ than teachers. Their role resembles the grandmother or aunt who, in older working-class neighbourhoods, helped out within the framework of the extended family. This level of provision might represent an improvement on a situation where a single parent has difficulty in coping with a young child in a small flat with no relief.

With cheap staff housed in public premises, children could spontaneously and safely develop certain areas of functioning. They could practise their gross motor skills through climbing, swinging and pushing objects around. They could learn to do up their buttons, tie their shoe laces, play with other children and use materials such as sand, water, paint, clay and world toys (models or animals, houses, and so on). Although there is educational potential within such activities, both the educational possibilities and actualities need to be articulated clearly before the activities can count as educational.

Most adults who work with young children, whatever their qualifications, are caring and wish to advance the well-being of individual children. It does not require advanced training to appreciate some of the 'common-sense' aspects of child-care listed above, and most parents learn how to 'look after' children 'on the job'.

It is possible to have high-quality custodial care that has a component of education. However, true 'education' must be concerned centrally with the transmission and reception of worthwhile 'knowledge'. This will be discussed in greater detail presently. Historically, provision for young children has reflected concerns other than children's intellectual or cognitive development, and there have been practical and theoretical reasons for this.[3] However, it is now in the interests of children, parents and professionals for early education to concern itself with issues such as 'thinking', 'experiencing' and 'representing'.

Teachers in early education are in a powerful position to make advances of a pedagogical nature on how children learn. Teachers have it within their power to develop more powerful diagnostic skills and become more conscious of their educational practices and the theories that inform them. A more conscious pedagogical knowledge can lead towards a concern with how quality of mind in young children can be cultivated.

Quality Education Requires Qualitative Descriptions

Many studies have shown that early education increases children's later achievements in specifiable ways. This evidence is mainly statistical; and quality, as inferred from figures, is seldom defined or described.

Most British studies reveal a conceptual weakness that permeates accounts of education at all levels. Not enough attention is paid to how children learn most effectively and consequently how teachers can teach most effectively. There is very little attempt to develop a theory on the relationship between an offered curriculum and how the offered curriculum is received by individual learners. Although there are exhortations from many people outside teaching for teachers to improve the quality of the education they offer, there is an anomalous accompanying denigration of the role of educational theory.

An erroneous idea is being perpetrated, by politicians rather than professionals, that standards in education can be increased and that the increase can be measured objectively via tests without a concomitant increase in teachers' understanding of the learning process as it occurs in individual learners. Professional advancement necessarily requires the development of a pedagogy. Pedagogy is for the teacher what medical knowledge is to the doctor. The problem in Britain is not an absence of excellence in early or primary education. What is lacking is a professional vocabulary that can clearly articulate the nature of excellence. Descriptions of quality must precede attempts to measure it. Measurement without description and conceptual understanding can capture only the organizational, surface or trivial features of situations. Sutton-Smith (1970) suggested that it is the conceptual cement in which trivial observations are placed that provides explanatory power.

Illuminative educational writing must contain information on the details of learning as well as teaching. Detailed accounts of observation, interpretation, curriculum experimentation and evaluation are badly needed. Teachers could take on the role of teacher/researcher because daily classroom events provide an ongoing source of data that can be professionally interpreted and shared with other teachers.

What is needed is information on the patterns of cognition children bring to educational situations. What is also needed is more evidence on how children receive or do not receive offered curriculum content. Questions on the nature of 'learning', 'knowing', 'understanding' and 'experiencing' are psychological and pedagogical rather than political and are of central concern to teachers. They are also of interest to many parents during the years of child rearing.

THE CONCEPT OF EDUCATION

As this book is about early 'education' it is necessary to consider the meaning of the term. The white paper, *Education: A Framework for Expansion* (DES, 1972), unambiguously promised an increase in 'education'. 'Education' was to be provided for all children of 3 and 4 whose parents wished them to benefit from it (para. 17). Since the white paper, the meaning of the term 'education' is used (when referring to young children) as though it is synonomous with 'care' just as, at the secondary level, the term 'education' is increasingly being used in juxtaposition with the term 'training'. Wood, McMahon and Cranstoun (1980, p. 1) point out that values towards child-care and education change systematically in relation to the gross national product: 'The government which promised expansion seemed determined to preside over the atrophy of early education.'

Earwaker (1973) suggests four ways in which the term 'education' is used in professional and non-professional writing and discussion. Concept A indicates 'education' at its weakest. This concept refers to any process, not necessarily desirable, of 'bringing up' or 'rearing' that can be applied to children, animals or even plants. This use of the term entails no necessary connection with knowledge. Earwaker dismisses concept A as the least adequate, most undifferentiated concept of education. As it includes neither knowledge nor value it has no relevance for people working within the educational system.

Concept B represents an advance on concept A in that it includes the development of desirable states but it still lacks a knowledge component. For instance, successful 'toilet training' may be desirable but does not involve 'knowledge' in the learner. Many broad and general aims of teachers are at a concept-B level in that the aims contain desirable values but do not specify the route of knowledge necessary for pupils to arrive at these desirable states. The aim of encouraging autonomy in children or the belief that 'education' should involve 'the whole child' are cases in point. Concept B might be 'worthy' from a desirability point of view but 'woolly' from a knowledge point of view (*ibid.* p. 251).[4]

Concept C involves knowledge without specifying its desirability. This is illustrated in some early-childhood programmes aimed at teaching specific items of knowledge or information without a consideration of values. The most notorious of these programmes is the one directed by Bereiter and Engelmann in the USA.[5] Its most criticized component consists of a didactic lesson on weapons.[6]

Concept D is the most elaborated and complete concept of education and is defined as follows: 'Education is a process of bringing up children that develops their knowledge and understanding in depth and breadth in worth-while directions' (*ibid*. p. 254).

As can be seen, concept D amalgamates all the earlier notions but requires that the development of knowledge and understanding should be firmly based on desirable values (*ibid*. p. 246). Whenever there is a serious discussion about the nature and purpose of 'education' as distinct from 'schooling', 'upbringing' and 'rearing', it is concept D that is being employed with its emphasis on cognitive content and worthwhileness.[7]

Kohlberg (1968, p. 1035) suggests that if it were known how to bring about fundamental cognitive structural change in children as opposed to the relatively minor changes that result from learning specific bits of information, then bringing about such fundamental change would clearly be the main objective of nursery education. The process of initiating children into worthwhile knowledge and thus bringing about fundamental cognitive improvements is probably widespread in nursery schools and classes, homes, play groups, day nurseries and reception classes. What is lacking is evidence that this happens.

Bruner (1980) described the ties between psychological research and teaching practice as tenuous and fragile. He wrote that a chasm exists between research findings and classroom observations. He found that research findings arrived at via laboratory experiments had little or no relevance to the classroom. This conclusion points to the desirability of developing more illuminative research.

When the researchers in the Oxford study (*ibid*.) found they could not interpret, to any degree of usefulness, the worthwhileness of what the children were doing, they brought in 'experts' to read transcripts of observed play episodes and to assess them as being either 'complex' or 'simple'. These are extremely general categories of evaluation and have no explanatory value. They offer no advance on the evaluations of Susan Isaacs half a century earlier. Susan Isaacs always amalgamated theory, however tenuous, with her observations of young children. By co-ordinating theory and observation, she began to develop a pedagogy of the early years that was not continued because of a shift in research methodology.

Many writers and researchers, mainly non-British, have pleaded for greater attention to be paid to theoretical notions that inform observation, practice and evaluation.[8]

EVALUATING COGNITIVE GAIN IN EARLY EDUCATION: SUMMATIVE AND FORMATIVE EVALUATION

'The end product of education or schooling is someone who has been improved by what has happened to that person' (Moore, 1982, p. 87). Any general theory of education must start with how improvement might be brought about and how it might be assessed. Educational inquiry does not yet have the status of a science in which clear postulates can be tested for support or refutation. Therefore there is, as yet, no obvious and uncontroversial way of plotting the process of improvement of individuals throughout schooling, particularly in relation to different areas of the curriculum.

Awareness of this problem is dawning. In discussions on accountability and appraisal, teachers and headteachers are asking important questions on the degree to which they can guarantee that individual children, who have been in a class for a year or a primary school for six or eight years, are 'on the inside' of essential or desirable knowledge in relation to the many areas of the curriculum. Although general levels of knowledge can be measured by comparing children with each other on tests, the process of diagnosing conceptual knowledge in individual learners is in its infancy. This could be one of the most exciting aspects of professional development in the years ahead.

From infancy, there are basically two ways in which improvement can be monitored:

1. Summative evaluation consists of tests given before and after educational programmes. The best-known and most controversial form of summative evaluation is the standardized intelligent test (IQ test). The IQ test was designed within a psychometric rather than a pedagogical framework. This will be explored presently. Psychometrics developed from the heredity aspect of Darwin's theory.[9]
2. Formative evaluations are descriptions of cognitive advances recorded regularly as an accompaniment to a programme. Formative evaluation requires professional skill in diagnosing concepts or skills in the process of being formed in the learner. The most effective evaluations are where both go on side by side.

Darwin's theories embraced both a heredity and an environmental explanation of intelligence. The environmental aspect has been incorporated into Piaget's theory of the 'functional invariants', which assumes that 'intelligence is adaptation to environmental circumstances' (Elkind, 1969, p. 319). This concept is of particular interest to teachers and will be explored in more detail in the next chapter. However, it is worth stating that 'intelligence as adaptation to environmental events' may be what the educational process is about, but it is difficult to record the process, much less to evaluate it.

The heredity aspect is of particular interest to testers and to people who would like to gain social control over populations. Standardized tests give a measure of a general standard of a given population. By definition, given the procedures of testing, a section of the population will be below the general standard and a section will be above. This can easily be understood where the population consists of every potato on a market stall. Unless buying is highly selective, most potatoes will be around an average size – some will be small, some very small, some large and some very large. However, within the population of potatoes, tiny ones are not branded as failures. On standardized intelligence and attainment tests, children below the norm are branded as failures. The very description 'not up to standard' is pejorative.

Standardized tests have items arranged in a hierarchy of difficulty. A child's test results will show where that child is in relation to other testees. For instance, the test results of a group of 6-year-olds may show that some individuals have a mental age above the 6-year-old level and some below. Most of the 6-year-olds in an unbiased sample will produce scores at a 6-year-old level.

This cross-classificatory view tends to obscure individual improvements. For instance, all children of a given age might be given a standardized reading test two years running. It could be the case that all children tested made a healthy gain in their reading scores between the first and second test. Some children, and frequently the same children, will still be below the average of the total group even though they have improved significantly on their own previous performance.

The fundamental tenet of standardized testing is that populations can be categorized in relation to established test norms. Although 'below average' is simply a function of test construction, real causes are sought to account for low scores. There are two very well-known candidates for blame: the environment and assumed genetic potential. Blaming the environment includes parents as well as the general effects of poverty, such as poor food, poor housing, and so on. For many years the aim of a large number of early-education programmes was to educate parents so that they would better educate their children. More recently, teachers have been blamed for low standards. Standards in measurable aspects of the curriculum, as in limited aspects of reading and arithmetic, are rising but a case can be made that they are not rising fast enough for successful competition in world markets.

Historically, tests have been used primarily for selection rather than educational illumination. The original social purpose of standardized tests was to select children on stable and 'measurable' performance criteria for scarce educational resources.

Psychometric and pedagogical concerns have always sat uneasily side by side. IQ tests can be used to measure the starting and end points of different educational treatments and the treatment that leads to higher scores can be deemed to be a success. Explanations for success can only be at the level of informed hunches because changes in measured scores are only statistics. It is the researcher who indicates the reasons for improvement, or lack of it. The informed hunches of a researcher may be true but they need not be.[10]

STABILITY AND CHANGE IN TEST SCORES AND EARLY DEVELOPMENT

In everyday parlance the description 'stable' implies a positive judgement. Similarly, psychometricians perceive stability of test scores over time as desirable. While scores vary with chronological age, IQ, the measure derived from scores and age should (within the tenets of psychometrics) remain stable. As already mentioned, 'stability' from a tester's point of view means that tests will be highly predictive of future performance. Long-term educational planning would be facilitated if future educational resources could be reliably predicted from the test scores of young children.

However, professional educators, particularly those directing remedial programmes, do not aim at producing stability of test scores. On the contrary, the central aim of education is to bring about cognitive improvement in individual learners. It is incongruous that educational programmes aimed at improvement use intelligence tests that have a built-in bias against change. Test items that produce unwanted variations are discarded. For instance, girls are known to be more advanced than boys in some areas of functioning. Over the years, items on which girls did better were eliminated. This process is referred to as making the test 'sex fair'. Kay (1974) points out that this means 'more fair for boys, less fair for girls'. Measuring educational improvement with IQ tests is, therefore, like using dice biased to come up with the same number. In the light of this it is likely that improvement in early-education programmes may be greater than recorded.

Tests have achieved stability in that IQ does not change much for the majority from the age of 7 or 8. After 10 it is pretty well stable.[11] However, stability of scores is found where there is stability, or no change, in environment. Education, particularly early education, can transform the symbolic aspects of environment through facilitating the symbolic functioning of children.

As long ago as 1920 there was evidence of increases in IQ as a result of nursery education.[12] When Skeels *et al.* (1938), in their now famous study, produced evidence that orphanage children had acquired a much higher IQ as a result of a dramatic change in environment, Goodenough, a leading psychometrician of the day, poured scorn on the findings because, at that time, IQ was generally regarded as being stable over time.[13] Skeels discovered that drastic changes in IQ can come about as a result of a drastic change in environment. The psychometricians were so critical of these findings that most investigators, who were starting to suspect that IQ could be altered, withdrew from the field.[14]

Most evidence of increases in test scores have been as a result of environmental enrichment before the age of 5. However, Bayley and Jones (1937) discovered many years ago that cultural and socio-economic differences are not reflected in baby tests. This may mean that baby tests are not sufficiently refined to detect environmental differences or it may mean that most babies are potentially sound until privilege or poverty bring about the differences reflected in later test scores. Ordinal scales of infant development based on Piaget's six stages of sensorimotor behaviours have been found to be more sensitive to environmental variation than other standardized baby tests (Uzgiris and Hunt, 1975). Unfortunately these tests have not been extended beyond infancy and, therefore, they lack the continuity of cross-classificatory IQ tests.

The use of IQ tests is still widespread because formative evaluation of improvement arising from enrichment programmes is more problematical than cross-classificatory testing. A persistent research problem in programmes designed to improve cognitive functioning in young children is how to describe ongoing aspects of improvement. What cannot be measured by tests are fundamental cognitive shifts from early motor and sensory behaviours to later symbolic functioning. The important developmental shift from action to thought is still being worked out at a descriptive level.[15]

There is little doubt that certain basic brain mechanisms are genetically specified from birth. The expression 'hard-wired' refers to the basic structure of a computer that cannot be changed by any amount of software input. In the body, reflexes, such as sucking, swallowing and breathing, are said to be 'hard-wired' in that these cannot be varied or recombined in subtle ways (Young, 1978, p. 72). The computer analogy is not a particularly useful one for teachers as educational improvement presupposes 'plasticity'. Almost from birth, very few structures are unaffected by input from the environment for better or for worse. Long before children start school 'plasticity' becomes superimposed on specificity (Rose, 1971, p. 227).

Evidence of the effects of environment on early brain development comes from modern biology. There is a 'critical period' which extends for at least the first few years of life (Rose and Chalmers, 1971, p. 247). During this critical period aspects of cognitive functioning, related to experience and symbolic functioning, can be enhanced.[16]

Many tests given to older children are still closely related to original IQ tests in that they 'tap' general cognitive functioning. Tests generated by the Education Reform Act 1988 (ERA) are supposed to 'tap' the degree to which curriculum content has been assimilated by individual children.[17] It is worth repeating that attempts to find a 'match' between an offered curriculum and diagnosed forms of understanding in individual learners is a most exciting area of development in education.[18]

Professionals working in early education have a particularly important part to play in the search for pupil understanding between the ages of 2 and 5. These are the ages at which basic concepts are formed. Professional knowledge of 'continuity of learning' cannot fail to be furthered by knowledge of patterns of cognition in children under 5 in that knowledge of early learning illuminates later learning.

RESEARCH AND COMPENSATORY EDUCATION

As mentioned in the Preface to this book and elaborated in Appendix III, the Froebel Early Education Project was concerned with the education of children and their families from socio-economic groups four and five. The Plowden committee (Central Advisory Council for Education, 1967) advocated measures to compensate for adverse socio-economic circumstances and, therefore, research on compensatory education was consulted.

If someone from another planet were to study research literature on earth in order to find out about early education, they might well conclude that compensatory education of the underprivileged was one sort of human endeavour, and that educational research aimed at finding out more about young children was another, and that the twain never met. This would be largely true. Most compensatory education programmes have consisted solely of ameliorative action that has not illuminated learning or advanced pedagogy. (An exception to this is Weikart (1972), discussed in Chapter 2.)

Different motivations generate different kinds of educational programmes, which are evaluated in different ways. These differences have persisted since the beginning of public education. Robert Owen, who opened the first infant school at New Lanark in 1816, focused on high-quality education. He was an environmentalist and believed that each child could be formed into an inferior or superior human being by the long-term effects of 'early external circumstances'. He was influenced by the theories of John Locke and Pestalozzi and, therefore, recognized that a stimulating environment had to be suited to the age and interests of children: 'His school can be described as the first in the developmental tradition of primary education' (Whitbread, 1975, pp. 9–10).

Samuel Wilderspin (1792–1866), who later competed with Owen as to who was the originator of the English infant school, employed different methods that stemmed from his motivation to 'rescue' as many poor, city children as possible from the streets and to put them into school. He focused on 'quantity'. Largely through his efforts, 150 infant schools were opened in about ten years. His rote-learning teaching methods were very different from Owen's. In order to facilitate didactic instruction to large numbers of children and to keep them quiescent, he invented raised galleries in classrooms. Teachers in these schools needed training in crowd control and in the 'one-way' transmission of knowledge to the masses. As is always the case, mass teaching mitigates against anything as refined as the study of the individual child. 'The lack of any unifying pedagogical theory was Wilderspin's great weakness' (*ibid.* p. 13).

Twentieth-century research and development has echoes of Owen and Wilderspin. Very little useful information on high-quality teaching or the processes of children's learning (Owen's concerns) has arisen from compensatory programmes. Modern compensatory programmes share Wilderspin's motivation, summed up in the first line of a chapel hymn: 'Rescue the perishing'. Concomitant with the rescue motive in education is political expediency and social control.

Most fundamental research has been carried out in privileged or high-quality environments, the kind Owen tried to create. Most of Piaget's findings came from the study of privileged children as did Susan Isaac's. The motivation behind fundamental research is to find new knowledge. In compensatory programmes, on the other hand, remediation of underfunctioning is the aim and is usually tackled by applying what is known.

In the 1960s, the purpose of many Headstart and Urban Aid programmes was to compensate for supposed defects in homes. The 'rescue' motive was still apparent but the children were rescued from inadequate homes and parenting rather than the streets. It was generally accepted that IQ gain as a result of these programmes would provide the best form of evidence for the environmentalists' cause. However, as a result of the over-hastily produced evaluations of these programmes, such as the Westinghouse Report (1969), professionals learnt not to rely too much on standardized test results.[19]

Recently, the many and wider benefits of early-education programmes have been documented in detail and IQ is no longer the sole criterion of improvement (Schweinhart and Weikart, 1980). Nevertheless, formative evaluation of cognitive gain in the early years remains relatively unexplored. Some educationalists think that improved IQ scores, or scores of any description, should not be an important criterion at all when considering the provision of early education. Blackstone (1971), for instance, argues that early-education provision should be related to the needs of parents and children. She argues that this is socially and politically safer than the criteria used for both the selection of disadvantaged populations and the evaluations by which compensatory programmes are judged.

Debates on the proportion of intelligence that is innate or the results of environment have been found to be arid and socially divisive. A truce exists at present in that both are acknowledged to be important. Where children are underfunctioning, professionals and parents working together can facilitate the growth of intelligence during its period of maximum plasticity.

Education must necessarily concern itself with environmental factors, since little can be done about hereditary influences. Evaluating improvement therefore ought to be more specifically linked with the curriculum of the school.

A PROSPECTIVE AND RETROSPECTIVE VIEW OF YOUNG CHILDREN

Piaget's writings have had the most influence on educational research this century. Almost all his studies were directed towards detecting a 'match' or 'mismatch' between levels of understanding in children and concepts from different areas of the curriculum. Greatest progress has been made in 'matching' curriculum content with cognitive form in mathematics and science. Constructivist research into early literacy has also produced new information on young children's understanding of language.

As an epistemologist, Piaget asked questions central to education, such as 'What is knowledge?' and 'How do we come to know?' Unfortunately, Piaget abandoned the research method he used so successfully while studying infancy. Initially he searched for the invariant features of child thought rather than for individual differences. He interpreted detailed and continuing observations of infants within available theory, mainly his own. By adopting this method he was able to document patterns of thought in infants from birth to 2 and, later, in children from 6 to 11. He did not, however, trace even an elementary map of invariant forms of thought in children aged 2–5.

One reason for this is that he shifted from formative evaluation, which consisted of systematic and ongoing observations of individuals, to cross-classificatory test situations where groups of children of different ages were asked the same questions. Consequently, young children were persistently asked questions that were too difficult and their answers were at an earlier level than those deemed to be correct (Elkind and Flavell, 1969, p. 43).

Asking children from 2 to 5 'concrete-operational' test questions produced evidence that they could not conserve, categorize or put things in order. The large databank of wrong answers or, more accurately, partial answers, led to the idea that young children are cognitively incompetent. Deficit descriptions were applied to young children, which have persisted. It is said that they are 'egocentric', 'idiosyncratic', exhibit static or pre-operational thinking and flit 'from pillar to post'. In literature interpreting Piaget, such deficit descriptions are presented as characteristic of young children's thinking. However, teachers are not helped by such descriptions in that the process of 'matching' suitable curriculum content to forms of thought requires knowledge of what children know rather than what they do not know.

Interestingly enough, having established the positive characteristics of children's thinking from the age of 6 or 7, somewhat at the expense of younger children, almost all Piaget's later studies were concerned with 'match' or 'mismatch' in key areas of the curriculum. Current National Curriculum documents reflect both the substance and the importance of his findings.

Susan Isaacs was the first researcher to challenge the usefulness of Piaget's deficit view of cognition in young children. In the 1920s she used theories derived from many sources in order to analyse children's thinking in the Malting House School. She co-ordinated observation of children with psychological theory and subsequently introduced the children to worthwhile curriculum content. This was followed by analyses of the children's responses. The success of this approach of co-ordinating observation, theory, teaching and evaluation can be measured by the continuing demand for Susan Isaacs' books over half a century.

Susan Isaacs and Piaget had great respect for each other. They visited each other's schools and were creatively critical of each other's ideas. Although they both observed young children closely, they drew different conclusions on early cognitive competence as they adopted different viewing positions. Put briefly, when assessment is carried out from a 'top-down' point of view, negative conclusions arise because younger children are seen as less competent than older children.

A 'bottom-up' perspective, that taken by Susan Isaacs, is founded on initial positive descriptions of cognitive competence in young children. When the more advanced thinking of older children is analysed, cognitive advances are apparent but do not detract from earlier competence.

The 'bottom-up' or 'prospective' approach to assessment is appropriate for teachers in that it leads to the identification of the positive aspects of thought at different ages and stages as they appear during development. As these are identified, steps can be taken to enrich or extend through education. The 'top-down', or retrospective, view identifies the positive characteristics of older children by reference to earlier deficits. This issue is of considerable interest to present-day teachers given the current emphasis on assessing children's achievements at different ages.[20]

Recently, some researchers have challenged the view that young children cannot 'decentre' – that is, that they cannot understand situations from points of view other than their own. Where test situations have been designed to relate to the concerns and experiences of young children, it has been found that they can decentre (Donaldson, 1978; Light, 1979). In other words, in familiar situations, the young child may not be as 'egocentric' as he or she appears to be when confronted, for instance, with abstract spatial relationships between mountains seen from various points of view (Piaget and Inhelder, 1956, pp. 209–45).

The findings of these studies, while important, mainly serve to push back the age at which there is evidence of concrete-operational thinking as opposed to pre-operational thinking. What seems to be lacking is evidence of systematic behaviours that characterize the positive thinking of children between the ages of 2 and 5. This search requires a 'natural-history' approach of observation and interpretation. Although this was bypassed for a long time in favour of the 'cross-sectional' approach, there is now a return to 'illuminative research' (Hamilton, 1980).

Prospective and Retrospective Assessments

Recently, the prospective and retrospective view of cognitive functioning has been given prominence because of the emphasis in the ERA on assessment. Mortimer *et al.* (1988), in their study of the progress and development of 2,000 pupils over four years in relation to important background variables, took achievement at 7 as their starting-point. They 'collected data about each child's attainments in assessments of reading, mathematics, and visio-spatial skills and obtained a class teacher's rating of behaviour at entry to junior school' (*ibid.* p. 4). They show the importance of school in relation to pupil achievement and they pinpoint areas of school effectiveness that will be useful in future curriculum and pedagogical development.

The researchers claim that the information gathered at the age of 7 'enabled account to be taken of differences in the past achievements and development of pupils which, they hypothesize, may have been influenced by their previous infant classes and nursery schools' (*ibid.* p. 4).

It is true in a general sense that measurement at 7 can be considered as a starting-point for future gain or, alternatively, as an overall summation of the first seven years of life. However, initial assessments at 7 cannot provide retrospective information that is sufficiently specific to tease out the efficacy of early educational provision from the general effects of social class and IQ. It is difficult enough to evaluate and account for improvement prospectively, even with the benefit of standardized tests and detailed daily records.

TEACHER AS RESEARCHER:PARENTS AND PROFESSIONALS

A teacher of young children stands as much chance of detecting new knowledge as a researcher who is not a teacher, however, the teacher must have an explanatory theory within which his or her observations can be interpreted.

Traditionally, teachers have been placed in a passive position in relation to research. They are frequently studied as objects rather than treated as active participants in research projects. They are also expected to apply in the classroom research solutions engendered elsewhere. This situation need not be accepted in that educational research problems are those encountered by teachers in classrooms inhabited by children, and there is no reason why teachers should not play a more active role in furthering professional knowledge. A more immediate reason for the teacher becoming teacher/researcher is the present lack of resources for fundamental research. 'Do it yourself' in the home and garden is a booming business. 'Do it yourself' in school could generate a new dynamism.

As already suggested, some forms of research have valid purposes and methods but are not particularly useful for teachers working, as they do, within particular constraints of time, space and circumstances. Research problems likely to sharpen professional concepts are those to do with pedagogy, the curriculum and timing. Timing governs whether there is a match or mismatch between an offered curriculum and understanding in the learner. Teachers need to advance their own theory and to become their own experts for various reasons:

1. To increase professional knowledge of children.
2. To assist the process of accountability that requires an articulate rather than an intuitive professional knowledge.
3. In order to communicate more effectively with parents who now want to know more than hitherto about what their children are being taught, how they are being taught and whether their children are working at an appropriate level. These three parental concerns embrace pedagogy, the curriculum and timing – the very issues listed by teachers as being the most important issues to be investigated in future research (Cane and Schroeder, 1970).

The National Curriculum clearly defines what is meant by a broad, balanced and differentiated curriculum to which all children will be entitled. The clear delineation of what is meant by a 'worthwhile' curriculum in ERA documents means that teachers can spend less time inventing a curriculum and more time than hitherto on 'fleshing-out' broad areas of study with appropriate content (this is pursued further in Chapter 7).

More attention can now be given to 'how' the curriculum can best be delivered. 'Delivery' is different from the 'delineation' of curriculum areas, which is different again from 'displaying' what is on offer. Display, for the illumination of parents and governors, for instance, will probably involve the selection and co-ordination of programmes, the organization of school time, class time and pupil time. The delineation of programmes of study is now out of the teacher's hands. Display will require a logical or sequential organization of subject-matter. The delivery of the curriculum and formative evaluation of what children have actually received from what is offered will remain the central concerns of the teacher. A more conscious and articulated pedagogy can be expected to help teachers to be more aware of how to extend children's thinking with worthwhile curriculum content and how to evaluate outcomes.

Over the last thirty years there has been a shift in emphasis in parent-professional relationships. Early studies documented the psychological benefits to parent or child as a result of involvement in early education. In the 1980s, in the UK, parents have been given considerable political power within the educational system.

A typical early study linked parent personality with children's IQ. It was found the IQ of children who had hostile or neglectful parents decreased (Baldwin, the IQ of children who had hostile of neglectful parents decreased (Baldwin, Kalhorn and Breese, 1945). During the 1950s, research findings showed that the quality of parenting during the first five years of life was of great importance for future intellectual development and mental health (Bowlby, 1953). Subsequently, a few studies emerging from Headstart programmes in the USA showed that where parents had been involved in early education programmes, the children had made considerable IQ gains.

Most research in the 1960s and 70s was designed to assist the 'inadequate' parent. Where mothers were taught to teach their children at their home, the children's progress was as great as children in nursery school and the cost was lower (Gray and Klaus, 1970). Where parents were taught how to help their children educationally in conjunction with half-day nursery programmes, the children showed mean IQ gains up to 30 points (Weikart and Lambie, 1969). Where mothers were involved in an educational programme, subsequent babies flourished (Klaus and Gray, 1968).

When the Froebel Project was being planned during the 1970s, there was very little parental participation in early-childhood education. It was the findings of the few studies listed above and a wish to improve the cognitive competence of children that led to the decision to involve parents in the Froebel project (see Chapter 3).

Parent participation has moved from the psychological to the political arena. Parents are no longer simply fund raisers, general school helpers or part of a psychological support system for themselves and other parents. Their position in law as school governors places them in a central position of managerial power. It is not yet known whether parents will avail themselves of increased power and if they do what effect it will have on the education system.

Legislation cannot decree that parents and professionals should work together to increase knowledge of child development or to work out ways of how an offered curriculum might more effectively become a received curriculum, but perhaps an increased managerial role for parents will lead into a concern with some of these central issues in education. It is within this context that it has become highly inconvenient to many teachers not to have a clear theory of education to improve effective communication with parents about advances in children's learning.

NOTES

1. The basic sample consisted of 5,413 children with pre-school experience and 3,719 without. This large sample of children attended a variety of different pre-school situations. These children have been followed up and tested. Variation in progress has been evaluated and correlated with different types of pre-school.

2. Osborn and Milbank (1987, p. 219) found that child:adult ratios of more than 10:1 occurred in 36 per cent of LEA nursery classes compared with only 3 per cent of LEA nursery schools. Curtis (1987) points out that there is a need in some LEAs to improve staffing ratios and material resources, as well as recognizing in the curricular provision made for 4-year-olds that there are important developmental differences between 4- and 5-year-old children. Osborn and Milbank (1987, p. 206) also make this point most forcibly.

3. Tizard, Mortimore and Burchell (1981, p. 28) describe the social conditions of less than a century ago, when Margaret Macmillan founded one of the first nursery schools in 1911. 'The children for whom her school was started were malnourished, ragged and verminous' (*ibid*. p. 28). These conditions, however, represented an improvement on what had gone before in that these children had survived. Sixty years earlier, in a typical inquiry for the period, it was found that 68 per cent of children born to 62 working mothers died under the age of 5 (cited in Dally, 1982, p. 26).

Where physical conditions are poor, a concern with health and hygiene necessarily takes precedence over a concern with quality of mind.

4. Van der Eyken, after examining the aims and objectives of nursery teachers (*Schools Council Working Paper 41*, 1972), criticized teachers who operate at the low level indicated. He suggests that what legitimizes existing nursery practice is 'received wisdom' rather than professional knowledge (cited in Roberts and Tamburrini, 1981. 'Received wisdom' or a 'bag-of-virtues' notion of education typifies concept B.

5. The main features of this programme are reproduced in *Deprivation and Disadvantage*, Open University, 1973, E262, block 8, pp. 52–8.

6. Leaving aside the ethics of teaching young children about weapons, Kohlberg (1968) challenged the educational worth of such programmes. His tests showed that the children were able to reproduce a learned verbal response to number problems such as 'six plus two equals eight', but they were unable to solve a conservation problem where they had to pick the row that had more sweets. He maintained that didactic teaching produced only minor cognitive changes. (For Bereiter's unrepentant evaluation of his programme, see Stanley, 1972, p. 7.)

7. For detailed discussions on 'four concepts of education', see Peters, 1966; Hirst and Peters, 1970; Earwaker, 1973.

8. Shapiro and Biber, 1972; Kamii and De Vries, 1973; and, by implication, most of Piaget's writings.

9. Darwin's cousin, Frances Galton, helped to found the Eugenics Movement in 1908 and wrote an influential book called *Hereditary Genius* (1869). The hypothesis, that IQ is largely genetically determined, appeared to be supported by evidence that brilliant families tend to produce brilliant children. What Galton did not consider was the possibility that brilliant parents could create brilliant environments, in which case high intelligence could result from adaptation to a particularly stimulating environment.

10. Oddly enough, the inventor of the original standardized intelligence test, the Stanford–Binet Intelligence Scale (Terman and Merrill, 1976), was more skeptical of the value of such tests than many present-day professionals and politicians.

Binet wrote in 1908, 'Our examination of intelligence cannot take account of all those qualities ... attention, will, popularity, perseverance, teachableness and courage which play so important a part in school work, and also in after life; for life is not so much a conflict of intelligence as a struggle between characters' (cited in Brierley, 1987, p. 108).

11. In only about 10 per cent of children are there changes of thirty IQ points over the primary- and secondary-school years (Brierley, 1987, p. 105).

12. Wooley (1925). Later, similar improvements were reported by Barrett and Koch (1930) and Ripin (1933).

13. These studies are cited in Hunt (1961).

14. Jones (1954) wrote: 'It is to the credit of the Iowa group [Skeels *et al.*] that they maintained a persistent interest in the possible effects of nursery school education and formulated an extensive and versatile program of research' (Hunt, 1961, p. 28). Psychometricians have never conceded the claims of environmentalists (see Jensen, 1969).

15. See Smith and Franklin, 1979; Forman and Fosnot, 1982; Matthews, 1988.

16. See Rose (1978) for scientific evidence from animal studies on the importance of early stimulation for later development.

17. Various reports generate optimism. The Task Group on Assessment and Testing (DES, 1987b) and the National Curriculum Science Working Group interim report (DES, 1987a) show that professional fears summed up in a leader in *The Times Educational Supplement* (1987): 'If it moves, measure it', may be unfounded. The reports, if acted upon, could lead to the illumination of learning processes and the evaluation of real educational outcomes.

18. See Blenkin and Kelly (1988) for papers on a developmental curriculum related to early education.

19. Neary (1970) discusses the sinister situation that followed the Westinghouse Report (1969). Because environmentalists appeared to have lost ground to the supporters of genetic determination, funding began to be directed towards 'behavioural genetics'.

20. The two different developmental viewpoints of Isaacs and Piaget are discussed in detail by Smith (1985).

2

PEDAGOGY

PEDAGOGICAL MODELS

'Pedagogy' is frequently defined as 'the art and science of teaching'. More specifically it refers to *how* children and curricula are taught. There are three theories on the nature of teaching and learning that have informed different pedagogical approaches from antiquity, and the focus in this book is towards the development of a 'constructivist' pedagogy as it can be applied in early education. 'Constructivism' embraces all the features of Earwaker's most complete definition of 'education' and contains an elaborate system of concepts on how children learn and, therefore, how teachers might best teach. The word 'pedagogy' is not as widely used in the UK as it is throughout Europe. Most British teachers would feel faintly embarrassed in using such a theory-laden term apart from the difficulty of pronouncing it.[1]

It would be possible to use alternative terms such as 'educational theory' or 'educational theory and its relations to practice', but these terms include issues that are not specifically to do with pedagogy. British and American teachers avoid using the term 'pedagogy' by referring to 'teaching styles'. David Weikart (discussed presently) refers to different pedagogical approaches as 'curriculum models'.

Stukat (1976), reviewing European research into pre-school, concluded that Continental researchers are more influenced by educational theory than their British counterparts in that reference is usually made to the psychological and educational theories that have guided the choice of the contents and methods of the programmes. Because of this, hypotheses generated from within theoretical systems can be tested in action. The results of empirical studies thus serve to support or modify theories as well as to be of use in the practical activities of teaching and learning.

All teachers have a pedagogy or, more accurately, a cluster of pedagogical notions. These may be held consciously or unconsciously. During the course of a school day, different pedagogical approaches are required. Crowd control in the playground requires one approach, an individual tutorial requires another. Some school situations may merely require a custodial role or a managerial role, and so on. A teacher's pedagogy permeates his or her thinking on practically every educational issue from the most general to the most specific.[2]

Weikart, in his Perry Project, 'High Scope' (1972), evaluated three pedagogical models by outcome and process. From a measurement point of view, he found that 'Different kinds of treatment ... provide little or no evidence that one kind is better than another as long as age and duration of treatment is held constant' (Brown, 1978, p. 33).

The three pedagogies investigated by Weikart correspond to Earwaker's (1973) analysis of different levels of 'education' as follows:

1. Child-centred (Earwaker's concept B).
2. Programmed (Earwaker's concept C).
3. Open-framework (Earwaker's concept D). This concept, and Weikart's implementation in Ypsilanti, Mich., correspond to a 'cognitive develop-mental' or 'constructivist pedagogy'.

Weikart admits to backing the cognitive-developmental, open-framework model (these are alternative terms for constructivist or interactionist approaches). He, along with many others, thought that constructivism must be the way ahead. By criteria other than the standardized measurement of end-products, this probably remains the case. As already mentioned, 'intelligence as adaptation' is at the heart of constructivism as well as life in general, but intelligence as an IQ score is what can most easily be measured (Elkind, 1969). As most important aspects of human functioning elude measurement, the choice between pedagogies is between systems of values rather than measured outcomes. Weikart's (1972) study has the virtue of describing in detail important features of the programmes being measured.

Earwaker and Weikart both agree that custodial care (concept A) is inappropriate for any endeavour that aspires to be 'educational'. Weikart suggests that, in such programmes, adults act as caretakers. Their responsibility is to 'mind' or 'look after' or 'take care of' children for their own good as the adult sees it, and such programmes have minimal educational value.

Having disposed of custodial care as a candidate for serious consideration, Weikart divides functionally retarded children of 3 and 4 years of age among the other types of three programmes: child-centred, programmed and constructivist. Two teachers were assigned by their own choice and preference to each programme. The children were taught as a group every morning and a tutorial was given to each child in his own home for 90 minutes every other week in the same style as the school programme.

Child-Centred Pedagogy

This model, according to Stukat (1976), is the pedagogy most widespread in Europe and the UK. It may also be the most widespread in the USA, but it is difficult to find evidence on this. Weikart sums up this approach as 'child initiates, teacher responds'. Within this model, teachers focus on social and emotional growth. Aims are vague, intuitive and very broad. There are many references to 'the development of the whole child'. Weikart points out that these aims reflect positive values in society such as independence, creativity, self-discipline and constructive peer relations.

A 'child-centred' pedagogy has its roots in a progressive movement that views the pupil with respect and that regards him or her as a unique individual to be kept happy and interested. It is assumed, without being explicated, that the pupil's stage of development entitles him or her to certain treatments that correspond with his or her development. The aims of 'child-centredness' can be implemented, but it is difficult to evaluate improvements or outcomes resulting from this pedagogical approach.

Programmed Pedagogy

This consists of stimulus-response training where 'teacher initiates and child responds'. Weikart is particularly critical of this type of programme. He writes (1972, p. 32): 'The program developers show little respect for traditional education at any level ... these curricula tend to be rigidly structured, with the teacher dominating the child and with a heavy emphasis on convergent thinking'. The child is expected to give correct answers in the right manner and to learn through repetition and drill.

The best-known example of an extreme stimulus-response approach is the programme directed by Bereiter and Engelmann (1966). Knowledge is conveyed irrespective of its desirability. It is neutral regarding value, but specific as to content. Kohlberg has criticized such programmes because there is no attempt to 'match' programme structure to cognitive structure in the learner. Bringing about fundamental cognitive change for the better is unlikely in such programmes (Kohlberg, 1968, p. 1035).

Bereiter has said that he does not consider it worth comparing the content of programmes 'because there is very little evidence that learning one thing does more good than learning another' (Stanley, 1972, p. 7). Such a 'value-free' approach excludes 'worthwhileness' as a criterion for the selection of curriculum content. Few British teachers would be likely to accept such a viewpoint.

WEIKART'S EVALUATION OF DIFFERENT PEDAGOGIES

The constructivist programme in the Weikart study corresponds to Earwaker's concept D (see p. 9). In this model, the programme is worked out by the teacher, not by a programmer. Because it is assumed that learning comes about through the direct action and personal experience of the child, the teacher attempts to focus on underlying processes of thinking or cognition. 'Her task ... is to find ways in which to help children to get to know things better ... to diagnose which knowledge, or form of knowledge, will most immediately help in the structuring of children's experiences' (Wilson, 1969, p. 114).

Weikart (1972, p. 35) describes the main characteristics of the constructivist approach as follows:

> These curricula [pedagogy and curriculum content] are based upon a theory of child development, the most popular is that of Piaget ... The learning process, structured by the teacher ... is usually paced by the child himself, with adaptation of the activities by the teacher to match the child's needs and interests. In general, these curricula are organized to accomplish cognitive and language development based on a theory of intellectual development. An open framework is provided for the teacher as a context within which she develops a specific program for the children in her classroom. Learning by the child is the product of his active involvement with the environment structured by the teacher.[3]

At the end of the first year of the Weikart experiment, all three programmes showed substantial IQ gains that were uniformly sustained at the end of the second year. This led Weikart to conclude that it did not seem to matter which pedagogy was employed, as long as staff motivation was high. Staff knew they were taking part in a research venture and each, presumably, wanted the children in their programme to do well.

The Child-Centred Programme

At the end of the third year there was a drop in the IQs of the child-centred group. This 'wash-out' effect, found in other studies, has given rise to criticisms of this pedagogical approach. In a compellingly interesting account, Weikart (1972) re-examines background features of the child-centred programme and highlights issues that beset most real-life experiments but that are seldom reported.

In the middle of the first year, the child-centred class had to move from their building and 'box and cox' near the constructivists. This arrangement interfered with their programme but, more disturbingly, they realized how many visitors the constructivists were receiving. The child-centred team suspected that they were merely a control group. They became depressed, staff began to arrive late and were frequently ill. These factors rather than the difference in pedagogy could have accounted for the third-year losses in test scores.

The Programmed-Learning Programme

The teachers in this programme also had problems. Weikart described them as working hard and diligently but they worked separately, they did not consult with the director and they were too detached from the children. Both teachers became extremely involved with the content of the programme because this was what they were concentrating on.

The Constructivist Programme

The problems of the constructivist team are the most interesting of all from the point of view of advancing theory and practice. One of the teachers was described as 'brand new' and 'confident'. She was warm and concerned for the children and appeared to pick up the basic ideas of the programme very quickly. The other teacher had been very successful in a different setting but was finding difficulties with the constructivist model.

Although both worked hard, they remained too rigid in the implementation of plans. Being new to Piagetian theory would account for the rigidity in that knowledge has to be assimilated before it can be applied successfully: 'Insecurity in knowledge leads to rigidity in teaching' (DES, 1983).

GENERAL RESULTS OF THE WEIKART EXPERIMENT

The pedagogical implications of the final results of the three programmes are not clear. They all worked if a short-term increase in IQ is the main criterion. The long-term results of Weikart's project, however, showed that when the children were aged 15 and 21 they were ahead of control children in a variety of important ways. The programmes were found to be 'cost-effective' in that fewer children who had early education needed expensive remedial help later. They stayed at school longer and therefore achieved useful qualifications that increased their earning power. This, in turn, increased the likelihood of them becoming contributing members of society (Schweinhart and Weikart, 1981).

The Weikart experiment is best thought of as a striking and instructive social experiment where an attempt was made to apply different pedagogies and to record results. Beilin (1972) suggests that it is not a scientific experiment in the true sense because in no 'real-life' educational enterprise is it possible to control crucial variables because they are all beyond the investigator's control.

Weikart himself reflects a dilemma. He remains critical of programmed learning on the grounds of values in spite of IQ gains. He retains constructivist hopes even though the objective results were equivocal and problematical.

HIGH/SCOPE IN BRITAIN

Aspects of Weikart's High/Scope project in Ypsilanti, Mich., have been generalized to children in other countries including Britain. A lively debate on the merits (or otherwise) of courses organized by the High/Scope Foundation in London and in Scotland has ensued. The training programme has gained support from Voluntary Organisations Liaison Council for Under-Fives (VOLCUF) that, in turn, has attracted money from influential benefactors. The Nuffield Foundation, for instance, financed an independent report on the High/Scope programme in Britain (Sylva, Smith and Moore, 1986).[4]

The programme claims to have adopted Piagetian theory that has been encapsulated into a motto. 'Plan, Do, Review'. A serious criticism of the programme, taking the report as an accurate representation of the course, is that there is no information on children's planning, doing or reviewing. There are, in fact, very few examples of children's behaviour or thinking before or after High/Scope training.[5] The authors of the report write (*ibid.* p. 68): 'Supporting and extending children's play are definite objectives of High/Scope but there is little evidence that they have been met in any serious way'.

Sylva and Smith were both researchers in the Oxford Pre-School Research group. They experienced the difficulties involved in measuring the relationship between even limited psychological research findings and classroom practice. It would appear that, in monitoring the High/Scope training programme, similar problems arose of evaluating children's spontaneous behaviour as were found in the Oxford study.

The spontaneous behaviour of young children is difficult to record whether in the home or in various nursery settings. Because of weak theory it is even more difficult to interpret spontaneous behaviour – much less 'tap' its educational potential. Difficulties lie in detecting cognitive structure below the surface features of spontaneous behaviour because the cognitive structures have not yet been identified by means of theory.

Cognitive structure is what children at a certain stage have in common. Where children at a concrete-operational stage of development have had similar experiences, they are likely to share cognitive structure as well as experienced content. Where experiences have been different, there will still be similarity of form but the content of experience will be different.

If the High/Scope training helps teachers to diagnose 'cognitive form', with a view to extending and enriching with worthwhile curriculum content, then the training will be worth supporting. However, it is doubtful whether this depth approach is a feature of High/Scope training.[6] Teachers can best decide what ought to be taught by finding out what children already know. Training must aim at deepening teachers' understanding of children's learning. Without evidence of improvement in children, short cuts in training will turn out to be of little long-term value to teachers.

As there is lack of evidence of a deepening professional understanding in the Sylva, Smith and Moore report (*ibid.*), particularly on the 'plan, do review' aspects, it will be useful to examine the comprehensive manual for teachers arising from the famous High/Scope project in Ypsilanti, Mich. (Hohmann, Banet and Weikart, 1979). It is presumed that the manual is used in High/Scope training to 'flesh-out' details of children's learning.

The manual is useful and informative in many ways. It is clear that the High/Scope teachers are experienced in that they record observations that suggest curriculum extensions. However, there is a discrepancy between their accounts of children's behaviour and the explanations they abstract from existing deficit theory. The manual demonstrates that much existing theory is holding back rather than enabling advancements in early education. For example, 'Tania put wheels on a stick and spun them round. Mike stuck sticks into every hole on a wheel and called it a "flower" ' (*ibid*. p. 244).

Following this type of example, familiar to many teachers and parents, Hohmann, Banet and Weikart search for illumination from the literature. This gives information on 'pre-operational' thinking where the focus is on what children do not know or understand. Having presented the 'party line' on deficits, the authors make skilled and practical suggestions on how children can transform materials by performing different actions on them. This positive aspect of constructivism could have been developed within the High/Scope programme but development was held back because 'teaching' is introduced too hastily and too often. More professional conceptualization of what children are doing and saying is needed before teaching prescriptions are made and adopted.

The Froebel project findings given in Chapters 5 and 6 illustrate an interesting difference between Tania's spinning wheel and Mike's flower. The diagnoses of schematic differences lead to differentiated and meaningful curriculum extensions. Tania's 'spinning' wheel would appear to be a working model of something that *rotates*, and rotators have different functional effects. But Mike's 'flower' is an expression of a different type of schema in that it has a fixed configuration. Curriculum extensions, therefore, can be usefully geared to concepts that are being explored by children. These concepts (or schemas) are revealed in the differential use of materials. The relationship between action and the effects of action is a central concept of constructivism. In the High/Scope manual, teachers endeavour to increase children's consciousness of the transformations they make on materials.

They do this by talking with the children about what they are doing. For instance, a teacher observes a child and then makes the following comment: 'Oh, I see, you're taking a straight pipe cleaner and bending it into a circle and then you are twisting the ends together'. Here, as Forman and Fosnot (1982, p. 207) point out, 'both the initial and final states are labeled as well as the procedure of transformation'. This intervention is positive in that it elaborates verbally on what the child is doing. It is employing a principle of helping the child to become more conscious of his or her own doing. But, as already suggested, professional theory needs to be advanced by conceptualizing in greater detail the type of transformation the child is bringing about and the cognitive level at which he or she is operating.

Buried in Piaget's writings are suggestions that the child with the pipe-cleaner might be interested in transforming a line into a closed, two-dimensional curve. If this is so, there are specific curriculum implications stemming from the observation. This particular transformational act can be extended with curriculum content from aspects of 'space' or 'geometry' (Piaget and Inhelder, 1956).

In the High/Scope manual, levels of understanding are diagnosed accurately, but only where the characteristics of thought are already known, as in 'concrete-operational' thinking. New patterns of positive thought are not identified. This results in an over-emphasis on acceleration towards later and recognizable cognitions. More detailed information is needed on the positive aspects of thought in children under 5, so that these can be extended.

TOWARDS THE DEVELOPMENT OF CONSTRUCTIVISM

Constructivism and Child-Centredness

There is a close relationship between well-run child-centred and constructivist programmes. It could be said that constructivists are child-centred teachers who are trying to become more conscious and more theoretically aware of what is involved in the process of 'coming to know'. Constructivists are interested in the processes by which children construct their own knowledge.

Unreflective child-centredness has led to the false belief that every child requires a unique educational programme. Constructivist teachers know that many children share similar cognitive concerns. Teachers who have taught 6-year-olds, for instance, will know that it is not unusual for over half the class to have reading to an adult at the top of their agenda. During this period of maximum motivation, which is linked with cognitive development, many aspects of 'reading' can be discussed with groups as well as with individuals.

In programmes where the focus is on a one-way transmission of information, teachers find it difficult to advance their knowledge of child development because so much time is taken up with the content to be transmitted. It is easier for child-centred teachers to make theoretical advances because listening to children is central to the pedagogy.

Stukat (1976) characterized child-centred pedagogy as follows:

1. Staff had broad objectives that were not explicitly formulated and that emphasized general personality development rather than training in narrow skills.
2. The curriculum embraced free play, social events, creativity and activity linked with interest. Adaptation of tasks to the child's maturational level was stressed.
3. Certain recurring features gave a regular rhythm to the day. The first hour was usually devoted to free play or some optional activity, such as drawing, modelling, handicraft or doll play. This was followed by discussion in groups, story-telling, singing and acting. Discussion was usually on a topic of current interest, for instance, Christmas, traffic, food or being ill. A typical pre-school programme included frequent study trips (pp. 22–3). This general description applies to most nursery schools and classes in the UK.

Bruce (1987) shows how research evidence from Bruner, Kellmer-Pringle, Piaget and Vygotsky supports what have been traditions in early childhood. She suggests (*ibid*. p. 182) that the way ahead is for teachers in early education to have a 'better conceptual articulation of what good early childhood education is, with appropriate assessment and evaluation which does not cut across its valuable traditions'.

A constructivist knows that experience of teaching is necessary but not sufficient for professional advancement. There is a great difference between 'know-how' and consciousness of 'know-why'. Volpe (1981), pp. 41-51) suggests that an ideal teacher is one who combines practical 'know-how' with the conceptual understanding which can come only from study and reflection. There are indications that, in spite of the politically motivated, anti-theoretical *Zeitgeist* of the present time, many teachers of young children wish to evolve from intuitive knowledge towards a more articulate system of professional understandings.[7]

Even with the qualification that constructivist theory is weak as it applies to children from 2 to 5, it is here that illumination can be found on how to assess levels of action, perception and symbolism in children. Of course, it is more difficult to give information on how individual children have thrived within programmes than it is merely to document the surface characteristics of intended programmes.

The Constructivist Teacher

Within a constructivist pedagogy, the teacher seriously considers what the child brings to the learning situation as well as what he or she wishes to transmit. Because the teacher observes children closely and attempts to evaluate their valid contributions to the negotiation of meaning, the teacher is able to accumulate deep understanding of stage levels of cognition in children as well as other aspects of development. There are other advantages for the constructivist teacher. Within limits determined by values and theoretical notions, each teacher creates his or her unique programme, which engenders commitment because it is self-generated. Teachers who are intrinsically motivated do not lack enthusiasm.

To a constructivist, the process of learning consists of an active construction of knowledge. The teacher, therefore, must arrange things so that knowledge is actively constructed and not simply copied. One problem arising from an 'open-framework' form of organization is that it may be 'invisible' to a casual observer (Bernstein, 1974b). For instance, to the uninformed observer, early writing may appear to be mere scribble or a mass of mistakes. Research into children's writing development, however, shows that children as young as 3 are systematically testing out hypotheses on the nature of print and the process of writing (Ferreiro and Teberosky, 1982). Because the teacher plans according to observed developmental levels of children, procedures can be used effectively with children of varying abilities and from diverse ethnic and socio-economic backgrounds.

Children's achievements also need to be construed conceptually, not simply perceived. Parents who find it difficult to understand what is going on in school during brief visits need information and explanation. In a stimulus-response situation, for instance, children may be copying the teacher's writing from the blackboard. The educational value may be minimal but the product will be visible and will appear to be correct. Parents who are not informed of the research basis for certain approaches to teaching may find the appearance of correctness desirable.

Teachers of young children who are working with parents need refined professional constructs. The concepts of constructivist theory, such as 'action', 'schema', 'assimilation', 'accommodation', 'stages', 'match', and so on, can be thought of as working hypotheses that can illuminate the learning of young children during the process of 'coming to know'.

GENETIC EPISTEMOLOGY: THE SOURCE OF CONSTRUCTIVISM

Piaget developed the discipline 'genetic epistemology' that deals with the development of knowledge. Constructivism concerns itself with the processes by which knowledge evolves in the learner. Current trends towards testing the crystallization of knowledge at fixed ages will continue, but a more fundamental issue in education is how 'the course of development succeeds in passing from a state of lesser knowledge to one which is more complete and effective' (Piaget, 1972a, p. 5).

British teachers who do not object to being described as 'child-centred' may avoid the term 'constructivist'. In the present 'anti-theory' climate, it is certain that scant acknowledgement will be given to a discipline called 'genetic epistemology'. This is despite the fact that most research on cognitive structure and functioning for the last fifty years has been discussed within the constructs of genetic epistemology. Consequently, many of its central notions have become common currency.

Piaget's work has illuminated cognitive structures in children from the age of 5 or 6 and in infants. Most professionals are familiar with terms such as 'permanence of the object', 'classification', 'seriation', conservation of length, area, volume, weight, and so on. Little is known about the course of cognitive development in children from 2 to 5. There must be stages from lesser knowledge to more complete and effective knowledge that are not yet known. Teachers in early education have a great opportunity to embark on a 'do-it-yourself' identification exercise, on how the children they teach construct knowledge.

Piaget (1969) claims that, at every stage, a child assimilates perceived content to cognitive structures. Cognitive structures should not be thought of as empty baskets labelled with the names of particular structures such as *one-to-one correspondence*. Neither should particular content be thought of as having the cognitive characteristics of the cognitive structure. For instance, 'six eggs and six egg cups' may be assimilated into a *one-to-one relationship* at a certain stage, but at an earlier stage, given the opportunity, these objects would be systematically dropped in order to inspect the trajectory and point of arrival. Later the cost of free-range versus battery eggs might be assimilated to still other concepts and values. External objects do not have cognitive structure. Cognitive structure is a feature of mind. Environmental content either can, or cannot, be assimilated into developing cognitive structures.

To the constructivist the description, 'structuring the environment', is a misnomer. Environments can and must be organized to enhance learning but 'structuring' is essentially a biological/psychological feature of mind.

All the constructivist ideas introduced in this chapter are discussed in depth in Piaget's work. They are introduced briefly here because they were the conceptual tools used by the professionals in the Froebel Early Education Project. Meanings will be elaborated and illustrated within specific situations in Chapters 4, 5 and 6.

Action

Piaget approved of 'new methods of education' by which he meant a constructivist pedagogy as opposed to 'traditional methods'. He noted that almost all the great theoreticians in the history of pedagogy have 'caught a glimpse' of the central feature of successful learning that is 'the active participation of the learner'. What William James, Dewey, Baldwin, Bergson and many others have in common with Piaget is the idea of action: 'The life of the mind is a dynamic reality and intelligence, a real and constructive activity' (Piaget, 1971b, pp. 139–46).[8]

The associated notion (at the heart of Piaget's theories), that 'thought' is 'internalized action', has been slow to be adopted as a research hypothesis probably because it is difficult to test.[9] Although a start has been made in mapping out the relationships between action and thought in controlled experiments, the progression has not yet been explored within an early-education setting (see Chapter 6 for evidence of the developmental route 'from action to dynamic thought').

Stages

Most writers who describe Piaget's theories give a great deal of space to the 'sensorimotor' stage of development, which lasts from birth to approximately 18 months. This detailed account is usually followed by a very short section on the deficits of children's thinking from the age of 2 to 6 – the so called pre-operational stage of development. This is typically followed by a detailed description of the positive characteristics of the 'concrete-operational' stage of development, which lasts from approximately 6 to 11 years.

The unequal attention given in the literature to these three broad stages of cognitive development reflects the paucity of existing knowledge of children from 2 to 5. Schwebel and Raph (1974, p. 46) summarize this situation as follows: 'Between two years and seven years is the stage of pre-operational thought during which the change from sensorimotor to operational thought is gradually prepared. The pre-operational period is usually negatively characterized by lack of reversibility, a lack of decentration and the absence of stable, quantitative constants'.

Opinions vary about when the so-called 'pre-operational' stage begins and ends. Most writers, particularly mathematicians, regard the emergence of 'one-to-one correspondence' as the beginning of a cognitive renaissance after the dark ages of pre-operationalism. The positive characteristics of thought between 2 and 5 have been discussed in general terms in the literature. However, detailed documentation is lacking of developmental increments in thinking and behaviour typical of studies on infants from birth to 18 months.

The end of the sensorimotor stage is heralded by 'symbolic functioning', although sensorimotor behaviour persists to some degree right through life, particularly while new skills, such as learning to drive a car or to ski, are being acquired. Many skills begin with sensorimotor action although internalization of action is speeded up by verbal (symbolic) instruction.

During its first months, a child has certain elementary motor behaviours such as *sucking, banging, looking, smelling, waving*, and so on. Each of these behaviours, when applied to objects, brings sensory feedback. Banging on the table produces an interesting sound similar to banging on a chair and different from banging on a cushion. A child's understanding of the relationship between his or her motor actions and the sensory or perceptual feedback that follows is central to the constructivist view of learning.

At the stage of symbolic functioning, it is not just the relationship between motor action and effects that give information. 'Internalized actions' lead to transformations on material and persons. Feedback from action assisted by 'thought' suggests that the thinking is either okay or that it needs to be modified. For instance, at a sensorimotor level a child may fit together 10 hollow bricks in a size series. Because the action consists of fitting one thing inside another with only a dawning notion of *size seriation*, the series may need 30 or 40 fitting-together actions. The actions of fitting together with follow-up perceptions of success (good fit) gradually become internalized and more efficient. Actions become speeded up and redundancies are eliminated. This leads to a more economical success and the series is constructed in fewer moves.

'Operational' thinking takes place when the child evolves from the relationship of action to effect and 'knows' that there is an invariant correspondence between certain kinds of actions (operations) and certain kinds of effects (trans-formations).

The most important aspects of constructivism, examined by Forman and Fosnot (1982), are the relationships between transformations and static states. All the 'conservation' experiments illustrate that 'knowledge is the coordination of correspondences and transformations', and what is required for 'operational' thinking is the ability to relate a transformation to a 'state' (*ibid*, pp. 93–135). For instance, for the pre-operational child, the initial 'state' of water in a jar is 'perceived' to lack correspondence with the final 'state' of water in a differently shaped jar (the amounts look different). 'Conservation' is achieved when the apparent transformation of the two different 'states' is compensated for by the understanding that the action of pouring is equivalent and, therefore, the quantity of water must be equivalent in spite of apparent figurative differences. The pouring action did not include *adding* or *subtracting* action, and therefore the two 'states' must represent conceptual equivalence.

Presumably the so-called pre-operational stage is where actions are being developed, increased, practised and internalized, and where differentiated actions are being associated with various kinds of sensory and perceptual effects. What is needed is a documentation of the actions.

Forman and Fosnot (*ibid.* p. 197) propose a new unit of knowledge or a new professional concept for early education that is 'the coordination of correspondences and transformations'. The pedagogical implication of this is that the young child would be encouraged to know 'not only what is (the effect) but also the procedure by which it became that way and, equally important, the procedures that can bring about this or that correspondence' (*ibid.* p. 209).

Schemas

There are many different definitions of 'schema', and there is no single definition with which all will agree.[10] In Piaget's early work he uses 'schema' to mean 'general cognitive structures in children under the age of 5'. Later, while exploring the mechanisms of perception (1969), he began to differentiate between 'schema' and 'scheme'. He states (*ibid.* p. ix): 'The terms ''scheme'' and ''schema'' correspond to quite distinct realities, the one operative (a scheme of action in the sense of an instrument of generalization) and the other figurative'. From that time when he used the term 'schema', he meant 'figural thought'. When he used 'scheme' he was referring to 'operational thought'.

If the problem is to discover how early sensorimotor systems develop into symbolic systems, a conceptual teasing-out of 'scheme' and 'schema' would seem to be necessary prior to carrying out an actual investigation. However, most of Piaget's writing of greatest use in the study of young children was written before he differentiated between the two terms. The task of re-interpreting the early work, even if possible, would be a major undertaking. It will be convenient therefore to start with a generalized meaning of the term 'schema', and to see whether a further differentiation is possible or useful.

Bartlett (1932), while discussing 'schemas' or 'schemata', pointed out that motor actions have consequences that lead to adjustments (accommodations). A tennis player, for instance, will adjust his or her stroke if the ball does not take the route intended. Skilled actions, therefore, become modified and linked with each other. As Neisser (1976, p. 56) puts it, 'A schema is a pattern of action as well as a pattern for action'.

'Pattern' can be defined as any sequence of events in time and space. In other words, 'pattern' can apply to dynamic sequences of action as well as static configurations. Patterns of either type in the brain can correspond with, or be discrepant with, dynamic or configurational patterns in the environment. Aspects of environment provide either a 'match' or a 'mismatch' with inner patterns.

All organisms exhibit behaviour that implies inner structure. Animals go round actively searching for things to see and they 'see' mainly what they expect to see. This is because they have 'plans' or 'schemas' that function as built-in hypotheses as to how things are. At a very simple level, fish that swim in caves or moles that live underground will interpret light as something to turn away from. Certain stimuli are approached and other stimuli are avoided (Young, 1978, pp. 117–20).

Cells are sensitive to certain aspects of environment and allow stimuli in the environment to be coded and to be given meaning at some level. Functioning improves with use. Where biologically determined cell assemblies are prevented from functioning, the coding and interpretive functions of these cells disappear (*ibid.* p. 126). Kittens, for instance, have specific cells at the back of the eyes that become activated at critical periods. Features in the natural environment of kittens 'feed' these cells. Where the kittens are artificially deprived of the correct stimuli, for instance, horizontal stimuli, both the perceptions and action patterns of the kittens are damaged. They can no longer jump onto horizontal surfaces. They are permanently damaged (Hubel and Wiesel, 1963).

In humans, the patterns in the brain that are compared with patterns in the environment are complex and developmental and are affected by experience. A general feature of 'plans for action' or 'schematic action' is that schemas are 'dynamic, active, information-seeking structures' (Neisser, 1976, p. 111). In humans, schemas (or cognitive structures) acquire content from experience that modifies hypotheses. There is a strong motivational and affective aspect in both the search for meaning and in the confirmation or disconfirmation of hypotheses.

Piaget's definition of a 'schema' is anchored in the definitions given so far but his particular contribution was to tackle the developmental route of schematic behaviour from birth right through to the advanced cognitive structures of the adolescent. He describes the general features of schemas and concepts as follows: 'Cognitive structures contain within them elements of "perception", "memories", "concepts" and "operations". These are linked together in various types of connections. The connections may be spatial, temporal, causal or implicatory. Structures can be organic, as in very early behaviour, or static or dynamic' (Piaget, 1971b, p. 139). The function of a schema is to enable generalizations to be made about objects and events in the environment to which a schema is applied (Piaget and Inhelder, 1973, p. 382).

The most easily understood meaning of 'schema' is as follows: 'schemas of action [are] co-ordinated systems of movements and perceptions, which constitute any elementary behaviour capable of being repeated and applied to new situations, e.g., *grasping, moving, shaking* an object' (Piaget, 1962, p. 274). Schemas are patterns of repeatable actions that lead to early categories and then to logical classifications. As a result of applying a range of action schemas to objects, infants arrive at the generalizations that objects are 'throwable', 'suckable' and 'bangable'. An infant may perform one schema on a range of objects, or a wide variety of schemas on one object (Foss, 1974, pp. 208–9).

Like most of the constructs within 'genetic epistemology', 'schema' must be understood in relation to other notions within the system. What enables a schema to function in a satisfactory way depends on its history. If early schemas are applied to a diversity of events in the environment, then they will have assimilated many contents (Piaget, 1953, p. 384). Piaget suggests that the extension of schemas, like the extension of action itself, consists of all the objects or contents to which the schema has been applied.

As Hunt (1961, p. 279) puts it, 'At each age and level the environmental circumstances must supply encounters for the child which permit him to use the repertoire of schemas that he has already developed'. Experience is thus assimilated to cognitive structures and this is how knowledge is acquired. This would appear to be a useful hypothesis in the study of underfunctioning children. Increase experiences, and schemas will be enriched. A schema, therefore, is a pattern of repeatable behaviour into which experiences are assimilated and that are gradually co-ordinated. Co-ordinations lead to higher-level and more powerful schemas.

Two early schemas are *tracking* objects and *gazing* at objects. Gazing leads to knowledge of configuration. Tracking leads to knowledge of the movement aspects of objects, including self and other persons. Initially, gazing and tracking are two separate forms of behaviour. If an experimenter makes a stationary object move, a very young infant will continue to gaze at the blank space. Similarly, if a moving object is stopped, the infant will continue to track. One of the first great accommodations takes place when infants realize that objects can be stationary or that they can move (Bower, 1974; 1977a).[11]

Co-ordination of Schemas

Co-ordination of sensorimotor schemas are the practical equivalents of concepts and relations (Piaget, 1969, p. 357). At a later point in development, a toddler moving between points *a* and *b* is co-ordinating, at a motor level, *points of departure* and *points of arrival*. He or she will not be able to 'imagine' this *group of displacements* because sensorimotor co-ordinations consist of successive perceptions and successive overt movements and there is no all-embracing representation. Sensorimotor intelligence has been likened to a slow-motion film in which all the pictures are seen in succession but without fusion.

A 5-year-old may be able to co-ordinate, at a representational or 'thought' level, the distance between *a* and *b* with the distance between *b* and *a* and arrive at equivalence. As schemas are co-ordinated into more and more complex amalgamations, the environment is comprehended at higher levels by the child.

Probably the most important accommodations, or steps forward in knowledge, are where there is a new co-ordination between two separate aspects of knowing. Some of these are dramatic and give rise to exclamations such as 'Oh, yes!' 'Eureka!' 'The penny dropped!' 'I suddenly saw the light!' 'I put two and two together!' and so on. Such co-ordinations have an agreeable affective or emotional component. What is 'known' leads to what becomes 'better known'. It would be useful from the point of view of assessing incremental learning if the component parts of co-ordinations could be described.

Struggle, Practice and Play

Each important advance in cognition is synonymous either with learning something new or realizing something for the first time. Sometimes an advance follows the cognitive discomfort that accompanies an unsolved problem. Piaget's theoretical model of the 'functional invariants', consisting of the processes of accommodation and assimilation, explains the mechanisms involved in cognitive advance. Each aspect of functioning has its affective component. Functioning ranges from struggle through practice to play.

The relationship between stage-level characteristics and different kinds of functioning can be illustrated from a typical behaviour of the first year. *Permanence of the object* (Oates, 1979, section three) develops from 'out of sight, out of mind' to 'absence makes the heart grow fonder'. Before *permanence of the object* is well established the child will be distressed if a toy is hidden. There is a conflict (or a struggle) between permanence and impermanence. When permanence is sufficiently established, through practice, *permanence of the object* enters its play form – best seen in the 'peek-a-boo' game. The form of the cognition is: 'now you see it, now you don't, but you know it is still there'. The child knows something so well (that objects are permanent) that he or she can even play with it (Chukovsky, 1966). Similarly, it is only when staying upright has reached a high degree of competence that the game of 'Ring-a-ring a roses' can be enjoyed. When toddlers fall down they are usually furious because falling down means failure to stand up. Having fun with pretend falling down signifies real competence in staying upright.

Theoretically, cognitive competence could be studied by reference to the affective accompaniments of behaviour. Struggle would indicate new knowledge or skill, playfulness would indicate the well assimilated. Cognition in infants is frequently assessed in relation to their affective responses.

Stages of Perception

Bower (1977a) describes six stages in the perception of configuration during the first seven months of life. His stimuli resemble the human face represented in different degrees of complexity from a few simple lines to a complex representation of two faces (*ibid.* p. 79; Figure 2.1).[12]

If the configuration of a stimulus is too simple, the infant will opt out and doze (habituation). If it is too complex there is also an opting out (too much struggle). The level of stimulus must 'match' the stage level of the child for absorption, interest or delight to be shown. In infant studies 'playfulness' is used as an index of something well understood.

Piaget (1962, p. 91) gives an example from one of his children that shows the child's active attempts to increase the interest of a perceptual feedback by varying action. The child was 2 months old (sensorimotor 2) and had developed the ability to throw his head back in order to look at familiar objects from a new position. Piaget (*ibid.*) describes this as follows: 'He repeated this movement with

Description		Age
Simple dots or angles.		Under 6 weeks
Eye section alone; under portion of face unnecessary.		10 weeks
Eye section still suffices, but under half of face must be present even though mouth movements only fleetingly noticed; motion facilitates.		12 weeks
Eye section still suffices, with wide individual differences. Mouth gradually noticed, its movements particularly effective. Wide mouth best. Plastic model of adult effective.		20 weeks
Effectiveness of eyes lessens; mouth movements generally necessary, especially widely drawn mouth. Still no differentiation of individual faces.		24 weeks
Attention to face as such lessens; recognition of facial expression begins, with interest in other children. Progressive differentiation of individual faces.		30 weeks

Figure 2.1 Six stages in the perception of configuration during the first seven months of life Source: from *A Primer of Infant Development* by T.G.R. Bower. Copyright © 1977 by W.H. Freeman and Company. Reprinted by permission.

ever increasing enjoyment and ever decreasing interest in the external result. He brought his head back to the upright position and then threw it back again time after time laughing loudly. This behaviour ceased to be "serious" or "instructive" and became a game'.

The child was generating his own experience in that he was varying his motor actions in order to vary the perceptual effects of those actions.

Symbolic Functioning and Symbolic Representation

The stage of cognition from approximately 2 to 5 years can be described positively as the stage of symbolic functioning in that children become able to represent known events symbolically. Representation can remain internal as in representational thought, or it can be made manifest in drawings, symbolic play or speech. At this stage, children symbolically 're-present' objects and events that have been experienced. Representation means being able to 're-play' in the mind the 'look' of objects or the movement patterns of objects or other features of objects that have been experienced. Action or movement 're-play' can be seen when the child uses some simple object (such as a stick) to represent objects moving, such as an aeroplane or a car. Action images are most clearly recognizable in symbolic play.

Action images are based on the perception of the movement aspects of objects. Iconic, or figurative, images are based on the perception of the figurative aspects of objects. Speech representations can signify all known motor behaviours, how things look, how things feel and a range of motivations – provided the child has learned the words necessary for expressing experiences and desires.

Different writers refer to these three forms of representation by different names. Bruner (1974) describes the three modes of representation as 'enactive', 'iconic' and 'symbolic' (speech). Piaget differentiates between 'operational', which has a basis in action, and 'figurative', which is based on perception. He refers to speech as a system of signs.

Processes involved in representation are not easy to understand. Forman and Fosnot (1982, p. 186) describe representation as follows:

> Constructivism assumes that we have no direct accessibility to an external world. We therefore, have to construct representations that have more to do with acts of knowing than they do with the external object per se. To Piaget ... what we represent is our own mental activity and not some static external object. We then externalize this mental activity as if it were a static external object.

The difficulty lies in understanding the constantly changing relationships between 'our own mental activity' and 'external objects'. *Permanence of the object* is a mental activity applied to objects in the first year of life. *One-to-one correspondence* is a mental activity applied to a range of objects at around 5 or 6.

The notion of different levels of mental activity can be illustrated by children of different ages playing with pebbles on a beach: a 3-year-old might place the pebbles in *a linear order* because that is a form of order typical of 3-year-olds; a 4- or 5-year-old might place the pebbles in a *one-to-one correspondence*, one pebble next to one shell, for instance; and a 6-year-old might arrange the pebbles into two lots of six, or six lots of two, or three lots of four. Such motor actions are clearly guided by cognition. Piaget showed that actions reflect symbolic thought from the second year, but more recent research has shown that the symbolic process starts earlier (Bower, 1974; 1977a). Symbolic functioning evolves from the sensory and motor stage of development.

Becoming 'operational' means that actions can be carried out intellectually. Operational thought has certain characteristics such as 'reversibility', which is essential for 'conservation'. For the stable mathematical operation of *addition*, the mental action of grouping together must be able to be cancelled out by reversing the process. For instance,

$$2 + 5 = 7$$
$$7 - 5 = 2$$
$$7 - 2 = 5$$

Subtraction cancels *addition* and *division* cancels *multiplication*.

There is no point in continuing to perform physical actions on stones after the actions have become internalized, operational and permanent. Fundamental learning lasts for life. The process of internalizing action is facilitated by speech, although speech alone cannot generate fundamental learning. (This is discussed further in Chapters 3 and 6.)

Seriation and *classification* have their origins in early actions applied to a wide range of objects and, later, to events. The common-sense world contains sufficient information to feed *seriation structures* such as *size*, *height*, *weight*, *strength*, *temperature*, *porosity*, *number*, and so on. Even if children did not go to school they would still make statements such as 'I'm taller than Charlie' or 'I have more marbles than Jenny'.

An important role of the teacher is to feed spontaneous structures with content not necessarily found at home, street or playground. In other words, worthwhile curriculum content can be offered that, if received, will extend cognitive structures educationally. Within the highest concept of education, teaching facilitates and 'fleshes-out' spontaneous and natural concepts with worthwhile curriculum content.

A problem in early education is a lack of knowledge of spontaneous concepts that can guide the search for appropriate curriculum content. This is not to say that appropriate curriculum content is not offered in early education but that evaluation of what has been received is weak. The weakness in diagnosing cognitive structures has led to demands for external structuring. This merely deflects from the need to study mental action as expressed through representation. Mental representation cannot be studied directly but it can be construed from symbolic play, drawing, brick constructions and the like.

Knowledge consists of internal constructions that have 'form' (schemas and concepts and constructs). The content of experience 'feeds' the forms of thought. Improvements, or modifications in functioning, are brought about by psychological processes such as 'accommodation' and 'assimilation'.

Form, Process and Content

Three important aspects of professional knowledge on learning and development are as follows:

1. Cognitive 'form'.
2. The 'content' of experience.
3. The processes by which content can, or cannot, be assimilated to cognitive form at different stages of development.

Because the characteristics of later forms of thought are better known than earlier forms, there is a temptation for teachers of young children to accelerate development towards the known. Teachers who try to respond appropriately to children's existing behaviour have little option but to focus on content.

A focus on content can be illustrated in Lowenfeld's (1957) advice to teachers on how they might extend a child's thought in relation to a drawing. He suggests that, if a child draws his or her mother, the teacher might ask questions such as 'Where is your mother?' 'Is she alone?' or 'What is she doing?' Such questions, suggest the author, are aimed at enlarging the experience of the child in relation to the subject-matter of the drawing. Similarly, if a child draws an aeroplane, he suggests that questions might be asked about its size, where it lands, whether there are people on the plane, and so on (*ibid.* p. 67).

Such extensions encourage associative rather than conceptual thinking in that the child is encouraged to associate content with content: 'sun' will be associated with 'sky'; 'houses' with 'roads'; 'aeroplane' with *size*; 'person' with 'place'; and so on. The children's attention is drawn only to thematic or proximity relations between 'unlike' things.

Attempts are being made, mainly in mathematics and science, to 'match' worthwhile curriculum content to prevailing cognitive structures. These attempts are mainly in relation to children older than 5 because the cognitive structures, such as *seriation*, *classification* and various *conservations*, are known (Harlen, Darwin and Murphy, 1977).

The search for the relationship between 'form' and 'content' has been going on for a long time. In the following example from Katz and Katz (1936), the difference between 'content' and 'structure' (or 'form') can be illustrated. The 'cognitive form' is *seriation of size*. The 'content' or 'stuff' of thinking is that of natural science, more specifically, 'elephant', 'mouse', 'snail' and 'flea'. The child is an intelligent and experienced 5-year-old who is having a conversation with his father, who is a natural scientist:

Child: The elephant is the biggest animal and the mouse is the smallest.
Father: The mouse isn't the smallest.
Child: No ... it's the snail.
Father: There are still smaller ones.
Child: The flea is of course the smallest.
Father: There are still smaller ones but you don't know them. They live in water.
Child: I know them but I don't know what they are called.

If this conversation took place in class, the teacher might decide to ask questions on where elephants live, how a snail protects itself or what kind of food a mouse eats. These questions may interest the child and they are worth asking, but they have a 'hit-or-miss' quality. The responses the father gave show that he is aware of the prevailing concern of the child, which is *size*. A size continuum is an invariant cognitive structure that links individual objects in the world with each other. Schemas and concepts facilitate a cognitive organization of disparate content.

Sinclair (1974, p. 46) refers to the search for invariants of behaviour, or thought, as the search for 'cognitive constants' – schematic patterns that exist beneath the flux of personally experienced content. Teachers who initiate a 'search for schemas' will subsequently find it easier to select appropriate curriculum content to enrich those schemas.

To advance a pedagogy of the early years, more research into schemas (cognitive forms) that are self-generated rather than other-generated is needed (Forman and Fosnot, 1982, p. 194). The identification of fundamental cognitive structures in young children will lead to a greater rationale for a pre-school curriculum.

Constructivism, Experience and the Curriculum

Central to constructivism is the idea that the teacher should 'match' worthwhile curriculum content to diagnosed cognitive structures. It must be stressed that the aspiration to 'match' is a professional ideal. All teachers who listen to children know that there is many a slip between what is offered and what is received.[13]

The curriculum is a heading under which many issues are discussed, such as the organizing of environment, the provision of concrete materials, managerial matters and curriculum content. Curriculum content is knowledge given educational validity by people 'in the know' and by people in power.

The central feature of the curriculum is knowledge. This exists objectively in encyclopedias, and so on, and it remains external to the knower until constructed psychologically in the individual. External knowledge, once validated for 'truth', 'worthwhileness', 'relevance', 'usefulness' and 'generalizability', must be discovered, assimilated and mastered by the learner. If knowledge is to be successfully assimilated it must fit in with the learner's 'lived experience' (Greene, 1971, p. 30). As 'lived experience' is itself, according to Piaget, subservient to the cognitive structures that assimilate experience, then the most important aspect of 'psychologizing' curriculum content is to identify the cognitive structures to which the curriculum content is to be assimilated.

Until recently, individual teachers had too much responsibility for deciding on appropriate curriculum content for their own class. This was wasteful of effort. Reform came with a collective rather than individual effort towards planning and articulating whole-school programmes. There are dangers in the drastic shift from the judgements of individual teachers to the implementation of a National Curriculum. Programmers will try to sell curriculum content organized into neat, logical programmes of instruction. Blenkin and Whitehead (1988) have criticized such programmes because they remove control of the learning process from the child. They maintain that the imposition of a subject-based curriculum runs counter to 'developmentalism', which is learner-centred. They suggest (*ibid*. p. 34) that teachers should aim at refining their judgements in action rather than relying on a tight prescription for action.

The idea that the child should be in control of his or her learning does not mean that the child can choose to study content in school that is not 'worthwhile'. Although there is enough information in the common sense world to 'feed' all spontaneous cognitive structures, qualifications for higher education require more specialized knowledge. Each society considers some knowledge to be of particular importance. Sub-groups within society may have different hierarchies of importance. As well as issues of content, there are issues of timing and the means by which agreed content should be introduced to children.

In very early development, sensible adults tend to follow the natural proclivities of the child. Adults who try to re-route natural baby behaviours are on a losing wicket. The energy of the infant throwing things out of the pram exceeds that of the exasperated adult.

Unless early education is to remain both static and apart, teachers must try to work out appropriate content for the early years that has some kind of continuity from infancy towards primary education. The chances are that more accommodations of a worthwhile nature will take place in a classroom containing materials from various curriculum areas than in a classroom that simply echoes a common-sense world. From a curriculum and a continuity point of view, the search for patterns of behaviour is simultaneously a search for the foundations and future of both scientific and mathematical thinking (Piaget, 1977, Preface).

Piaget (1969, p. 364) claims that, as experience increases, development itself is provoked because 'New schemas are endlessly constructed by the subject assimilating the content of experience to schemas'. The more that is assimilated, the more extensive the schemas and the more coherent are resulting 'networks of schemas'. From an affective point of view, Piaget maintains that the more a person knows the more he or she wants to know.

NOTES

1. Pronunciation is made easier by making the final 'g' soft, as in 'psychology'. It then becomes possible to pronounce 'pedagogical' without too much glottal strain.

2. The decision to use the term 'pedagogy' in this book is linked with a quarter of a century's teaching at the Froebel Institute where education courses were based on a co-ordination of theory, observation and practice. The philosophical and psychological roots of most theory found useful at the institute stemmed from Europe rather than Britain. The term 'pedagogy' reflects this European bias.

3. Americans do not always differentiate between the curriculum, meaning 'what' is taught, and the more specific meaning of pedagogy, meaning 'how' content is taught.

4. The report deals mainly with two aspects of the programme: what teachers appear to have gained from it from their point of view, and matters of organization.

Success in the first year was gauged by the fact that most of the agencies sending or financing participants plan to continue with the programme (p. 86). This is a debatable criterion of success in that people continue with plans of action even when evidence suggests they should do otherwise.

5. Ten children were observed for 40 minutes in a pre-training setting and for 40 minutes in a post-training setting. A few differences were recorded in the amount and type of adult involvement in the children's play. The report gives no information on the effect of a Piagetian programme on children, but concerns itself with the perceptions of adults.

6. A group of lecturers from the Froebel Institute suggest that the 'teaching' aspects of the programme may be bypassing a necessary natural-history level of investigation (Makins, 1987).

7. Indications are from conferences, in-service courses and responses of nursery teachers to surveys (Cane and Schroeder, 1970; Morsbach, 1982).

8. There is considerable empirical evidence for the premiss that successful learning depends on the active participation of the learner. Support comes from animal studies (Hubel and Wiesel, 1962; Held and Hein, 1963; Young, 1978) and from studies of children (Bruner, 1971; Bailey and Burton, 1982; Forman, 1982; Newell and Barclay, 1982).

9. This is now being remedied. Forman (1982a) has edited a collection of research studies on this theme, called *Action and Thought: From Sensorimotor Schemes to Symbolic Operations.*

10. Oldfield and Zangwill, 1942; Oldfield, 1954; Vernon, 1955; Skemp, 1962, 1971; Neisser, 1976; Anderson, Spiro and Montague, 1977; Norman, 1978.

11. Recently, several books have been published with seductive titles that promise information on 'concepts', 'schemas', 'cognition', 'action', 'perception' and 'representation'. Interesting though these books are, they are of doubtful use to teachers of young children because the emphasis has shifted from the human, biological and psychological aspects of the above concepts towards the logical. They may lead to advances in information technology that may, at some point, help in the study of human cognition but this stage has not yet been reached. (See Rumelhart and Norman (1985) for more information on this line of development.)

12. As is shown in Chapter 4, these stages correspond to an evolution in children's drawings between the ages of 2 and 5.

13. For the most illuminating and entertaining account of 'match' and 'mismatch', see Harlen, Darwin and Murphy (1977).

PART II

PART II

3

AIMS AND FINDINGS OF THE FROEBEL EDUCATIONAL INSTITUTE PROJECT

PART A

The Aims of the Froebel Educational Institute Project

The Froebel Early Education Project had three main aims:

1. To produce information on the ways in which knowledge is acquired by young children within home and school situations. This entailed developing a new approach to the description and interpretation of cognitive behaviour. Interpretations were based on the Piagetian notion of cognitive structures (schemas). The aim was to search for commonalities and continuities or 'cognitive constants' in spontaneous behaviour and thought. Efforts were made to document the route from sensorimotor action through to 'thought' via figural and action representation.

2. To provide an effective enrichment programme for children from a disadvantaged section of the community. The programme was based on a new kind of collaboration between parents and professionals. The professionals did not deny their own specialized knowledge but made it freely available to parents without fear of loss of status. The approach and the concepts referred to under aim 1 were central to what was shared.

    A comparison group was also studied consisting of advantaged children educated at the Froebel Institute Kindergarten.

3. To document a number of developmental sequences of behaviour from early motor behaviours to 'thought', in sufficient detail to allow professionals to evaluate the data and the usefulness of interpretation. Aspects of theory found useful during analysis are presented in sufficient detail to be useful to teachers and parents who may wish to experiment along similar lines.

General Information about the Froebel Project

It is generally accepted that the most extensive (and expensive) investigations into child behaviour are those that employ both formative and summative evaluations (White, 1969, p. 255). During the Froebel project, summative evaluations were carried out at regular intervals and hundreds of hours were spent recording observations on the spontaneous behaviour of twenty children over a two-year period.

It was not difficult to record the spontaneous behaviour of the children but it was difficult to interpret it. It was not easy to find as yet undiscovered commonalities underneath the surface features of recorded behaviour. (The main findings on 'cognitive constants' (schemas) are presented in Chapters 4, 5 and 6.) The results of the summative evaluations are given in this chapter. The total length of time of project planning and implementation was five years. Following up families for final testing, evaluating the data with the help of computer analysis, linking outcomes with illuminative literature, working out curriculum implications and writing up the study took several more years.

Project families attended the project for two years (six school terms), for three hours each morning. This amounted to 1,020 hours of education for each child – similar to the amount of time many children spend in early education. Many people were involved in collecting observations: the project teacher, teaching-practice students, students attending various education courses at the Froebel Institute, parents and the writer. Observations were made on most children most days.

The kindergarten children, who were highly intelligent, competent and confident, were studied by the writer one morning most weeks during which video- and audio-recordings were made of spontaneous behaviour and speech. Audio- and video-recordings preserved a richness of detail. Increasingly detailed interpretations of project and kindergarten behaviours were made possible as points from professional literature illuminated the raw data. Decisions on what to record were based on informed 'hunches' that time and effort would reveal high-level cognition that was not immediately obvious at the time of recording. This material formed the substance of long, intensive meetings of project and kindergarten staff and students.

The aim of staff meetings was to clarify and make more specific intuitive evaluations. In spite of the high professional qualifications of staff, early evaluations tended to consist of 'grunts' of approval rather than clear and articulate evaluations of the cognitive level of the children being observed.

All information was transcribed in triplicate by a full-time secretary. One set was organized as a record of the whole programme on a day-to-day basis, with management and planning features incorporated. Another set was organized into twenty longitudinal studies, one for each child. The third set was cut up into individual observations, each containing basic information such as name, age, date, and so on. As patterns of behaviour were 'discovered', these individual observations were categorized conceptually. Using a computer it was possible to trace through the 'schematic' development of each individual child over a two-year period, as well as to discover age-related patterns of behaviour in the group as a whole.

Sub-divided into ten variables, 5,333 observations were analysed within programmes taken from the Statistical Package for the Social Scientist (SPSC). Every observation, starting from the youngest child at his or her youngest age, was studied with reference to available theory and a decision was made as to its schematic or cognitive structure, type of speech use, and so on (the analysis was tackled from a prospective point of view as discussed in Chapter 1).[1]

Ongoing analysis of observations during the project provided the main substance of communication with parents. The frequency of each schema, however, and the chronological ages at which new schemas appeared, emerged from the computer analysis carried out after the children had entered primary school.

The main aim of the computer sorting was to find out the frequencies of observations that had been placed in nominal categories. The frequencies of schemas at different age intervals indicate a developmental scale of schemas. However, although the 'search for schemas' was the main focus of the project, it was only when a schema had been conceptualized that particular behaviours were recognized to be instances of that schema. It is fairly clear that earlier instances were overlooked because they were not recognized. When the project teacher had her own children, she found schemas appeared much earlier than in project children. This may be because they did appear earlier, but it may have been partly due to her increased skill in recognizing them.

A more important reason for not 'scaling' schemas in a developmental hierarchy is that they 'cluster'. Schemas and concepts are 'systems' of thought and perception. In this study, no way could be found to measure co-ordinations, although examples of co-ordinations have been given at the end of Chapter 6 and are discussed further in Chapters 7 to 11. Theoretically, co-ordinations of schemas have greater power to 'embrace' an increasingly larger number of events. We therefore describe co-ordinations of schemas even though they defy measurement (a more detailed account of the different stages in the analysis of observations is given in Appendix I).

Selection of Families

The project was funded within the ethic of 'positive discrimination' so there were constraints on the selection of families who could be invited to participate in the programme. Professionals in the area, headteachers, teachers, health visitors, social workers and play-group leaders gave their help in finding twenty suitable families with 2-year-old children. All families lived near each other in an Educational Priority Area (EPA) within twenty minutes travelling distance of the institute.

Because of the intention to study the children in depth over two years and to test them for longer it was necessary to find families who were relatively stable although disadvantaged. As the local school consisted of an ethnic mix, families were chosen to reflect this situation. The health workers were particularly helpful and twenty families were contacted. After the proposed project was explained in detail all parents wanted to participate. Attendance figures show the initial selection of families to be successful (see Appendix II).

During home visits by the writer, parents were told that the Froebel project had been set up in order to investigate how children think, learn and develop between the ages of 2 and 5. The need for testing was explained. In order to allay possible test anxieties, test materials resembling play materials were shown and discussed in general terms.

Parents were invited to attend the project as often as possible. Information was given on educational projects where children had made educational gains that were thought to be the result of parent and professional co-operation.

Approximately four home visits were made to each family before the educational programme began. After her appointment, the project teacher joined home visits where she worked with, and got to know, each child.[2] This enabled the writer and parent to communicate over initial project questionnaires in a relaxed, uninterrupted atmosphere. All the parents were enthusiastic about the venture. Mothers answered the questionnaire, except in Asian families. During the home visits, much useful information was exchanged.

Certain practical problems were encountered in testing the Asian children. Four of the children spoke Urdu only, so all the tests were translated into written Urdu by a Pakistani student in her first year at the Froebel Institute who worked closely with the Asian families throughout the project. Her assistance was invaluable.[3]

The method adopted when testing Asian children was as follows. The writer would ask a question in English. If the child did not respond, Mariam would ask the question in Urdu. This does not conform to a standard testing procedure but the three alternatives would have been to have the Asian children appear as low scorers, not to have tested them or not to have had any Asian families. As it turned out there was no significant difference between the mean IQ scores of the English- and Urdu-speaking children. End-of-project tests were given in English.

The parents were carefully briefed on appropriate behaviour during testing but afterwards they had much to say. They became aware that this was a different kind of evaluation from the kind they habitually employed. They tended to evaluate their children's actions in terms of good or bad behaviour rather than by cognitive criteria. It was clear from parents' comments that they provided more educational materials for their children after the tests than before. Initial testing started a shift towards educational evaluation. In initial tests children frequently began to yawn soon after the start of testing. During the project, the majority became enthusiastic about being tested.

As testing proceeded some of the older siblings became aware that they were being compared unfavourably with the younger children by their parents. This did not improve their test motivation.

Towards the end of the first term of the project, four families had to leave the project. Two moved to another area. One parent could not cope when she had a new baby and one family had reasons for avoiding publicity. This left 16 families, which was not as serious as might have been imagined at the start of the project because, by the end of the first term, it was realized how important four younger siblings were to the study. The younger children brought the number studied in depth over two years to 20. As well as this, 28 older siblings attended the project during school holidays. During these times they were tested and given a range of educational experiences by interested members of the Froebel Institute staff. These included art, movement, music, drama, natural science and environmental studies. The older siblings provided a second comparison group for testing purposes.

Two questionnaires, consisting of 300 questions, were given to parents in their homes before the start of the programme.[4] (A summary of information on the project families abstracted from the questionnaire is presented in Appendix II.)

The Project Environment

The project building was situated in the grounds of the Froebel Institute in a building that had been previously used as the kindergarten of the Institute's Demonstration School. A large upper floor contained video and audio equipment and all research material. A full-time secretary worked in this room near a small office used mainly for testing. The project classroom was on the ground floor adjoining a science laboratory used by junior children from the Froebel Preparatory School. Project parents were often invited to look at work being carried out by the older children. The size of the project classroom was modest compared with most State classrooms. Parents used all areas, except the office, quite freely.

The classroom was typical of the British nursery school. It contained a wide range of materials such as paint, clay, wood, sand, building bricks and other construction materials, water, dressing-up clothes, home-corner materials, cooking equipment, books, mathematics and science materials, and a wide range of world toys such as dolls' houses, farms, zoos, and so on. Outside there were climbing frames, slides, cars, perambulators, tricycles, trolleys, a sand pit and a great deal of movement equipment.

The children were free to move between the classroom and the playground most of the time. The playground led straight onto a large sports field. The parents appreciated the country atmosphere, the fresh air and the relative peace and quiet. The project setting was very different from the drabness and pollution of the inner-city area in which the families lived.

As in most early-education situations, the teacher led group activities such as stories, poetry, rhymes and singing. During the first term children often sat on their mothers' laps for these sessions. On most days, the teacher or, increasingly, a parent, organized small group activities such as cooking or sewing. Although the children were free to choose what they wanted to do, having chosen they were encouraged to stay with the activity. This presented few difficulties.

Information on Comparison Groups Studied in the Froebel Project

For conceptual, practical and ethical reasons, a comparison rather than a control group was used for the purpose of evaluating similarities and differences between the two groups of children studied in the Froebel project.[5] It was decided to study a comparison group of twenty children attending the Froebel Institute Kindergarten at the same time as the project children attended the project. Although the children came from opposite ends of the social scale in terms of wealth, educational qualifications of parents, housing conditions, parental employment, and so on, they were to be given similar opportunities in the two school situations. The project and kindergarten teachers were both trained at the Froebel Institute and they had a similar pedagogical approach. The two groups were in different buildings and had no physical contact with each other. The kindergarten children were, on average, six months older than the project children. Observations on the kindergarten children, therefore, provided useful cognitive indicators for the ongoing assessment of the project children.

Because of the compensatory dimension of the project, the comparison group provided a safeguard against lowered staff expectations. As the project progressed, the comparison-group children provided useful 'ceiling' levels of schematic functioning. As Piaget (1971a, p. 227) advised, 'Knowledge of the terminal point of a development helps set the beginnings in perspective'. The high-level cognitive functioning of the comparison group is apparent in test results.

Where there is stability of environment, IQ within families tends to be stable (Schaefer, 1970). Where a change of environment is brought about, a measurable difference in IQ within families has been shown. As it was intended to change project children through an enrichment programme, the older siblings of both kindergarten and project groups served as a second comparison group. The intention was to test for initial stability of IQ within families and to see whether there were changes related to the enrichment programme given to the project children. Standardized test results showed that as the test scores of project children increased, so did the difference between project children and their older siblings. The standardized scores of kindergarten children and their older siblings remained similar.

PART B

Standardized Tests and Results

Project and kindergarten children were measured before, during and after the project on a range of standardized tests. Initial tests were given to all children in their homes. Because of the decision to measure older siblings, the Stanford–Binet Intelligence Scale (form L–M) (Terman Merrill, 1976) was used (test one). Although many criticisms have been levelled against this test, it has the advantage of measuring IQ from the age of 2 to superior adult level. It is, therefore, extremely useful for comparing children of different ages within families.

Other standardized tests used in the project are as follows:

Test two: the Reynell Language Comprehension Test; the Reynell Expressive Language Test (Reynell, 1969). (The Reynell tests could not be used after the initial tests because the range of test scores was too narrow for repeated testing of children with high scores.)

Test three: the English Picture Vocabulary Test (EPVT) (Brimer and Dunn, 1962).

Test four: the Harris–Goodenough 'Draw-a-Man' Test (Harris, 1963).

The children were tested in their homes two years after they left the project. At this point most of the children were 7 years old. During this final home visit, the Neale Analysis of Reading Ability (Neale, 1966), was given to the experimental children and their older siblings.

Results of the Tests

Tests were given to:

1. evaluate the progress of twenty project children;
2. compare test scores of the project children with the comparison group; and
3. measure all older brothers and sisters of project and kindergarten children for consistency of IQ within families.

Tests 1, 3 and 4 were given to the project group and the kindergarten comparison group two years later; tests 1, 3 and 4 were given to the project group after they had spent two years in their primary schools; tests 1, 3 and 4 were given to the older siblings of the project children; test 3 was given to the older siblings of the kindergarten comparison groups; and tests 1, 3 and 4 were given to the younger siblings of the project group.

The Neale Analysis of Reading Ability was given to the project children after they had spent two years in their primary schools. Older siblings were also given the reading test during those visits.

The Stanford–Binet Intelligence Scale was given to the project group at home before the education programme started, at the end of the first year, at the end of the second year and again at the end of the first two years in primary school.

Test results: project and comparison groups

The initial tests showed that the kindergarten comparison group was significantly ahead on all tests (at the .01 level), except for the 'Draw-a-Man' Test (which was at the .05 level).

On the Stanford–Binet Intelligence Scale the kindergarten comparison group (mean chronological age 3:7) was 34 mean IQ points ahead of the project group (mean CA 3:0). The mean IQ of the kindergarten group was 124. The mean IQ of the project group was 90. Differences between the two groups were expected because of the initial selection criteria.

During the programme, the children who were receiving the experimental programme made significant gains on all tests. There was, for instance, an increase of 27 mean IQ points between the first and third Stanford–Binet test results. These gains were not 'washed out' during the first two years in the primary school. The initial IQ differences between the two groups were significantly reduced.

Project children and younger siblings

Two years after the end of the project it was found that four of the younger siblings had higher IQs and 'Draw-a-Man' scores than their experimental group siblings. This may be a reflection of the parents' extra focused attention on their younger children during the critical early years as a result of attending the project.

Project children and older siblings

At the end of the educational programme, the mean IQ of the experimental group was 20 points ahead of the older sibling group whereas initially the scores were similar. The initial mean score of the experimental group was 90 and the older sibling group 93. Although tests tend to be unreliable when used on young children, the initial equivalence of scores probably indicates that 90 was a fair measure.

Reading-test results

After two years in the primary school, the experimental group children were six months ahead of their chronological age on 'accuracy' of reading, and three months ahead of their chronological age on 'comprehension' of reading. The test used was the Neale Analysis of Reading Ability (Neale, 1966).

On the same test the older siblings 'lagged' one year and two months behind their chronological age in their mean accuracy score. There was an equivalent 'lag' in their 'comprehension' scores.

Explanation of gain

The gains made by the experimental group indicate that the educational programme affected the children's performance on tests. It was probably a combination of three major aspects of the programme – parents participating with professionals within an articulated pedagogical approach (the three 'p's).

A general explanation of the large and sustained gains of the project children may lie in the considerable change in the lives of the project children and parents brought about as a result of participation in the project. The environment was more complex than hitherto and, consequently, greater adaptation was required for all the participants.

Although it is not possible to produce direct evidence on how the parents exerted their influence differentially on their older and younger children, the difference in all test scores, with the youngest children being highest, suggests (as mentioned previously) that the parents practised on their youngest children what they had learned during the project.

Early testing and inequality

The summative results of the Froebel project show that initial wide differences in cognitive functioning can be narrowed by early education. Increases in 'intelligence as adaptation' in underfunctioning children, as opposed to the shifting distributions of IQ scores, benefit society. Long-term results from the High/Scope programmes (Schweinhart and Weikart, 1980) show that early education is cheaper than later welfare benefits.

Our findings simply add to the large amount of evidence that children under 5 who are underfunctioning intellectually can be helped to function more effectively by good-quality early education. Given that this is so, increasingly effective means of evaluating the day-to-day educational progress of young children need to be found. Until such formative evaluations are refined, starting-points will continue to be ascertained by summative evaluation.

PART C

Results of the Content Analysis of Symbolic Representations following Project Visits

Enrichment: experiences gained from weekly visits

As part of the enrichment programme, project families were taken to places of interest one morning each week in the project bus accompanied by project staff and students. The project teacher arranged 71 visits over the two years of the programme. Of the visits, 19 were within the grounds or departments of the Froebel Institute; 12 visits were from outside people including police, doctors, a dentist and a book publisher; and 40 visits were organized to places of interest outside the Froebel Institute.

The psychological process of 'experiencing' or 'acquiring knowledge' cannot be observed directly. Therefore, a simple if laborious method was adopted of assessing the experiences of the project children by the 'content' of what they chose to represent: 'The whole problem is to find out how the subject records the data of experience' (Piaget, 1953, p. 360). To this end, every symbolic representation was analysed in order to find out whether it had a connection with project visits or whether the content could have been equally well acquired in the home or neighbourhood. Two examples will make these two criteria clear.

Example one   During a visit to the police stables, Jock (2:6:6) saw a policeman mount and dismount his horse several times. Later, Jock climbed a metal structure, cocked one leg over the top and said, 'Me policeman "orsy"'. This representation was repeated several times.

Example two   Amanda (4:2:1) painted a *rectangle*, filled it in and said, 'This is a window with curtains across.'

Example one was classified as an action representation arising from a project event. Example two was classified as a figurative or graphic representation that could have risen from experiences at home.

Much of this book illustrates the way in which 'experiencing' contains at least two important factors:

1.   The 'content' being experienced.
2.   The 'concept' or 'schema' (cognitive form) to which content is assimilated.

Carrying out a 'content' count as a measure of experience was separate from the analysis of the cognitive forms to which experiences were assimilated. (Chapters 5 and 6 illustrate the relationships between form and content.)

Results of the content analysis of symbolic representations following project visits

There were 1,968 clear, unambiguous representations of content: 1,191 (60.5 per cent) were related to project visits and related events that included preparation and follow-up work in the project organized by the teacher; 777 (39.4 per cent) could have been experienced in the home setting.

These figures offer some support for the critical importance of first-hand experience in providing the content of representation. Experience thought of in this way could be called the 'stuff' or 'content' of mind, as opposed to the 'form' or 'structure' of mind.

Experience is what 'feeds' schemas and extends them

The visits that stimulated the greatest number of representations were the zoo (no. 232, 11.7 per cent), boat trips up the River Thames (no. 177, 9 per cent), London Airport (no. 130, 6.6 per cent), trips to the common or park (no. 131, 6.6 per cent), the railway (no. 90, 4.5 per cent), the police (with dogs and horses) (no. 69, 3.5 per cent) and swimming (no. 52, 2.6 per cent).

All the places visited were sufficiently 'rich' to be experienced at different schematic levels. Two different levels of representation following a repeated visit are as follows. After a first visit to police stables, Lois (3:5:5) represented 'Horse with legs' (Figure 3.1). After a second visit, when she was 4:5:12, she painted another horse (Figure 3.2). She called this painting 'This is the back of a horse. He's carrying things on his back'. A careful examination of her early representations showed her interest in content that could be expressed with *grid-like* graphic schemas. In the later representation she shifted to a *projective space* concept, where objects are represented from different points of view. She used the semi-circle (*an open curve*) that emerges later than *grid*. (It is worth mentioning at this point that speech use reflects schematic concerns as well as describing content.)

Figure 3.1 'Horse with legs'   **Figure 3.2** 'This is the back of a
                                           horse. He's carrying
                                           things on his back'

Even when some offered experiences appear to have less potential than others (Westminster Abbey compared with the zoo), the children found situations that 'matched' their existing schemas. Children who were drawing or making clay models of *semi-circles* absorbed the *semi-circular* structures in the abbey and represented 'arches'. Children who had started to represent objects from different points of view (*projective space*) represented *horizontal* statues.

As the project progressed, the professional's became increasingly skilled at predicting the aspects of environment on which certain children would focus during visits. Parents became engrossed in this aspect of their children's learning.

School visits shared by professionals and parents provided an important symbolic continuity where adults were able to refer back to shared experience. This kind of continuity is expressed most clearly in the question, 'Do you remember when?' Another important aspect of continuity lay in the different levels of reality being received by the children. For instance, sensory and motor experiences, gained during a visit to a 'helter-skelter', provided a basis for the further study of the *helix*. Scientific toys were introduced with this kind of extension in mind. Continuity is a vital component of conceptual development.

PART D

The Development of Parent and Professional Collaboration

A conceptual gulf exists between parents and professionals on issues such as play, creativity, messing about with raw materials, individuality, self-regulation, reading readiness, and so on (Tizard, Mortimore and Burchell, 1981). At the start of the Froebel project there was a conceptual gulf because of many factors, none of which were to do with 'high-handed' attitudes of staff or cognitive deficits of parents but rather to a lack of shared experiences typical of disparate groups of people who start to work together. The process of the growth of mutual understandings was central to the success of the project, although it remains difficult to document.

During initial home visits and the early days of the project, the parents treated the professionals with too much reverence because they were seen as experts on child development. In spite of this, initial interactions can best be described as tentative explorations of shared meaning. The project could be described as a physical environment in which parents and professionals worked together within a symbolic system that changed as people accommodated to the ideas, views and attitudes of other people. Initial differences became less and less important in the search for shared areas of agreement on how to help individual children.

At first the teacher concentrated mainly on interacting with the children but it became clear that it would be more economical in time, and of greater use to parents, if she focused on interactions between parent and child. As parents became more verbal they tended to be over didactic and unnatural, but this soon changed.

Throughout the two teaching years of the programme, children's interactions with adults were considered together with useful interpretations from educational and psychological literature. Information passed on to parents from a wide range of writers on education was usually prefaced by 'They say ...'. What 'they' had said provided much of the substance of daily discussions between the researcher, the teacher and parents.

There was much discussion on the importance of adult speech, particularly speech that accompanied the children's motor actions, together with the effects of those actions on materials. Adult speech support from the start was focused on what the children were doing.

Expressed formally, the interactive process was as follows:

1. Observation of children.
2. Interaction with children.
3. Analysis of outcome.
4. Shared reflection.
5. Modification of ideas.
6. More informed observation.
7. Interaction with children.
8. Analysis of outcome, and so on.

'Interactions' and 'analyses' inevitably involved some kind of theoretical assessment. Trying to establish this process required an attitude of reciprocity between professionals and non-professionals, not present at the start of the project but developed in action.

A genuine 'open-ended' type of enquiry was encouraged with everyone working together to find patterns of cognition. The parents were genuinely respected and recognized as experts on their own children in that they had had them full time from birth and therefore knew them better as individuals than anyone else. This knowledge did not include what they had in common with other children. The professionals were better equipped to initiate, to manage and to assess this aspect of the inquiry throughout.

The search for commonalities of behaviour necessarily relied on highly specific instances of behaviour. Most observations were made in the project or on visits and some were made in the home by parents. Each child had a 'home book' for the exchange of noteworthy information between home and school. Apart from the educational advantages of exchanging information, it made reading and writing both meaningful and affectively satisfying for the children. The usefulness of home observations depended on the degree to which parents became increasingly involved and informed.

Initially the project was too unfamiliar for the parents to understand what was entailed in helping with the education or research. Creative collaboration had to be carefully cultivated. Parental confidence required evidence of professional knowledge but the most important feature of the 'ongoing' collaboration was a genuine and, where possible, a clearly articulated interest in the children.

There were four main categories of parental participation (PP). These categories, with their absolute and relative frequencies, are shown in Table 3.1.

Table 3.1   Categories of parental perception

1.	No PP (no. 2,026; 38 per cent of observations). In most of these cases the parent was not present at the project when an observation was made
2.	Parent listening to, or copying, the project teacher (no. 852; 16 per cent)
3.	Parent recognizing, or trying to extend, the child's learning by making reference to content or material (no. 1,189; 22 per cent)
4.	Parent recognizing or trying to extend the child's learning with knowledge of the child's prevailing schemas (no. 1,189; 22 per cent)

Table 3.2 shows a decrease over time in the level of help described as 'listening to or copying the teacher'. During the first term, most parental help was at this level (no. 274). In the sixth term there were very few cases (no. 83). In the early days the teacher invariably initiated an interaction with a child, usually about what the child was doing. The teacher would make a comment such as 'This looks interesting, would you like to talk to me about it?' If the child continued with his or her action but remained silent the teacher would describe the actions and the perceptual results of the action. For instance, 'I see that you are squeezing that piece of clay. You can make it into different shapes, can't you?'.

Table 3.2 Frequency of different levels of parental participation over six terms

Project terms	(2)	(3)	(4)	
1	274	134	30	(438)
2	152	289	145	(586)
3	94	187	224	(505)
4	122	258	202	(582)
5	124	169	325	(618)
6	83	151	263	(497)
	(849)	(1,188)	(1,189)	(3,226)

By this simple approach the teacher was validating the action for the child and parent as well as employing a central aspect of constructivism – which is to assist the developmental route from 'action' to internalized action, which becomes thought (Piaget, 1952, Foreword, p. xi). Throughout the project the children were helped to become aware of two important aspects of learning:

1. The specific nature of the actions they were using.
2. The transformations or displacements that actions produced on objects, materials and events.

Table 3.2 also shows an increase of category-four instances (the highest level of parental participation) over six terms. There were only 30 instances in the first term. This rose to 263 cases in the sixth term. This increase reflects the success of the second aim of the project, which was to search for schemas. The parents became increasingly skilled at recognizing and extending schematic behaviour after they had been identified by the professionals.

The numbers of category-three cases do not differ systematically over the six terms. This is to be expected as 'help with content and material' is a 'common-sense' type of help typical of most adult–child interactions in home and school. This type of help probably becomes more skilled, but it is difficult to assess the level of skill. It is also difficult to convey the considerable excitement experienced by all the adults involved in the day-to-day exploration of these fundamental patterns of behaviour in the children.

Although the number of families involved in the Froebel project was small, the parents are probably typical of larger populations in inner-city areas. If this is so then the amount, level and commitment of project parents is an indication of the great source of untapped ability and energy that exists in working-class, multi-racial communities.

One term after the official end of the project the parents called a meeting in one of their homes in order to discuss how the children had settled in school. The home consisted of one room and a kitchen. Many issues were discussed at the meeting including what the children were focusing on now that they were at school and the different degrees of encouragement school staffs had given in response to offers of help from most mothers. In the main, schools were overcautious about letting the parents in. Where parents were allowed to help it was almost always with narrowly prescribed tasks.

Some of the parents were critical of the schools but in a good-natured way. One mother had astutely grasped the mechanism of a self-fulfilling prophesy. In her child's school the parents were put into a hut in the playground and were asked to make things for the school jumble sale. With such trivial occupations there was some back-biting and parental 'drop-out'. She noted humorously that the staff had taken this to be an instance of parent unreliability. She said she would be interested to see how many teachers would 'survive' the jumble-sale course.

The strength of the parents' interest and involvement can be measured by their attendance at the meeting. All mothers except one unsupported mother were present, including the Asian mothers with very little English. Three fathers who had helped in the project whenever they could also attended the meeting.

Examples of parental participation

Detailed descriptions of parental interactions with young children in early education are seldom given in the literature unless the interactions have been both highly structured and prescribed by the researcher, as in Gordon's (1971) study. The most probable reason for this is the difficulty of evaluating spontaneous interactions.

In the Oxford Pre-School Research Project (OPRP) (Bruner, 1980), interactions between adults and children were analysed for 'quality': quality of dialogue and quality of play. The criteria of evaluation were limited and general. Real dialogue was defined at a minimal level as A talks to B, B replies and A responds to B's response. Similarly, the length of a play session was taken to be an indication of quality. In spite of the generality of these criteria, the findings of the OPRP indicate the importance of the presence of parents in early education. It was found that even passive parents increased the time a child stayed with an activity and increased the likelihood of dialogue. Most adults know when they have 'struck a chord' in a child. The child's closely focused attention usually signifies that a good match has been made between an adult stimulus and some particular or general concern in the child.

Examples of the highest level of parental participation are given below to illustrate the way in which project parents used their developing knowledge of schemas to identify instances and to extend in various ways. These examples also serve as an introduction to the more detailed findings of the Froebel project in Chapters 5 and 6.

Jock's father demonstrated the *up and down* movement of the toy crane to match Jock's (2:7:7) *dynamic vertical* schema.

Lois (4:0:7) made 'traffic lights' and referred to the *sequence* in which the lights came on and what they signified. Mother reported playing the 'traffic-light' game, which consisted of the question, asked at every set of lights, 'Which one comes on next?' Lois (4:0:7) was *connecting* and naming three parts in her drawings. Her father took her to the library for a book on insects. They studied the drawings together and named the parts. The next day Lois reported to Mrs B, 'I just saw an ant'.

Shanaz (3:11:9) described a picture she had drawn as 'Big, big flowers growing up in a big, big house and the girl going down that' (pointing to a drawing of a ladder). Mrs K, who spoke very little English, understood Shanaz's powerful '*grid*' schema. Together they made a book at home that contained cut-out pictures and drawings of all the *grid-like* objects in the home.

Linda (3:6:28) walked round an *enclosure* in the park and reported to her mother, 'The ducks can't get out of there'. This led to a shared examination of various kinds of *enclosures*. The next day Linda made 'An island' and surrounded it with blue paint, which she said was 'the sea'. Linda's mother reported that she could not get her (3:9:2) past a junk-shop window because she was so absorbed by an old bed-spring. This led to an exploration of *helix* and *spiral* shapes. Linda's mother began to talk with interest about what was on the classroom walls of the school where she was a cleaner.

Brenda (3:9:16) showed her mother two straws she had interwoven, and said that the pattern was a *spiral*. Two days later she pointed out the 'pattern on a jelly mould' and said it was *spiral*. Later she drew the *spiral* 'stair case' she had seen at Kew Gardens.

Alistair's mother maintained that he really did understand the true nature of '*four*'. She said that long after Alistair (4:1:10) had eaten three biscuits he demanded the other one. When she teased him by saying he had had them all he held up four fingers. She also reported that he had an understanding of '*five*' because he had put five seats in his model boat and told her who the seats were for.

Stephen's mother reported the following instances that, in each case, she helped to develop further. Stephen (3:4:30), having examined their underground tickets, said, 'Your ticket is thick and mine is thin'. Stephen (3:5:3) standing in a bus queue, observed, 'There are three men and one lady in this queue'. Stephen (3:5:27) said, 'I like the dolls with the happy faces best'. His mother related this comment to the *semi-circle* mark he had started to use in drawing. When Stephen mistook a shoe for a handbag in a picture, his mother suggested that the source of his confusion might be related to the fact that they were both *containers*. While walking along the river bank, Stephen (whenever possible) varied his base level by, for instance, walking on top of walls. Stephen's mother knew that he had been paying attention to *height* and asked teasing questions, such as 'Who is the *tallest* now?' Stephen always referred to the *height* he was standing on.

The final example is given in greater detail to show that communication between Jack (3:11:4) and his mother demonstrated two different kinds of symbolic functioning. Jack was mainly 'enactive', his mother mainly 'ikonic'. These differences provided substance for communication between parent and professional. Bruner (1974b, pp. 314-24) uses the term 'enactive' to describe schemas that are abstractions from actions, as opposed to 'ikonic' schemas.[6]

Jack had had meningitis and his paediatrician was anxious for him to be included in the project because of underfunctioning. During the early days of the project, Jack was given concentrated help by Miss D, a third-year teaching-practice student. She was implementing the project policy of accompanying the children's actions with speech. As Jack played with a model train, the student used a range of space words in context, such as *up, under, on-top-of, over, near* and *round*. Jack's mother was very interested in this and communicated with Jack in a similar way.

The next day Jack accompanied his actions with speech. For instance, as he moved a toy car he said, 'Now it's going *straight*, now it's going *up*, now it's *going down*'. This rapid accommodation to the appropriate use of speech probably indicates the depth of his need. It may also explain the startling increase in his test scores. In two years, Jack's IQ increased from 75 to 112. His scores on the English Picture Vocabulary test increased from 91 to 126.

Although Jack's mother picked up Miss D's 'enactive' speech in the example just given, picking out these features of events did not come naturally to her. An analysis of encounters between mother and son shows an interesting mismatch that seemed to be due to her 'ikonic' view as opposed to his 'dynamic' approach to objects and events. For instance, when Jack was 3:9:12, his mother was showing him shapes and giving him the names. She said, 'This is a *circle*'. Jack replied, 'A *circle goes round*'. When she said, 'This is a *triangle*', Jack followed one of the lines with his finger and said, 'That goes *up there*'.

Jack's mother loved painting and drawing and often painted pictures for the project. Jack never painted. He spent much of his time playing action games, such as chasing and hiding (*trajectory* games).

In the following situation, which was video-taped, the mismatch between the enactive and ikonic approaches are clear, although there was some accommodation on both sides. The discussion was over features of a model farm provided by the teacher in preparation for a visit to a real farm. The interaction between mother and son can be described as 'enactive son, ikonic mum':

Mum: What are these animals called? [Request for Jack to name.]
Jack (3:11:4): The animals are *going in there* [his hand indicates the route between the animals and the enclosure].
Mum [Accommodating to Jack's reply and expanding on it]: Yes, they are *going in there* for a drink aren't they? What are they called?
Jack: They're pigs.
Mum: And what is in this little *enclosure*? [this is a request for naming and identity but his mother has recognized that Jack has a strong schematic interest in *enclosures*].
Jack: It's a lamb.

Mum looks closely at the very small model with genuine interest and asks, 'Oh, is it?' At this Jack becomes very animated. As he speaks he moves the toys about as an action illustration of what he is saying: 'Yes! You *open the gate* and *let the lambs out* and they go get a wash. They go in the water and get back'. In this example, three connected schemas are being described and enacted with gesture: *opening and shutting* (or *connecting* and *disconnecting*) *in and out* and *going through a boundary*. Mum shifts attention to another part of the farm and asks, 'Do you know who that man is?' (request for naming and identity):

Jack: He's holding those baby lambs [the man is defined in terms of what he is *doing*].
Mum: What sounds do cows make?
Jack: I don't know.
Mum [In encouraging tone]: Yes you do.
Jack [Using a *circular* hand gesture]: They go *running round the other* [the animals are defined in terms of movement].
Mum: How do they talk?
Jack [Accommodating obligingly]: They go mooing [at this point Jack gets in a quick sentence that reflects his *inside/outside* schema: '*Outside* the farm that man was'].
Mum asks: What is this lady doing? [This is her first action-based question, which is asking about the imagined movement of the farmer's wife.]
Jack: That lady's going and getting the buckets. That's her house [Jack makes a clear statement that matches the question].

Just to confuse the issue of enactive versus ikonic, which seemed fairly clear and which Jack's mother found extremely interesting, at the age of 6 Jack started to draw a great deal and became very good at it. It is difficult to know how to account for this change in emphasis.

The over-zealous parental help, already mentioned, developed into natural playful and teasing communication. An instance of this is as follows: Jack's mother asked two boys what they expected to see when they visited the zoo. The boys started a playful conspiracy of silence. 'Well,' she said casually, 'I know what we are going to see.' She allowed a suitably long pause: 'We are going to see cats and dogs'. This triggered a stream of disagreement from the boys followed by an interesting discussion on the difference between *tame* and *wild*.

Parents and professionals can help children separately or they can work together to the great benefit of the children. Parents can give practical help in classrooms (as many already do), but perhaps the greatest benefit to teachers in working with parents is the spur towards making their own pedagogy more conscious and explicit.

One of the most important outcomes of the project was that all the adults watched and listened with ever-increasing interest to what the children were saying and doing. Nothing gets under a parent's skin more quickly and more permanently than the illumination of his or her own child's behaviour. The effect of participation can be profound.

NOTES

1. Sutton-Smith (1970) suggests that trivial facts become dignified by the theoretical system into which they are woven.
2. Mrs T. Bruce, B Ed (Hons.).
3. Mariam Shera (née Abbas) now has her own nursery school in Karachi.
4. The questionnaires, with some modifications, were those used by Chazan, Laing and Jackson (1971) in their Swansea study.
5. Research respectability, until recently, has demanded strict controls against which experimental test results can be measured. The 'matched-sample' approach, however, is inappropriate for exploratory studies and is demanding on time, which can more usefully be spent in the investigation itself. There are also ethical reasons against using an underprivileged group simply for measurement purposes.

6. Explanations of ikonic modes of perception and representation are far from clear. Perception is clearly 'fed' by the surface characteristics of objects, such as colour, height, width and other 'perceptible features' (Bruner, Olver and Greenfield *et al.*, 1966, p. 169). This suggests that ikonic representations are abstractions from perception.

4

SCHEMAS FROM ACTION TO THOUGHT

GENERAL FINDINGS

Three sequences of 'repeatable behaviours' were found during the analysis of the 5,333 observations. Two sequences are documented in Chapter 5. One consists of ten graphic schemas with their 'ikonic' or 'figurative' effects. The other consists of eleven space schemas that include a shift from *topological* to *projective* space organization in representations.

The third sequence, presented in detail in Chapter 6, consists of nine 'dynamic' schemas, each sub-divided into four stages:

1. Motor actions.
2. Symbolic functioning.
3. Functional dependency relationships.
4. Thought.

Using Piaget's stage theory, each project observation was initially categorized as being at a 'motor', 'symbolic representation' or 'thought' level. Motor-level behaviour is where a child performs actions that do not appear to have representational significance even though they may have. Unless a child (by speech, product or action) made it clear that representation was present, the behaviour was coded at a motor level. Symbolic representation is defined on p. 40. 'Thought' is where a child gives a verbal account of an experience in the absence of any material or situational reminder of the original experience. For instance, if a child (after a visit) talked about events he or she had experienced on the visit, it was assumed that the child 'knew' what he or she was talking about.

Three different levels of functioning were found in relation to increasing chronological age. These three levels correspond to the three broad levels postulated by Piaget and Bruner. The frequencies of the three levels in relation to age are shown in Table 4.1. The largest number of motor-level examples occurred

Table 4.1 Differing levels of functioning

Level	No. of obs.	%
Motor action	1,107	22.8
Symbolic rep.	3,208	66.1
Thought	539	11.1
Total	4,854	100

at 3 years 1 month; symbolic representation at 4 years 1 month; and thought level at 4 years 5 months.

Symbolic representation examples consisted of three sub-divisions:

1. Graphic representations of the static states of objects (configurational or ikonic).
2. Action representations of the dynamic aspects of objects and events.
3. Speech representations of either the static or dynamic aspects of objects or events that accompanied representations of 1 and 2.

There was no significant age difference between these three sub-divisions of symbolic functioning.[1]

Although there are relatively few instances of 'thought', they are of particular interest because, in relation to every child, thought-level observations consisted of internalizations of earlier schematic concerns. Although it may seem obvious that what a child thinks and knows at any given time must reflect what has gone before – both in terms of cognitive structure and the content of experience – it was rather startling to find out how specifically the thought-level observations were related to a child's previous representations. (Examples of this continuity are given in Chapter 6.)

Piaget and Inhelder (1973, p. 51) have given theoretical guidance on this continuity between stages when they write 'The structures constructed at a given age become an integral part of the structures of the following age'. Very little evidence has been produced in support of this powerful hypothesis.

Two other groups of observations were named:

1. 'Recognition based on schematic concerns' (no. 254).
2. 'Functional dependency relationships' (no. 225).

It was initially thought that 'recognition based on schematic concerns' lay somewhere between 'motor action' and 'symbolic representation' because individual children noticed features in the environment that 'matched' prevailing schemas.[2] For instance, when Jock was struggling to draw *grids* he consistently pointed out *grid-like* structures in the environment. However, 'recognition' was found to be part of general assimilation. The children were spontaneously 'fleshing out' prevailing schemas by 'matching' environmental events to them. Observations in this category did not reveal an age or stage pattern in schematic development but were spread randomly over all ages as children acquired new schemas.

The category of *'functional dependency relationships'* is an important project finding because, although Piaget *et al.* (1968) have written a full-length book, *Epistémologie et Psychologie de la fonction*, the category has not been verified in observational studies.[3]

'Functional dependency relationships' immediately precede conservation. Before thought becomes reversible the child's thinking proceeds by *'functions'* in the modern sense of *'mappings'*. One-way mappings is where a function is treated as a mapping of one set into another. If there are two variables, *Y* and *X*, then a one-way mapping can be expressed as *Y* is a *function* of *X* ($Y = F(X)$).

In early education, *'functional dependency relationships'* are manifest when children observe the effects of action on objects or material. For example, *functional dependency* (FD) effects understood by project children are:

- the distance of a ball depends on the power of the throw;
- high and low notes are FD on the position of fingers on a guitar fretboard;
- getting to a higher level is FD on increasing the height of the base-line;
- melting wax is FD on heat; and
- the height of a typist's chair and the length of a fishing-line are FD on rotation.

Piaget *et al.* (1968c) gives an example of the route from functional dependencies to conservation as follows. While *rolling out* a piece of clay a child notices that the *length* of the clay is FD on his or her *rolling action*. He or she will then observe that length increases as width decreases and that both length and width are FD on his or her action of rolling.

In this example, variation in width is compensated for by variation in length. Both can be reversed or cancelled, at first on an action level by transforming the clay, and later at an operational *conservation* level. Piaget describes the single functional dependency relation (a one-way mapping) as *semi-logic* (Inhelder, Sinclair and Bovet, 1974, p. 9).

Functional dependencies not only herald imminent conservation but demonstrate continuity with earlier stages. They arise from the application of earlier schematic behaviours to environmental events. They develop from the sensory and perceptual information accompanying motor actions and lead to true operations that can be carried out in the mind.

Piaget *et al.* (1968) make a large, general claim for the importance of FD relationships when they write (p. 199) 'Function appears to us more and more as the common source of operations and causality'. This suggests that such relationships have a healthy future in the primary-school curriculum. In the Froebel project findings, the category of 'functional dependency' relationships is presented as a sub-division of 'thought level' examples. Both are illustrated in detail in Chapter 6.

One detailed 'thought level' will be given at this point to try to bridge the gap between the rather bare information on frequencies of occurrence and the real substance of examples as they were gathered during the project.

Lois (4:7:7) was tape-recorded having a conversation with the Urdu-speaking student who helped with the project on a regular basis. Every schema included in this thought-level example had been used by Lois at an earlier stage level. (Other examples showing developmental continuity are given in Chapter 6.) The internalized action displacements, described by Lois, are in relation to her pet cat, Polly, and later, a dog. The whole conversation is reproduced except for some repetitive sentences. During the discussion, Lois used 530 words, Mariam 152.

Mariam: What does she [Polly the cat] do then?

Lois: She don't do nothing. She won't go outside any more. Every time you leave the door open, she going out. She'll come back in. She'll run upstairs and go to bed cos she's scared of ... she won't even go out there.

Mariam: Does that mean she plays with you more?

Lois: Yea, and she plays with all the other cats but she doesn't like cats. She runs upstairs but she don't go out any more, she stays indoors, so that's why we don't let her go out but she's very naughty really. She goes in the bin and if there's a leg of bone in there, all raggy, she goes in the bin and takes it out in her mouth and puts it on the floor and leaves it there and goes in my room and goes to sleep.

Mariam: Oh dear! That's naughty. I bet mummy doesn't like that?

Lois: No, we chuck her out. We just throw her out and bang the door quickly.

Mariam: Does she take the bone out with her?

Lois: What? No, she left it indoors.

Mariam: That's just like a dog, isn't it?

Lois: Yea, dogs do that sometime. Jack's got a dog.

Mariam: Has he?

Lois: Yea, and it's called Glenda, and it's all yellow and sometimes she goes out in the garden and she lays on the floor and you actually stroke her tummy sometimes. She's a girl.

Mariam: Is she?

Lois: Polly's a girl too. One day we took Polly up Nanny's place and Glenda was there.

Mariam: How did they get on? Did they fight?

Lois: No, he did bark sometimes but see we hadded a lead so we clipped it on there and she hadded a lead and a collar so we put the collar on, clipted the lead on and tied her up so she couldn't get away. Jack took Glenda home so we had to let Polly run around ... cats are nice really so are dogs.

Mariam: That's true, we've got two dogs at home.

Lois: Nanny's got a dog too. Guess what his name is? It's Whisky ... Whisky! Guess what he does to me when he comes in the gate? He jumps over me and knocks me over.

Mariam: Does he really? Is he a big dog?

Lois: No, he's about that size. I shut the gate now. I don't let him come in.

Mariam: Don't you?

Lois: No, I shut the door and go indoors, but I still let it in sometimes though, not most of the time. Guess what Whisky does to Jock? Unless I'm playing with him or joking, he bites me.

Mariam: Does he? That's rather naughty, isn't it?

Lois: Yea, so I shut the gate and leave him out and you know those bushes? Well, he comes through there, through a tree and he can come from Nanny's place.

Mariam: And what happened?

Lois: Well, he knocked me over but I letted him out but Polly, Polly's always running away from us, she keeps running away.

Mariam: Does she come back?

Lois: Yes but Polly ... well! When dogs come along and she runs away but cats that are

black she runs away. [The meaning of this is not clear: the pause suggested that she
was searching for the words 'from them'.]

Mariam: Does she run away and hide? Where does she hide? Do you know her favourite
hiding place?

Lois: Yea, she hided into a bushes.

Mariam: Does she really?

Lois: A little tree by our window, she hided in there and she got a gate so she bends that
on her. I bang in on her and in case the cat can't get her, but her does and she comes
along and when I open the door when I come home, she comes in, she's nalf [not half]
nosy. When I go 'pss pss' she kisses me like that.

(The last comments are less well organized than the rest of the conversation,
probably because Lois was tired as a result of such a sustained communication at
a *'thought'* and speech level.)

The general structure and dynamics of the conversation show that Lois has
internalized certain spatial notions. Moving, living objects (cats and dogs) move
about in a three-dimensional world of different kinds of spaces that are now
understood to be related. The *trajectories* of the cat and the dog link up these
spaces. In earlier examples, Lois's own *transporting* behaviour linked various
spaces at a motor level.

Lois now understands that movements can be defined in terms of *direction*.
Spaces are also known to be *separate* but *connected*. She knows that cats and
dogs *go through* doors and gates and *through* trees via branches. They *go through*
boundaries in order to *get into enveloping* spaces, such as the 'house' or the
'dustbin'. They can get into spaces where they can hide. They can climb trees and
stairs in *vertical directions*. They can move *horizontally* or *straight ahead* as on a
walk to Nanny's. They can *reverse* their direction in order to find the way home.
She knows there is a relationship between a *container* and the *contained*. The
'dustbin' *contains* bones. She knows there is a rule attached to this particular
container in that the dog must not take rubbish out of the bin. She knows that a
dog can knock a person down from a *vertical position* into a *horizontal position*.
She can mentally change Polly's position from *upright* to *upside-down*. She can
mentally construct tickling her tummy while she is lying on her back.

As well as *going through* boundaries she can mentally construct *going round*
boundaries as in the case of a collar around the dog's neck. She can mentally
connect one thing with another, as when she puts the dog on a lead.

This conversation was held in the absence of any concrete reminder of the
events being talked about. In other words, all her earlier action displacements at a
motor level and all her earlier representations that required material aids are now
the co-ordinated structures of her thought to which her experienced objects and
events have been assimilated.

Mariam adopted the role of a quiet, interested listener who made pertinent but
short comments and asked genuine questions. This maximized Lois's
contribution to the conversation. This approach would not have been appropriate
at an earlier motor level. Adult speech, meaningfully linked with a child's
actions, helps 'action' to become symbolic. Symbolic functioning detaches
'thought' from 'action' (Piaget and Inhelder, 1969). Sigel (1970) calls this process

'distancing'. Other 'props' are also required for symbolic functioning, such as paint, clay, wood, dressing-up clothes, and so on. In the example above, Mariam is helping Lois to reflect on the events that are being communicated through speech. Before this could happen Lois must have acquired the appropriate speech.

It would seem that the role of the adult should change from providing a great deal of speech to accompany children's early actions to being more of an interested and active listener when the child is able and wants to talk. Ideally, if adults could recognize and give verbal support to new behaviours or thought patterns as they appear, this would ensure that language and thought would develop simultaneously and in co-ordination with each other. The glee shown by the younger children when adults gave running commentaries on their actions would indicate that this was a welcome and appropriate form of adult support.

PROJECT RESULTS ON THE RELATIONSHIP BETWEEN SPEECH AND SCHEMAS

Of the 5,333 observations made during the project, 1,490 (28 per cent) did not involve speech. There were, however, relatively few 'symbolic representations' that were unaccompanied by speech. This indicates that, given the opportunity, children like to talk about what they are doing or what they have done.

Of the observations, 1,279 (24 per cent) could not be related to schematic concerns. There were 114 (2.1 per cent) instances of speech recognition but no speech used. There were also 'where', 'why' and 'what' questions and 'executive' speech (telling other people what to do), and speech used to attract attention.

Speech Use and Graphic Representation

Of the observations, 1,319 (25 per cent) were classified within this general category. These were sub-divided into 'form' (schemas), 'naming' and 'content'. If, for instance, a child drew a *grid* and named it 'milk-crate' then the observation would be categorized as 'naming' 'content' that had been assimilated to the schema *'grid'* and had been represented graphically.

Drawing is one way of symbolically representing the relationship between form and content; speech is another. Drawing is 'isomorphic' (it has a configurational equivalence) with the shapes of objects. Speech does not resemble objects and events, it is arbitrary, except in the limited case of onomatopoeia. In the analysis of observations, a word such as 'milk-crate' was assumed to mean content conveyed in the normal use of the word. Form is best illustrated with many examples (as given in Chapter 5) where form is invariant and content differs.

Taking the group as a whole, there was a close correspondence and continuity in the relationship between speech use and schematic development. The following observations from one child on the relationships between speech and schemas support the 'cognition hypothesis of language acquisition' (Cromer, 1979). The name given to the schema is given in brackets followed by the age of the child. The age is followed by the speech that accompanied the representation. As will be seen, naming reflects both the 'form' of the schema and 'content'.

(*Grid*) (3:7:13): See-saw.
(*Two circles joined with a horizontal line*) (3:7:13): Two headlights.
(*A downward arc*) (3:8:19): A bridge.
(*Core and radial*) (3:9.10): A spider.
(*Zig-zag*) (4:0:11): Stairs.
(*A downward arc*) (4:0:11): A tunnel.
(*Two connected arcs*) (4:0:11): A camel's humps.
(*Core and radial*) (4:0:14): An octopus.
(*Two circles*) (4:0:14): These are wheels on a bike.
(*Three rectangles connected*, forming a horizontal line) (4:1:19): These are train windows.
(*A small rectangle* placed '*on-top-of*' a *large rectangle*) (4:2:19): This is a house with a chimney on top.
[The last two examples also illustrate topological space notions of *connection* and *on-top-of*.]
(*A spiral (helix)*) (4:3:19): It's a spiral staircase [after visiting Kew Gardens].
(*A circle*) (4:3:20): This is a toilet.
(A three-dimensional *grid on-top-of* a cylinder) (4:4:5): This a windmill [This was a working model and will be considered further when 'functional dependency' relationships rising out of schemas are discussed].
(*A horizontal line* with *arcs connected underneath*) (4:4:28): This is a clothes line.

Illustrations used in Chapter 5 will make the relationship between speech and graphic schemas clearer.

Speech Use and Action Representation

After graphic representation the next most frequent speech was used to express 'actions and the displacement of objects' (1,072 observations; 20 per cent of all observations). These action schemas are illustrated in detail in Chapter 6 under specific 'actions' and 'displacements'.

At a motor level there was an interest in objects that moved *vertically*, *horizontally* or in various other directions. These movement features were central to later symbolic representations. (They are also central to children's early writing. This will be illustrated in Chapters 6, 7 and 8.) Examples:

(*Dynamic vertical*) (3:3:21): London Bridge is falling down.
(*Dynamic vertical*) (3:6:2): You pour milk all over it.
(*Rotation*) (4:0:6) [Using a hoop as a signifier of a driving wheel]: I'm driving the bus on my holidays [she was aware that the direction of the bus was functionally dependent on the direction in which the wheel was turned].
(*Dynamic vertical*) (4:1:6) [Referring to an owl]: When he stops flying his wings go down.
(*Dynamic vertical*) (4:1:19) Whales jump.
(*Dynamic vertical*) (4:3:29) [Referring to a tape recorder]: I've turned this off and on [off and on functionally dependent upon up and down of switch].
(*Dynamic vertical*) (4:4:18) [After drawing three, connected semi-circles named it]: A bouncing ball.

Speech and Concepts

Of the observations, 526 (10 per cent) showed a close relationship between speech and concepts. These concepts included *number, size, time, fractions, distance, class* and *ordered series*.

> Brenda (4:8:18) [While investigating the relationship between an object, the distance of a light and a shadow]: Put the light nearer.
> Salam (4:2:11) [About the water in the sink]: It goes higher and higher.
> Stephen (4:8:7): There are five bricks down one side and five bricks down the other that makes it even.
> Clare (3:7:30): A giraffe has a long neck. A rabbit has long ears.
> Lois (3:4:20): This is a fruit bowl where all the fruit goes. This is an apple and a banana.
> Lois (4:1:19) [About the tortoise in the Natural History Museum]: I don't think it was real was it? It was stuffed.
> Lois (4:1:19): Sea-lions go in the water like dolphins ... A hippopotamus lives in the water.

Derrick (1977) reviewed the literature on how parents assist their children's speech development. It was found that parents seldom expand their children's utterances from a grammatical point of view. They focus almost entirely on meaning and attempt to expand that (*ibid.* p. 19).

Speech help related to schemas resembles help in logic. Inhelder and Piaget (1964) point out that the 'intension' of a class consists of the features that define the class. For instance, the class property of a container is that it contains. Adults help children to extend or 'flesh out' classes by providing instances that help the children to make distinctions within the class. For instance, if a child holds something up and says 'A box', the adult is likely to say, 'Yes, that is a box for chocolates'. The child's classification is validated and the *class of containers* is extended (*ibid.* pp. 44–6).

The highest level of adult help in the Froebel project was where the children's speech was extended in relation to their schematic concerns.

ENRICHMENT, EXTENSION AND CATEGORIES OF 'AFFECT'

Usually, when teachers respond to positive or negative affect in children, they are interested in accompanying cognition. Piaget (1968b, p. 33) writes: 'Affectivity and intellectual functions are two indissociable aspects of every action. In all behaviour the motives and energising dynamisms reveal affectivity while the techniques and adjustment of the means employed, constitute the cognitive, sensorimotor, or rational aspect'.

Indissociable though they may be, until relatively recently, cognition and affect (emotion) have been studied separately.[4] Only in a few studies of 'play' and 'humour' are cognition and affect considered simultaneously (Chapman and Foot, 1977). This is in spite of wide agreement in psychological literature that 'playfulness' signifies knowledge that is so well assimilated that it can be played with (Athey, 1977).[5] One of the pedagogical implications of this view of affective functioning is that enrichment and extension are likely to lead to greater success than teaching aimed at acceleration from diagnosed deficits. Most training experiments designed to speed up forms of thought have not succeeded (Tamburrini, 1982).

In the Froebel project it was initially intended to record relationships between different kinds of affective response and diagnosed schemas. This proved to be too difficult. Even had it been possible to co-ordinate schemas with degrees of affect, the information would have been too fragmented to show pattern.

These relationships are within everybody's personal experiences in that new knowledge is associated with struggle and well-assimilated knowledge is usually accompanied by feelings of confidence (competence generates confidence). Systematic evidence is only likely to be found in studies where the 'forms' of thought are already known.

In pursuing the first aim of the project (see p. 49), seven categories of affect were applied to each of the 5,333 observations that constituted project data (Table 4.2). The seven categories illustrate different positions on Piaget's 'functional invariants' model of cognitive functioning. In the list in Table 4.2, a description of each category is given, followed by the absolute frequency (AF), the relative frequency (RF) (given in percentages) and the rank (R) of each category, with the highest rank being first.

Table 4.2 Categories of affect

Category of affect	AF	RF %	R
Absorbed, focused attention	4,018	75.3	1
Surprise perturbation, struggle	487	9.1	2
Affective accompaniment not noted	387	7.2	3
Play manner or delight	189	3.5	4
Tired response	109	2.0	5
Humour	104	1.9	6
Extreme disturbance	39	.7	7
Total	5,333		

A combination of the first two categories shows that over 80 per cent of the children's affective responses were accommodatory (surprise, perturbation, struggle, absorbed or focused attention). One possible explanation is that the stimulating environment of the project generated struggle. Indirect evidence for this could be found in parents' reports of how tired and sometimes bad-tempered their children were in the afternoon until they had rested. The finding that there were only 293 instances of playfulness and humour came as a surprise because the focus of the professionals in the project was on assimilatory functioning.

In the following illustrations (Chapter 5) of each of the categories, an attempt has been made to illustrate simultaneously 'affect' and 'cognitive structure'. By definition there are no examples where the type of affect was not recorded. No specific examples will be given of 'tired response' as most of these behaviours were typical of earlier levels of affective development – pushing, poking, biting, and so on. Examples in this category were jokingly referred to as 'skid-row'.

NOTES

1. This finding supports Piaget's stage-level theory in that he maintains that the three types of symbolic functioning emerge simultaneously from sensorimotor functioning.

2. Piaget and Inhelder (1969, p. 7) point out that sensorimotor and perceptual assimilations precede real symbolic functioning. Action schemas relate signifiers in the environment with what is signified (putting a coat on signifies taking a walk). A perceptual assimilation (recognition) signifies meaning of a kind, but is best thought of as an 'indicator'. Recognition implies a match between a given object and a schema ready to assimilate it but recognition is, at first, only a particular instance of assimilation in that the thing recognized stimulates and feeds a sensorimotor schema. True assimilation is detached from immediate perceptual activity (Piaget, 1959, p. 6).

3. The book has not been translated into English. It was translated for the project by D. Brearley.

4. Even in the influential *Taxonomy of Educational Objectives* by Bloom, Krathwohl and Masia, *The Cognitive Domain* (Vol. 1, 1956) and *The Affective Domain* (Vol. 2, 1964) were considered separately and published eight years apart.

5. Chukovsky (1966, p. 103) subscribes to this high status of play and humour when he writes that 'the child has become so sure of truths that he can even play with them'. Huizinga (1949) took the same view when he suggested that the upper levels of civilization can be defined in terms of playfulness.

5

FROM MARKS TO MEANINGS: THE LANGUAGE OF LINES

Graphic ability, judged by whatever standard, will not develop unless the individual is in a social and educational setting which places considerable importance on drawing according to that standard.

(Harris, 1963, p. 235)

INTRODUCTION

In Chapter 2 it was suggested that there may be two kinds of cognitive patterning evolving from early action and early perception. When the general findings, given in Chapter 4, were analysed in detail, two kinds of representation corresponding to early action, on the one hand, and early perception on the other were found. Dynamic thought patterns, emerging from action, provide the substance of Chapter 6. Figural representation that appears to have developmental links with early perception are discussed and illustrated in this chapter. The materials of representation include drawing, brick constructions, clay and scrap-material models. The following few examples will help to establish a difference between the figural representations of this chapter and the action representations of Chapter 6.

Lois (4:0:9) made 'a pavement' with square mats and 'an aeroplane' with two pieces of wood stuck together. She would not be parted from a wooden tortoise. Soon afterwards she drew a *core-and-radial* pattern she named 'spider'.

Amanda (4:1:3) made a three-dimensional *grid* and named it 'scaffolding'. Although she described the actions she performed on the scaffolding (to be discussed in the next chapter), the *grid* represented the static configuration of the scaffolding.

Lois (4:1:8) drew *zig-zag lines* she named 'stairs'. She drew *circles* she named 'wheels'. She then drew small *open curves* that were called 'tunnels' and a *rectangle* she named 'This is a window with a curtain across'.

In each of these cases there is a correspondence or an equivalence between a graphic schema (*grid*, *core-and-radial*, *zig-zag lines*, *circles* and *semi-circles*) and experienced environmental content. Amanda's assimilated environmental content consists of 'scaffolding', 'spider', 'stairs', 'tunnels', 'pavement' and 'window'.

Of the 5,333 observations collected during the project, 46 per cent consisted of drawings, paintings and three-dimensional constructions. All observations were included in the analysis except where several drawings were virtually identical. Jock (2:2:1), for instance, produced 30 drawings in one morning when he was struggling to combine a vertical and horizontal line. In such cases only one drawing was included in the analysis. If a child repeatedly used the same graphic form and named them all the same (for instance, ten *grids* all named 'ladder'), only one example would be included. If the same form was used but named differently, all the drawings would be included.

Twenty-four marks were distinguishable from each other. To aid analysis the marks were sub-divided within two criteria – *straight lines* and *curves*. They were also sub-divided into 11 *space orders*, some of which are of more theoretical interest than others.

The three continua (with frequencies of occurrence) that are illustrated and discussed in this chapter are as follows:

Lines	*No.*
1. Vertical scribble (the effects of vertical action of the hand)	254
2. Horizontal scribble	80
3. Continuous horizontal and vertical scribble	97
4. Horizontal and vertical differentiated scribble	70
5. Open-continuous triangle	92
6. Horizontal line	36
7. Vertical line	49
8. Straight parallel lines	42
9. Grid	177
10. Stripes	90
11. Triangle	52
12. Rectangle	205
13. Right angle	45
14. Two right angles	48
Total number of observations	1,337

Curves	*No.*
1. Circular scribble	254
2. Circular enclosure, or core and radial	385
3. Oval	17
4. Enclosed curve with or without corners	75
5. Closed semi-circle	119
6. Open semi-circle	200
7. Helix	19
8. Plane spiral	14
9. Concentric circles	46
10. Multiple loop	17
Total	1,146

The following space orders were categorized in terms of space relations between things represented. If hair was placed *on-top-of* a head in a drawing it would be placed in a category described as *vertical order between elements*.

The following space order schemas, given with their frequency of occurrence, are systematically related to increases in age.

Space orders	*No.*
1. Proximity between marks	1,477
2. Vertical order of elements within figure	155
3. Horizontal order of elements within figure	41
4. Grid order within figure or within enclosure	143
5. Grid order inside and outside discrete figure	202
6. Proximity between figures but no order	114
7. Vertical order between figures	74
8. Horizontal order between figures	135
9. Grid order between figures	39
10. Projective space. Representative of 'in front of' or 'behind'	44
11. Representation of figures in different positions	56
Total	2,480

THE DEVELOPMENT OF DRAWING

As already discussed in Chapter 4, the sequences of representation presented here should not be viewed as scales typical of larger populations because the collection of data was influenced by increasing professional insights. There is little doubt that drawing development is sequential and it may be that the sequences are as listed in *lines, curves* and *space orders*. What cannot be generalized are the ages at which schemas appear, because symbolic functioning occurs earlier in conditions of privilege.

A careful study of the literature on drawing shows that there is a lack of firm research evidence on invariant sequences of drawing behaviour. Normative studies on large groups of children have shown that children typically produce marks and shapes at different ages. These are of limited use in the developmental assessment of individual children for the following reasons:

1. The norms are usually given in widely spaced time intervals such as years or half years.
2. In the interests of standardization, norms are usually arrived at by asking children to copy a standard (copying does not reflect spontaneous development).
3. Individual meanings attributed to spontaneous 'mark-making' are not considered in normative studies.

A typical norm is as follows: 'Child (2:6) imitates horizontal and vertical strokes' (Gesell, 1971, p. 330). While of some use in comparing children of very different abilities, norms do not illuminate important features of spontaneous development.

Kellogg (1968, 1969), who studied the drawings of young children from 30 different countries over a period of 18 years, is thought by many to have described a developmental sequence in drawing. She describes (1968, p. 1) her own broad findings as follows:

> Early drawing evolves out of scribbling and proceeds according to a developmental sequence scale. Regardless of ethnic, geographical and cultural influences, young children the world over make identical scribblings between the ages of two and five years.... The various scribbled forms occur in definite sequence, according to maturational levels, and therefore they should be viewed as products of biological behavior, rather than of culturally learned behavior.

Kellogg was in a powerful position to document the developmental sequence claimed above because she was the first researcher to study thousands of scribblings (starting with 2-year-olds) collected at the Golden Gate Nursery School in San Francisco. As a result of her time-consuming analysis, she identified 20 basic scribbles and demonstrated the universality of basic graphic forms in different cultures and at different times. What she did not show was a developmental sequence in which the 20 basic scribbles emerged. This was because she became increasingly absorbed in pursuing logical rather than developmental complexity; because she was defeated in her attempts to establish a developmental sequence in children's drawing by problems of measurement; and because she did not believe in talking with children about their drawings.

Kellogg is firm with teachers on this last issue: 'No questions need be asked ... comments can be restricted to such constructive ones like "very interesting", "nice colors", "I like that", "good work", "a nice scribble", "pretty"' and so on. (Kellogg, 1969, p. 156). Kellogg warned teachers on the dangers of accelerating children out of their biological art stage. Unfortunately these warnings became generally associated with adults talking to children about their art. There is now evidence that children who function well are those who are talked with, and one of the most satisfying topics for young children is what they are doing. This is not simply affectively satisfying, it also facilitates cognition: 'young children enjoy discussing their art work as they are in the process of creation and cognitive growth is assisted by the integration of language and motor processes' (Mann and Taylor, 1973, pp. 36-7).[1] Being interested in the representation of content was frowned upon as much as talking with children. Kellogg hardly considered the content of children's drawings so taken up was she with form.[2]

Lowenfeld (1957) also warns against adult attempts to accelerate graphic representation: He writes (p. 87): 'While a baby is still in the state of disordered scribbling, drawing a picture of something "real" is inconceivable. Such attempts would be similar to trying to teach a babbling baby to pronounce words correctly or to use them in sentences'. Many writers since Stern (1924) have used the analogy between scribbling and babbling. Without talking with children there is little information on whether children are investing their marks with meaning. The shift from 'motor' to 'symbolic' functioning is clearest when children describe the content they are expressing through marks.

What is left out of the scribbling and babbling analogy is extension. Good parents babble back to their infants. This has been found to increase the frequency of babbling (Dodd, 1972). Also, most good parents recognize that babblings have meanings. However, parents do not usually scribble with their children nor do they validate scribbles sufficiently.[3]

Kellogg and Lowenfeld view intervention as pushing a child on towards a future stage of development. They seemed not to consider intervention aimed at extending and enriching an existing stage ('match'). This is the kind of intervention used in the Froebel project and it was quite clear that the children thrived on this kind of adult verbal participation.

CONTENT AND FORM IN CHILDREN'S DRAWING

Eng (1959, first published in 1939) carried out a detailed developmental study of her niece, Margaret. It is interesting to compare her work with Kellogg's in that she paid great attention to 'content' at the expense of 'form'. Margaret drew her first mark, a vertical line, at 10 months but Eng was so influenced by the movement for free and spontaneous art where 'The history of graphic art is hidden in a scribble' (*ibid*. p. 19) that she attributed no importance to the line and waited for a scribble before she began to record progress systematically.[4]

Because Eng illustrated, wrote about and meticulously recorded background information, the drawings are still valuable to present-day readers. Her interpretations, reflecting the theories of the day, have been superseded but the drawings can be re-interpreted in the light of current theory. Eng was working with theories mainly concerned with individual differences rather than with the search for cognitive constants and, consequently, she did not document similarities of graphic form. She was particularly interested in changes in content, especially where they seemed to be related to emotional or moral issues. For instance, when Margaret draws 'jagged teeth' Eng speculates on why she is feeling aggressive. She does not point out that 'jagged teeth', 'stairs' and many other types of content are drawn with a common *zig-zag* form. Similarly, she does not point out that several drawings ('family on a sledge', 'a sitting figure' and 'an old fashioned letter F') are ways of using a newly acquired mark that resembles a *semi-circle*.

This is an important issue because focusing on 'content' at the expense of 'form' can lead to the conclusion that young children 'flit' from one theme to another and that they are unsystematic or even idiosyncratic. In fact, Margaret shows systematic experimentation of disparate content that can be expressed within particular forms, particularly as they appear in development.

One of the uncharted areas of early cognitive functioning is children's own search for commonalities. While it is true that children often name a drawing as one thing and then change it to another, it is also true that, more often than not, there is a common form underlying differences in content. In the Froebel project, for instance, it was observed that if a drawing was named 'wheel' at one time, followed by 'flower', it was because the child was representing those, and other objects, with a particular graphic form, such as a *circular enclosure*.

Thus, paying too much attention to content can prevent the perception of similarities of form. One project child, for instance, drew lots of 'apples' and 'clocks'. A teacher, focusing on content, might decide to develop a topic on either apples or clocks. If the teacher perceived, however, that the 'apples' had *radials connected* to the *outside* of the *enclosure* and that the 'clocks' had *radials connected* to the *inside* of the *enclosure* a different kind of provision might suggest itself, such as objects and creatures with a *core-and-radial* configuration. The extension of form rather than content is not yet widely adopted in early education.

TOPOLOGICAL SPACE NOTIONS

Before presenting the developmental sequences of *lines*, *curves* and *space orders*, we discuss five topological space concepts as early 'mark-making' takes place within these notions. In order to focus on the space aspects, 'content' will be kept constant. Drawings and models of 'faces' will be used to illustrate a topological space sequence. Although these particular space notions have received some attention in the literature they have not been employed in empirical studies.

Drawing and spatial organization appear to be closely related to earlier stages of perception. Goodenough, the originator of the 'draw-a-man' test, suggested, in extremely tentative terms, that 'Possibly in depicting a concept by drawing, the progression is the same as that observed by perception, from undifferentiated whole, to partial differentiation, to more complete differentiation' (cited by Harris, 1963, p. 202).

Most teachers who have taught intellectually impoverished children will know that their drawings are usually poor, stereotyped and undifferentiated. If children of 7 years, for instance, are still representing 'tree' by a lollipop form (*core* with *one* or *two radials*) it probably means that earlier perception has not been sufficiently well cultivated.

Bower (1977a) has demonstrated clearly defined stages in the development of perception during the first year and has suggested that each stage needs to be 'fed' with appropriate stimuli. He shows that under the age of 3 months infants respond as readily to the parts as to the whole of a stimulus. After this age, infants need a whole pattern. There is evidence that the whole face pattern begins to be perceived at about 3 months. By 5 months a face pattern must include a mouth if a smile is to be elicited. By eight months a baby can respond to subtle indicators of mood on adult faces (*ibid*. p. 79).

Bower (*ibid*.) cites Ahrens (1954), who illustrates a 'match' between stimulus and response at different stages of perception. These stages are shown in Figure 2.1. It is well known that infants at Ahrens' final stage begin to distinguish between faces sufficiently well to refuse to go to strangers. Six-month-old infants can also discriminate between different geometric forms (Ling, 1941, cited in Ruff, 1978, p. 294).

The representations of the Froebel project children followed a similar sequence to early perception. Individual marks, such as lines and dabs, were drawn within simple spatial organizations before aggregates or combinations of marks appeared. Only from the age of 4 did some children begin to draw two differentiated persons. This corresponds to the last stage of perception in Figure 2.1, where the 30-week-old infant differentiates between individual faces.

Lois (4:1:12) drew 'Two bears. The polar bear in the water has a sad face [Figure 5.1]. This bear has a happy face' (Figure 5.2). Here the differentiation between two 'face' configurations ('happy' and 'sad') was based on 'good' and 'bad' form. In other words, she knew that her marks inside the enclosure labelled 'sad face' were not correctly ordered topologically. The bear with a happy face has the 'eyes', 'nose' and 'mouth' *spatially ordered within the enclosure* although the whole figure is not yet represented in a vertical position.

After children managed to order features within enclosures and between elements in a drawing they sometimes temporarily lost the order. Lois (3:3:22), for instance, painted 'Mrs Bruce'. Instead of putting 'hair' *on-top-of* the head enclosure, she put it *underneath* so that it looked like a beard (Figure 5.3). Similarly, at 3:7:14, she put hair *on-top-of* instead of *underneath* a hat on a model (Figure 5.4). In both the above instances, on realizing what she had done, she laughed. As she looked at her model she said, 'Oh! His hair is on top of his hat'.

This example highlights a difference between 'perception' and 'representation'. Lois has 'known', on a perceptual level (since infancy), that hair is *on-top-of* the head. Now she is learning this on a representational level. In the above examples the spatial relationship is not quite stable. Bower (1974, pp. 205-8) has pointed out that behaviours recur at different levels of development and that what is learned at one level has to be 're-worked' at higher levels.

Lois differentiated between two people in three dimensions before she did so in drawing. Two early clay models were described as 'The man has a flat head and the lady has a round head'. This, and many other examples, show a growing awareness of the use of geometric form in representation. Later, Lois used headwear stuck *on-top-of* models to differentiate between 'king' and 'queen', 'man' and 'woman', and so on.

TOPOLOGICAL SPACE AND REPRESENTATION

Here we discuss one drawing from a project child to introduce topological space orders. Graphic schemas will be discussed later. Randolph (4:4:2) named his drawing 'Boy's skipping. He's happy. He's sad' (Figure 5.5). The spatial orders he uses are as follows:

Proximity The features of the face are near each other.
Enclosure Features of 'faces' are enclosed as are 'buttons' within 'body' shapes.
Connection The head, arms and legs are connected to the body.
Separation Different parts of the body are separated from each other.
Horizontal and vertical co-ordinates The features and all parts of each body are organized within an internalized system of horizontal and vertical co-ordinates.

Graphic schemas used to represent content are as follows: *dabs* (eyes), *circle* (nose and buttons), *horizontal lines* (arms), *vertical lines* (legs), *downward curve* (sad expression, skipping-rope and eyebrows), *upward curve* (smile), *rectangle* (body).

Randolph progressed systematically through marks and spatial orders. He first made *dabs* and *scribbles* and then began to *enclose* them. He advanced to *circular enclosures*, *enclosures* with *radials attached* and *enclosures* with *ordered marks* within. *Order* became increasingly elaborate. In Figure 5.5, for instance, *rectangular* bodies are placed *underneath circle* faces and *vertical-line* 'legs' are placed *underneath* heads and bodies. His developing repertoire of marks and spatial orders were not confined to the representation of people. Drawings, clay models and scrap-material models included plants, people sitting on chairs, mincers, spectacles, aeroplanes, letters, people at the pictures, and so on.

Proximity

Bower (1977a) has shown that *proximity* is the earliest perceived topological space relationship (first-stage stimuli of dots and angles). Piaget and Inhelder (1956, p. 450) write that 'Proximity is to space what resemblance is to logical classification'. At first, marks are *heaped together* rather like the heaps made by toddlers at the end of *transporting*. Resemblance between things in the heap is 'transportability' or 'I put them there'.

Proximity may be the earliest spatial organization used in representation in that marks and objects are placed *next to* each other at a very early age. However, determining *proximity* in drawing, model-making and brick play is difficult because there is little indication (before 'content' makes it clear) as to whether *nearness* is simply fortuitous. For this reason, *enclosure* was the earliest space order that could be meaningfully classified in the project children's representations.

Enclosure

In Bower's (1977a) experiments, positive affective responses were taken as indices of 'match'. Infants began to respond positively when marks were placed near each other. By 10 months they required a 'mouth' and 'eyebrow' configuration (*horizontal lines*) before showing pleasure. Later positive responses depended on partial and then complete enclosure of marks.

All the topological space notions that provoked interest in infants were featured in project representations. It is an interesting thought that if project infant, Jim, had been one of Bower's babies, he would have been excited by a stimulus of *dabs* and *horizontal lines* inside an *enclosure*, while his brother Alistair (3:1:11) was using those equivalent elements and space orders for representing 'Two eyes and a mouth' (Figure 5.6). In common with other children starting to *enclose*, he has not managed to get the 'mouth' (a pipe-cleaner) *inside* the clay *enclosure*. Similarly in two dimensions, Susan, at a similar age (3:1:6) (Figure 5.7), has not quite managed to get her *horizontal line* 'mouth' *inside* her 'face' *enclosure*. At 3:1:6, however, she has managed to *enclose dabs* in her representation of 'stone' (Figure 5.8).

The failure to *enclose* the 'mouth' is probably due to the fact that '*line*' does not yet entail the Euclidean notion of length. The length of line, therefore, would not be judged as equivalent to the breadth of the enclosure.

Horizontal and Vertical Co-ordinates

After *proximity* and *enclosure*, the third topological space relationship generating perceptual interest in infants is '*horizontal and vertical co-ordinates*'. In order to stimulate a 6-month-old, a 'face' must have two eyes above a nose and a mouth below the nose and eyes. In other words, the form must consist of *enclosed dab* and *line-like* configurations in a *horizontal* and *vertical relationship* with each other. The features are *separate* from each other but *connected* within the enclosure by an ordered space relationship.

Earlier, while discussing Lois's drawings of 'sad' and 'happy' faces (Figures 5.1 and 5.2), it was suggested that although her ability to order features spatially within a face enclosure was not quite stable, she could discriminate between her representations in terms of 'good' and 'bad' form.

This level of representation echoes experiments on 4-month-old infants who were found to prefer good face configurations to 'scrambled' faces (Mussen, Conger and Kagen, 1969, p. 162). In other words, at a certain stage infants reject or show an antipathy towards faces that lack good spatial order.

Two-year-olds have internalized a sufficiently wide range of faces to recognize familiar adults in photographs (Sheridan, 1975, p. 46). Because their knowledge is stable they show interest in discrepant configurations. They ask questions such as 'Did he fall off a bus?' (Fantz, 1961).

Three- and four-year-old project children rejected 'poor form' in their representations. It was quite common for them to stop brick *enclosure* play when the bricks were out of alignment in order to 'mend the hole'. They became capable of 'topsy-turvying' established orders for fun.

Separation and Connection

Children sometimes draw parts of an object *separately* before they correctly *connect* and *order* the parts. A staircase, for instance, might be represented outside a house. Luquet has described this as 'synthetic incapacity' (cited in Piaget and Inhelder, 1956, pp. 46–9). Figure 5.9 could be so described but this would miss all the positive features of the representation.

Pete (3:1:5) was excited by being given his first toothbrush and small tube of toothpaste by a dentist visiting the project. Pete cleaned his teeth for a long time. Later he drew 'toothbrush' (an elementary *enclosure*) and 'bristles' (short *horizontal lines*) (Figure 5.9). Deficits are a lack of *connection* and *order*. The following four points describe positives:

1. The drawing represents an exciting first-hand experience.
2. He has two available graphic schemas for representation, *enclosure* and *lines*.
3. He may not be able to *connect* but he can place marks in a *proximity* relationship.
4. He can express the meaning of the representation in speech.

From a teaching point of view, deficit descriptions can only suggest acceleration. Identification of positives can lead to curriculum extensions (this is discussed further in Chapter 9).

The following three drawings show a progression in the evolution of topological space notions. Lois (3:1:19) (Figure 5.10) has started to *enclose* marks. The marks are *near* each other but *separated*. There is no *order*. Lois (3:2:10) (Figure 5.11) draws a face *enclosure*. Hair is not yet *connected* to the head. An *order* is emerging in that the nose is under the eyes and the mouth is further down than nose or eyes.

Lois (3:7:29) (Figure 5.12) draws 'Humpty', which shows a clear advance on Figure 5.11 in that, pupils (*dabs*) are *enclosed* within eyes that are *enclosed* within the face. The circular scribble hair is *connected* to the head. The mouth (*horizontal scribble*) is *ordered* below nose and eyes. The *order* between the features shows an advance on Figure 5.11. *Horizontal* arms are *connected* to the enclosure. Having drawn the two eyes, with pupils for the first time, she held up her drawing and shouted out 'eye'. She then added the third 'eye' out of sheer ebullience.

The final stage of perception in Figure 2.1 shows the complexity level reached by 30 week-old-infants. They can recognize facial expression and differentiate between individual faces.

It has been said that pre-school children cannot distinguish between male and female forms in drawings (Harris, 1963, p. 208). However, in spite of initial selection criteria, several project children were able to represent, as well as to distinguish, differentiated male and female forms. Following a farm visit, Randolph (4:11:2) drew the farmer, who was differentiated from his wife in many ways including the wearing of spectacles: 'Mr and Mrs Braham and dog' (Figure 5.13). The configurational differences between the two heads reflects the differences shown in the most complex stimulus level (Bower, 1977a) for 30-week-old infants (Figure 2.1).

There seems little doubt that access to materials, as well as appropriate adult intervention, can facilitate graphic representation. Randolph's 'draw-a-man' test at the age of 3:2:0 was unscorable, which put him in the bottom 2 per cent of the population on which the test was standardized. A later drawing at 3:11:10 (Figure 5.14) placed him among the top 20 per cent. Although tests are known to be unreliable at the earlier levels, this increase was echoed in the 29-point IQ gain he made during the two years of the educational programme.

Figure 5.17 top shows, on the left-hand side, a set of 9 out of 20 'best' drawings by project children. On the bottom right are 9 'best' drawings from children matched for age, sex, ethnic background and neighbourhood during their first week of playgroup. The developmental difference between the two sets of drawings are obvious and give support for the importance of early education in developing representational competence.

LINES

It is not difficult to see how sensorimotor actions acquire symbolic meaning as when a child *moves forward*, imitating 'the movement of an ambulance'. Children's actions become signifiers of things that move. This type of signification is usually called symbolic play and is discussed in the next chapter.

In symbolic play, actions are used as symbols and the actions are carried out in a transient sequence. The products of drawing and model-making are not transient. The visibility of products may serve to deflect from the actions that gave rise to the products.

Piaget and Inhelder (1956) maintain that marks (and three-dimensional constructions) are the figurative effects of sensorimotor movements. These movements or *groups of action displacements* can be seen in a wide range of situations such as when the infant *throws things onto the ground* and the toddler *transports* objects and places them into *heaps*. Mark- and model-making emerge from groups of undifferentiated movements that produce differentiated groups of figurative effects.

In drawing, for instance, the hand moves about on surfaces in *horizontal*, *vertical* and *circular* movements. Each movement produces a different feedback. As motor actions become more controlled, one set will result in *lines*, another set in *circles*, *angles*, *quadrilaterals*, and so on. By co-ordination and differentiation movements become increasingly skilled and the figurative effects reflect this. Mark- and model-making, therefore, are abstractions from the child's own movements. Motor mechanisms and perception are both employed in mark- and model-making in that visual perception 'picks up' the graphic images that result from motor movements.

From an early stage, pleasure accompanies 'matching' internalized *groups of actions* with their known figurative effects. The pleasure of being able to perceive predictable effects from known actions sustains the activity of mark- and model-making.

Arnheim (1972, p. 35) describes the match between outer stimuli and inner processes as follows: 'The stimulus configuration seems to enter the perceptual process only in the sense that it evokes in the brain a specific pattern of general sensory categories which "stands for" the stimulation'. In other words, a pattern must already be in the brain in order to perceive external configurations that 'match' it. Piaget would maintain that the pattern becomes established in the brain through action and not simply by perception.

Even if the importance of action in drawing were appreciated, which it is not, it is difficult to know how the teacher can facilitate the relationship between skilled action and figural outcomes in individual learners. One possibility is to implement the constructivist idea, already discussed, of focusing simultaneously on the action and end-product, the figural effect, but to place particular emphasis on the action.

Here is an example from the project. Brenda drew a recognizable 'house'. After a short discussion on 'houseness', the project teacher commented on the interesting fact that the day before Brenda had drawn a 'box of chocolates' and the day before that had drawn a 'table' and that Brenda in each case had used a similar shape. Recognition was therefore given to the shape similarity between those objects as well as giving recognition to the recent advance in Brenda's motor skill in producing a *rectangle*. This developed into a discussion on a wide range of content that could now be represented with that group of motor movements. The motor movements were treated as a great source of interest. When an advance was made, as in making a corner with a continuous line, Mrs B commented on the advance.

As each form appeared it was practised spontaneously until a standard was created against which 'good' and 'bad' form was judged. The standards being built up through experiences of mark- and model-making had nothing to do with external 'standards' representing norms.

The following age-related sequence of developing actions is called '*lines*'. Given the opportunity, young children draw *lines*, make *lines* with any objects that can be aligned and run in *linear directions*. They construct *circular enclosures* and run in *circular directions*. They construct and draw *zig-zag configurations* and they run in *zig-zag directions*.

The issue of how one level of marks evolves into another level is considered below, starting with *horizontal*, *vertical* and *circular scribbles*.

Horizontal, Vertical and Circular Scribbles

Most early marks are the figurative outcome of bodily movements. Some arm movements knock things down, some produce interesting sounds and some produce marks on a surface. Of 3-year-olds, 80 per cent can copy a vertical line (Stanford–Binet intelligence test – Terman and Merrill, 1976, p. 95). Most 3-year-olds also make lines and towers with bricks. Although building actions (*connecting*) are different from drawing actions, there is a figurative correspondence between outcomes. There is an element of '*connection*' between paper and pencil. Young children obviously need to see the results of their actions because, from the age of 2, scribbling soon stops if no marks appear.

The following sequence of observations from one child cannot illuminate the whole process of how motor actions become signifiers for graphic representations. However, the observations suggest that the transition from action to graphic form does occur spontaneously. Kamal is an Asian child. When these observations were made, he had very little English. Kamal (1:11:28) tipped things onto the floor and *transported* objects from various places in the classroom and grounds to his mother. There is a formal resemblance between this and learning to walk with starting and end-points.

Kamal (2:0:4) placed four cars in a *line* on the slide. He knocked them out of place and then put them back in *line*. He repeated this behaviour with many different objects typically picking up two objects in each hand. Kamal (2:0:12) painted his first *circular scribble*. He followed this by making *circular arm movements*. These gestures seemed to be repetitions of his drawing action.

Kamal (2:0:19) put four trains in a line and moved them along. He held one end of the line with his left hand and the other with his right hand. His hands could be said to be at *end points of the line*. He alternatively gazed at the line then moved it along.

It is tempting to think that Kamal is representing the movement of trains because the children had just been on a train journey. However, the observation does not contain sufficient information for such an interpretation.

Kamal (2:1:1), on a three-wheeled vehicle without pedals, followed his brother, Salam, who was on a tricycle with pedals. They moved in a *forward direction*. At a certain point, Salam made a sharp turn on his tricycle and started to ride back over the same route. Kamal lifted his vehicle round and followed him. The two children rode back and forth along the *straight-line trajectory* for some time. Then Salam made a *wide arc*, followed by Kamal. After repeating this several times, Kamal left his vehicle, entered the classroom, painted a clear *arc* and named the product 'My bus'. The *arc*, coming as it did after his own *arc-like trajectory*, could be a graphic representation of his own movement. Kamal (2:2:23) made a row of bricks. He placed one car at each end of the line. He then built a tower of bricks. He carefully topped the tower with two bricks.

The literature is not very helpful on the significance of such behaviour. Statements are too general. Piaget (1968b, p. 14), for instance, has suggested that, in similar kinds of behaviour, 'objects are co-ordinated with each other and with the child's own body'.

Kamal (2:2:29), *matched a row* of four cars with *a row* of four shops. This could be a case of *one-to-one correspondence* but it is more likely to be an earlier *line-to-line correspondence*. Most of the project children drew *line-to-line correspondences*, the figurative effect being *parallel lines* or 'stripes'. It is of interest to note in passing that the two lines, consisting as they do of 'cars' and 'shops', are early spontaneous groupings based on similarity of configuration but placed in alignment.

For the next few days Kamal's favourite occupation was as follows. He would arrange cars in a long *row*, bunch them into a *heap*, *enclose* the *heap* within his *encircling arms* and then put the cars back into *line*. This may have been an exercise (an assimilatory form of functioning) in making a 'good form' (*a line*), before 'spoiling' it in order to reconstruct it, or it could be an early co-ordination of two schemas:

1. *Making lines.*
2. *Enclosing.*

He had been producing *enclosures* in painting. At 2:4:16, he named one *enclosure* 'Balloon' and another 'Face'.

Young children are said to evaluate quantity by two primitive topological notions, *heaping* and *length*, with *length* defined as an ordinal comparison of *points of arrival*. In a typical test situation, two rows of bricks are placed before the child, one spread out and one with bricks placed close together. Children of a certain stage judge the crowded one to be *more* by the criterion *crowded together*. But they also judge the line to be *more* because the *point of arrival* (*the end of the line*) is *further away*.

In the observations on Kamal, given so far, it can be seen that he *transported* and made *heaps*. He then made *lines* with the ends marked out that appeared to have a formal similarity with both toddling and transporting. He then spontaneously experimented with two topological space notions of *crowding* followed by *spreading out* lines. According to Piaget (1968a, p. 977), all of these behaviours provide the basic experiences on which later evaluations of *length* and *distance* are based.

So far, action appears to be related to action representation and also to configuration. Further information became available when Kamal began to talk about what he was doing. Kamal (2:11:2) spent a long time gazing at a caterpillar. His mother asked him what the caterpillar was doing. He said, 'He stretched ... he oped' (opened). His perception seemed to be related to schemas, discussed above, of *bunching* and *spreading-out*.

Kamal (2:11:2) painted a thick *horizontal line* with short *radials connected* with the *line*. He named this 'Crocodile'. The next day he painted a row of short *vertical lines*. When the paint began to trickle down he named it 'Raining'. He showed a picture of water spraying out of a watering can to Mrs B. He recognized the short, vertical lines in the picture as graphic signifiers of water. It seems clear that Kamal can interpret static lines as equivalents for something that moves.

One month later, his favourite game was making cars go up and down a slope, using speech such as *going up*, *going down* and *fallen down*. Several *grid* representations, such as 'aeroplane', followed. It looked as though the figurative aspects were paramount. However, while painting an 'aeroplane' Kamal made engine noises. After another *grid* painting he made cars run down a slope to car sounds. It is possible that, in early representation, configuration and movement are held in the mind simultaneously.

Kamal (3:2:23) drew a common graphic schema consisting of a *horizontal line* with an elementary *circular enclosure at each end*. The drawing was not named but earlier Kamal had been observed finger-tracing worm tracks that were visible through the glass sides of the wormery. Kamal was very absorbed in Mrs B's explanation of the worm tracks (*going through* is discussed in Chapter 6). A *line* may appear as a configuration but it may also represent *a trajectory with a starting- and finishing-point*.

Kamal (3:3:12) drew 'Crisps falling on the bus'. For this he used a *circle scribble*. His speech indicates the *dynamic trajectory* of what is being represented. The project bus driver had been having a vigorous campaign against crisp-eating on the bus and Kamal had received the message. Kamal became more competent in representing static configurations but he continued to represent the movement aspects of objects.

As children get older, configuration becomes more clearly recognizable to adults and dynamic representation in drawings less recognizable. It is possible that too much emphasis on figural resemblance will reduce the number of dynamic representations through lack of validation. This is, no doubt, what Kellogg, Lowenfeld and Bell (discussed earlier) were warning against.

Kamal had an IQ of 109 at the age of 3 after attending the project for one year. This was 10 points higher than his brother at an equivalent age before attending the project. (Kamal's IQ was much higher than his brother's at the end of the project.)

There appears to be a close relationship between mark-making and an increased perception of objects in the environment that have a figural equivalence. Also a great deal of language is used in describing objects that correspond with their available marks. Some of these correspondences are illustrated in the following short sequence. Jock began to draw *circular scribbles* at 1:2:0. At 1:8:28 he watched, at short range, people playing golf. Suddenly he shouted exuberantly, 'Football'. A few days later, on a visit to Teddington Lock, he gazed at a buoy for sometime, pointed and shouted, 'Football'. Mrs B explained, 'That's a buoy' – a reaction of disbelief. Two weeks later on a visit to Kew Gardens, he was absorbed by a *circular pattern* on the floor.

When he was 1:9:6 he spent almost the whole morning with his father selecting *spheres* from a range of other shapes. At 1:9:10 he named a *circular scribble* for the first time. He called it 'Football'. On a subsequent visit he spent a lot of time examining *spherical* door-handles. After seven months of absorption with *circles* and *spheres*, Jock had begun naming objects that had a perceptual correspondence with the visual effects of his *circular scribble*.

This sequence can be compared with another sequence from the same child, which suggests that the relationship between mark-making, perception and representation is not random. Jock (2:5:22) drew a *vertical line* and named it 'Crocodile ... a tail that's burning'. One month later he painted a strong *vertical line* he named 'Animal, one leg'. He repeated the *vertical line* the next day and called it 'Leg'.

Jock (2:7:8) painted a thick *horizontal line* with a *vertical line next to it*. He named this 'Aeroplane'. He was dissatisfied with this and struggled through thirty paintings trying to *intersect* a *vertical* with a *horizontal line*. He finally succeeded in producing a perfect *grid*. He became as absorbed with *grid-like* configurations as he had been with *spheres*. At 2:7:9, while on the project bus, Jock shouted to his mother twice on the journey, 'Look'. Once it was 'scaffolding' and once it was 'a fence'. On that same day he rolled out some long pieces of clay and called them 'Spider's legs' and, later, 'stripes'. This is an example of 'fitting' form (*parallel lines*) onto suitable content.

Jock (2:7:14) would not be parted from a tennis racquet. He hugged it and gazed at it alternatively. Two days later he pointed to a *grid* configuration and said, 'Windmill'. He followed this with a painting of *four vertical lines* named 'Horsey, Man, Sheep and Tree'. Jock (2:7:28) carefully inspected a hammock. Jock (2:8.0) made a model. He called it 'Tiger', pointed to the nails and called them 'stripes' (Figure 5.16).

These short sequences illustrate that, right from the earliest representations, content had a perceptual equivalence to graphic form and there appeared to be a heightened perception of objects in the environment that also matched existing form. Objects such as 'aeroplanes', 'fences' and 'scaffolding' were not represented with *circular scribble* but with *grids*.

It would seem that different acts of drawing, each with its figurative feedback, engenders interest in objects with similar configurations. Most people who have painted know that this subsequent perception of what has been painted has been transformed.

Horizontal and Vertical Lines Co-ordinated: Grids and Grid Orders

Subjects, human and animal, respond to the stimulus characteristics of objects that are equivalent to the cognitive structure on the subject (Hubel, 1963). Infants less than 1 month old can perceive stripes that are vertical or horizontal, one-eighth of an inch wide at a distance of ten inches (Fantz, 1961, p. 69). At 6 weeks, infants can see vertical and horizontal stripes better than oblique stripes (Leehey *et al.*, 1975, p. 579).

Again, there are interesting similarities between early perception and later representation. For instance, children can copy *vertical* and *horizontal lines* before they can copy *oblique lines*. Children draw *circles* and *stripes* simultaneously as earlier they perceived *circles* and *stripes* simultaneously.

As with the earliest mark-making, once a good *grid* form has been mastered, then poor form is disliked. Kamal (3:5:29) managed to draw perfect *grids*. The figurative effects suggested to him a variety of content, such as 'kites', 'window' and 'aeroplane'. At 3.5.29, his brush slipped. He named the product 'Pakistani aeroplane, broken' (Figure 5.15). The term 'broken' acknowledged bad form.

The day after this observation Kamal laid out a neat three-dimensional *grid* (a fire) for Mrs B, who intended to demonstrate transformation of matter brought about by burning. He went straight from this to examine the spokes of an umbrella.

When *parallel lines* were 'discovered' they were used in drawing, three-dimensional models and symbolic play. For instance, when a group of children found *parallel lines* painted on the floor of the movement hall, they played chasing games (horses and drivers) within them. They invented their own *parallel lines* in the form of reins. This kind of game had been stimulated previously by the tracks in the snow made by pram wheels.

The main mention of *parallel lines* in the literature is that they are first used to *connect* face *enclosures* to legs. Later they represent 'neck' (Cambell, 1958, cited in Harris, 1963, p. 162). Only one project child, Randolph (3:6:27), represented 'neck' before 'legs'. He drew a row of small *circles* between the *parallel lines* and named his drawing 'Lady with beads' (this was probably a two-dimensional representation of '*going round a boundary*').

The same day, Randolph (3:6:27) asked his mother to write his name, which he then tried to copy (Figure 5.18). As can be seen, he was constrained by his prevailing schemas. Of particular interest is the *core and radial* letter 'p' and the *parallel lines* he used for the lower part of letter 'R'. He was still drawing letter 'R' in this way at 3:7:22 (Figure 5.19). In Figure 5.19, he drew *parallel line* 'lips', 'hairs', 'legs' and upper-case letter 'A'.

The *rectangle* first appears as a figurative feed-back from *grids*, as can be seen in Joel's (3:8:9) 'Umbrella' (Figure 5.20). *Grid* structures have a great potentiality for extension. When children acquired the *semi-circle* they represented 'umbrella' with that. After a visit to the park, Adrian (4:5:15) made a flat, oval shape with clay. He drew a *grid* on the surface and said, 'Look ... a leaf' (Figure 5.21). Like

Randolph in Figure 5.18, he modified the *oblique* veins on the leaf towards *grid*.

At this stage children were particularly interested in comparing *grid-like* objects. For instance, during a visit to Hampton Court, the children were shown the earliest tennis racquets. Jack (5:2:2) said, 'My daddy's racquet doesn't look like this. This one is bigger'. He then asked, 'Is the net bigger?' Later, he showed his mother a knitted shawl. He said, 'This is like a cage but this one has round holes'. He was paying close attention to different *grid-like* configurations and comparing them. He was also paying attention to *size*. There are probably continuities between earlier schemas and later concepts that are, as yet, undiscovered.

Straight and Oblique Lines

There is uncertainty in the literature on when children can identify and when they can represent *oblique lines*.[5] Gesell (1971) did not include 3-year-olds in his test on 'copying a diamond' and this task only appears in the Stanford–Binet scale at the age of 7. Many project children used *oblique lines* from the age of 3. Just as the *rectangle* is a figurative effect of drawing *grids*, so '*triangularity*' is a figurative effect of drawing *oblique lines*.

Amanda (3:5:28) began to copy the letter 'A'. Like other children, she modified the 'A' towards *parallelism*, with a curious exception. She reported to Mrs B that 'Linda fell over when she came down the slide'. Outside, Amanda climbed to the top of the ladder (at an *oblique angle*), and shouted to Mrs B, 'You have to come down like this'. She then slid down (also at an *oblique angle*). When she returned to the classroom she drew two upper-case letter 'As'. One was *upright* and one was *on its side*. She laughed and said, 'Look, it's fallen over'. What was curious is that these letters were more *oblique* than many drawn later. It was as though her verbalized sensorimotor actions on the slide had helped her to achieve temporary *oblique* lines.

For several weeks Amanda practised *grids* and *oblique lines* with varying success. She made several static three-dimensional models, each named 'see-saw'. She then produced a working model of a see-saw after using a balance bar. She added weights to both sides and then removed the weights from one end. At first she enjoyed the crash down before making the ends move more slowly.

Amanda (4:6:9) followed this with a model of 'A gun', which could be moved up and down and followed by 'A boat' with a rudder that could be moved back and forth. At 4:7:20, Amanda aimed at getting *weight equivalence* with the balance bar. She made the bar *oblique* and then said, 'That's got to be even'. She then levelled it up. In the following observations, Amanda tried to modify her *straight-line* schemas towards the *oblique*.

At 3:5:28 (Figure 5.22 – 'Mum, dad, Nichola and me'), her letter 'As' are *grids*, but she also draws a continuous *zig-zag* (a section gives the figurative effect needed for an *oblique* letter 'A'). The next day she managed to draw *oblique lines* (Figure 5.23) but they are all going in the same direction. A *triangle* requires *oblique* lines going in opposite directions. She called this drawing 'Amanda's slide, Mum's slide, Nick's slide', so the action element is still there. As though 'worn out' with her efforts, Amanda followed with a spate of *parallel line* and *grid* drawings of which the following are typical.

'Railway line' (Figure 5.24) was drawn with two pens in one hand. Figure 5.25 was named 'This is a chipper for cutting carrots', which introduces a *function* for the *grid*. Formally expressed this would be 'The cutting of carrots [into those shapes] is *functionally dependent* on the *grid* shape of the chipper'. *Function* also comes into Figure 5.26, which she drew at 4:3:26 and is named 'A man and a ladder for climbing up'.

Function was usually defined initially in terms of personal action. Ladders, for instance, were 'for jumping off' as often as 'for climbing up'. Probably for two reasons: ladders were assimilated to dynamic schemas of *up* and *down*; and personal experience of ladders and slides provided the content for the judgement.

Adrian (4:7:18) described Figure 5.27 as 'Noughts and crossed' (not 'noughts and crosses'). 'Crossed' describes the action of making the mark. 'Crosses' would describe the figurative feedback from the mark-making.

Piaget (1971a, p. 139) has suggested that even the most elementary aggregates of behaviour are connected with each other. From an early age, marks are connected spatially. For instance, following a candle-making activity, several children represented 'Candle with a flame on top'. They *connected* marks in a *vertical order*. They placed the flame (*a dab*) on-top-of the candle, (*a vertical line*). Several researchers have found a preference for vertically organized objects in early perception, which is echoed in early representation.

Graewe (1935, cited in Harris, 1963, p. 14) found that children move from *vertical* to *horizontal* orientations, particularly in relation to drawings of animals. At first the same general schema serves for both animal and human figures. Later there is an attempt to differentiate the animal from the human by drawing the animal on a *horizontal* plane. An early example of this from a project child is as follows.

Amanda had been using *parallel lines* in a variety of representations. Her mother was a heavy smoker and several representations were of 'Cigarettes on an ashtray'. For this she placed thin, wooden cylinders side by side on a shallow container. At 3:4:22 Amanda represented 'Rabbit ... long ears' (Figure 5.28). Here she has used *parallel lines* to represent the long ears of 'rabbit' but, for the first time, she has also represented an animal on a *horizontal* plane.

As with the initial placing of marks, it is not always easy to differentiate between intended spatial orderings and orderings that are simply the fortuitous effects of drawing objects on a page. It is easier to see advances in *ordering within figures* than to see developments in *ordering between figures*. For instance, in the following two drawings, the children drew, pointed at and named the parts as though they were working within an internalized *horizontal and vertical co-ordinate system*. Brenda (4:7:11) pointed at and named each part of Figure 5.29: 'Police dog, leg, leg, leg, leg, head'. Similarly, Stephen (3:7:28) drew 'Elephant, trunk, eyes, ear, four legs, tail' (Figure 5.30).

The following observation illustrates an earlier stage of spatial organization. It also illustrates the close relationship between cognition and affect. Alistair (3:1:11) painted 'A horse'. The teacher talked to him about it within hearing distance of Stephen, who had just painted Figure 5.30. Alistair said, 'That's the head', pointing with his brush. Stephen saw this and quickly pointed to the opposite end and said, 'That's his tail'. Alistair was furious, pushed him away and said, or rather shouted, 'No, it isn't, that's the legs'. The legs were at an *oblique* angle, half way between *horizontal* and *vertical*. He had not managed to place his marks accurately within a set of *horizontal and vertical co-ordinates*.

When young children squabble they are often described as naughty or socially immature. It came as a relief to parents to realize that children, like adults, might have understandable reasons for being annoyed. In the example just given there was a lack of cognitive match between the two boys in relation to spatial ordering. Interestingly enough, when these two boys first made a positive social contact (Alistair was 2:10:10 and Stephen 3:2:0), it was on the basis of a cognitive match. They were both making *lines* with cars. When they noticed each other's *lines* they made them meet to their mutual satisfaction.

Circles and Enclosed Curves

Of 3-year-olds, 53 per cent can copy a circle (Stanford–Binet intelligence scale). Such norms of development were made available to project parents but they were not interested. What did interest the parents were examples from the children as shown in this and the next chapter. Some examples, such as the following, generated particular interest.

Meryl (2:3:0) drew an *enclosure* and named it 'Button' (Figure 5.31). Her mother reported, with excitement, that while Meryl was 'helping' to wash curtains she had handled a curtain ring and said, 'Button'. The experience followed by the representation indicates that a shape generalization has been made. After discussion on extension, Meryl's mother gathered together circular objects and played a 'naming' game, thus helping Meryl to differentiate between objects in the general class of *circular* objects.

During a home visit, after the end of the project, Meryl (5:7:2) drew 'My house' (Figure 5.32). The actual house is on a new, imaginatively planned estate, high on a hill with an attractive view. During the project the family had lived in one damp room in an inner-city area where the atmosphere was polluted by heavy and noisy traffic.

During the project Meryl's scores on intelligence, language and drawing tests went up by about 20 points and, two years after the end of the project, she was one year ahead of her chronological age in reading recognition and comprehension. Teachers will recognize that the drawing of the house is advanced for a 5-year-old.

Salam (2:11:26), following a project visit to a park, drew a *vertical line* and a *circle*. He named the *circle* 'Conker' (Figure 5.33). This was the first English word he had spoken in the project. The drawing may have suggested that he had a 'figurative' mental image except that in the park he had put conkers in one container and twigs into another. The sorting was *classificatory*. To collect objects on the basis of similarity and to differentiate those from others is to *classify*.

Pete (3:1:0) struggled to draw a *discrete enclosure* instead of his habitual *circular scribble*. When he achieved a fairly good form he named it 'Bubble'. Five days later, he used his new form to represent 'Hat'. At that time he could not be parted from a white bowler hat. Mrs B admired the drawing and asked, 'Where is the rim?' Pete looked at his drawing with interest and said, 'Oh!' He drew a *circle* next to the first one and said, 'That's the rim' (Figure 5.34). One week later, in the park, he collected pebbles and placed them in a neat *circle* around a hole.

Pete (3:2:17) selected buttons from a box of odds and ends. He stuck these onto the top of a carton and named it 'Bus and wheels'. At 3:2:30 (in a burst of effort) Pete did six *circular* paintings one after the other. At this point he began to show an obsessive interest in things that *rotate*. The figurative appearance of a circular hat may seem to be in a different category from an interest in *rotation*, except that *rotational actions* produce the figurative effect of *circles*. The widespread representation of 'wheels going round' indicates that children often represent *rotation* with circular action.

At 3:2:30 Pete watched Alistair pulling a toy bird, which made its wings swivel. He said, 'Look, that goes round'. Every day for weeks he borrowed Mrs B's keys and matched up keys with locks throughout the building. His two criteria for success were whether they would *rotate* and whether he could make the lock move. He was exploring a *functional dependency relationship* that, formally expressed, would read 'Opening the lock is *functionally dependent* on *rotating* the key in the lock'. This dynamic aspect of *one-to-one correspondence* has more curriculum potential than more static types of matching.

Pete (3:5:0) suddenly, and atypically, appeared to be both social and co-operative in offering to fetch water for a group of children playing in the sand. Further observation showed that this was a ploy for investigating the *functional dependency relation* between the force of water and the *rotating* tap. He discovered that the sharpened end of a pencil is *functionally dependent* on *rotating* the handle of a pencil sharpener; that he could make a bell ring by *rotating* the hands of a clock; that hinges on the oven door allows the door to *swivel* back and forth; that the *rotation* of a ratchet wheel-handle makes a driver's seat move *backwards* and *forwards*; and that a right or left *rotation* of a driving wheel steers a pedal car in a *right* or *left direction*.

On a project visit to a museum, Pete accompanied every right and left turn of the bus with an equivalent right and left turn of an imaginary wheel. He also represented the starting and stopping of the bus with a backward and forward movement of an imaginary brake.

Pete was taken into the project in response to a concerned paediatrician. Initially he was unstable and unpredictable. His IQ increased from 87 at 2:8:0 to 92 at the age of 4:8:0 and to 100 at the age of 7:1:0. He became much more stable emotionally and his social relationships improved.

Stephen (3:1:26) ran round and round in a *circular direction*, laughing. The next day he told his mother while having breakfast that his plate had two *round lines* on it. He also pointed to a tin and said, 'That has a *stripe* on it'. His mother wrote this information in his 'home book' and he took it to the project. Stephen (3:4:30) drew a *circle*. He called it 'Puddle and snow'. The snow was signified by *dabs*.

Newly emerged graphic forms were usually content-free and small modifications served to differentiate content. For instance, *a circle* with a small *radial* would be called 'apple' but not 'orange'. This route from generalizing assimilation to differentiation also took place with speech, as when Jock (1:8:28) assimilated 'golf ball', 'buoy' and 'beads' to a *spherical* schema, all expressed by 'Football'. Similarly, Meryl assimilated several *circular* objects to a generalized schema called 'Button'.

Much parental help was directed towards naming differences within schematic similarities, as in the following example. Alistair (2:9:1) pointed to a *circular*, numbered dial on a toy petrol-pump and said, 'It's a clock, mummy'. His mother replied, 'It looks like a clock, doesn't it? I wonder why a clock would be among the garage toys?' Together they explored and decided that it was more likely to be a petrol-pump.

Observations discussed so far show that graphic representations are based on schematic form combined with personal experience. Both the form and the content of experience can be extended by adult interest and help.

CORE AND RADIALS

Werner (cited in Harris, 1963) points out that the crudest drawings of 'men' are often just completed closed figures and that this central core soon acquires various radial appendages. There is some disagreement in the literature as to whether children begin to draw and model with global, undifferentiated wholes before adding particularized elements, or whether they begin with individual elements they then build up to wholes. This is probably an artificial problem in that cognitive development is seldom related to 'either/ors'.

The project children represented 'wholes' with simple enclosures, but they also represented 'parts' of an object from an early stage. A single *enclosure*, for instance, could represent 'apple', while a single *line* could represent 'stalk'. A single *enclosure* could represent 'brush' but a few unconnected *lines* could represent 'bristles'. The children represented the salient features of objects related to their existing schemas. Whether the prevailing schema was used for the representation of wholes or parts did not seem to matter.

Marks are co-ordinated and the *core and radial* is one result. In many cases, *radials* represent the appendages of main bodies. For instance, after seeing deer in the park, Clare (4:1:22) represented 'Deer with antlers' (Figure 5.35). The 'antlers' consisted of seven *radials* stuck through the boundary of a *core* of clay. Although the form is basic, the 'antlers' are not spread all over the core, they are clustered *near* each other as are actual antlers. Kellogg (1969) found the *core and radial* form to be universal and biologically determined. What is not determined is richness of content that can be assimilated through experience.

Enriching experiences cumulate. Young (1978), while working on nerve cells, found their 'tree-like' forms attractive because programmes in the human brain have a special affinity for such shapes. In the interests of continuity it would be useful to have curriculum materials based on schematic themes.

Much adult help can be received at different cognitive levels, during which children find their own 'match'. For instance, Amanda (3:3:15) drew a straightforward *core and radial* pattern and named it 'Spider on the grass' (Figure 5.36). Spiders, of which there were many in the project, had been examined under magnifying glasses. Amanda's 'spider' had eight 'legs'. Mrs B and Amanda's mother showed enthusiasm over the correspondence between Amanda's radials and the number of actual spider's legs.

It was known that Amanda was unlikely to have represented *eightness* because she was paying almost exclusive attention to *three*. She drew *three* see-saws and *three* letter 'As'. She told Mrs B that there were *three* ways of coming down a slide. She clung to *three* pens and tried to use them simultaneously to make *three* lines, and so on. The adults were validating *one-to-one correspondence* up to *eight* on a 'fingers crossed' basis.

The following example illuminates the action basis of *one-to-one correspondence*; it also dashes hopes that the figurative effect of early radials necessarily corresponds with perceived content. Adrian (4:8:19) drew 'It's an animal, it has four legs' (Figure 5.37). At this point it did have four legs. Mrs B admired the drawing and asked how many legs there were. Adrian said, enthusiastically, 'Four ... look'. He drew another four strokes saying, 'Look ... one, two, three, four'. The counting was a tally of his actions. He disregarded the altered figurative effects. The chances are that he was equally indifferent to the original effect of *'four'* legs. An explanation may lie in the fact that an interest in *radials* is spatial; an interest in *one-to-one correspondence* is logico-mathematical. The two aspects do become co-ordinated but it is an unsolved pedagogical problem as to whether co-ordinations can be helped along by intervention.

As might be expected, conventionalized 'suns' and 'hedgehogs' are common representations with this form. As with other schemas, perception is sensitized to similar things in the environment. For instance, while on a visit to Kew Gardens, Alistair (3:5:17) shouted with excitement when he came across three objects. One was a water sprinkler that *rotated* and produced a dynamic *core-and-radial* spray. One was a besom broom (a bunch of twigs tied round a handle). The third was an open pine cone.

Intension to a class (aspects that are common) begins in sensorimotor assimilations. For instance, objects are perceived to be *suckable* or *throwable* (Inhelder and Piaget, 1964, p. 283). Intension, therefore, is truly spontaneous.

'Extension', on the other hand, requires that the subject must be able to define specific members of a given class. Language is crucial to 'extension'. Although some aspects of language are spontaneous, names for specific members of a given class have to be taught. When project adults helped to extend the range of objects that shared a common property, by naming, they were 'fleshing out' form (intension) by extending content.

The earliest *core-and-radials* were simple and undifferentiated, as in the following. Meryl (2:2:5) stuck pieces of curved pasta into a lump of clay. This seemed to influence her perception as she became fascinated by a bubble pipe and a magnifying glass, both with *a core* and *one radial* configuration. This interest was reflected in her drawings and models. At (2:2:21) she drew an incomplete *enclosure* with *radials* next to it (*juxtaposition* rather than *connection*) (Figure 5.38). Meryl (2:10:8) amalgamated *core* and *radials* and named the result 'Flower' (Figure 5.39). She had been showing a lot of interest in flowers. Like many other children with this schema, she liked representing 'umbrella', using a configuration similar to Figure 5.39.

Jock went through a sequence similar to Meryl. When the schema was at its most powerful he became devoted to a large, soft model (Humpty-Dumpty) made by a mother, consisting of four lozenge-shaped radials sewn onto a *core*. After a few days he represented the model and called it 'Humpty-Dumpty' (Figure 5.40). He was also inseparable from a puppet made for him by a mother. He made his own puppet called 'Animal ... one leg' (Figure 5.41).

Pete (3:1:5) drew 'Plant in pot' (Figure 5.42). Mrs B asked if he had any kind of plant in mind and he replied, 'A bean plant'. The example of 'Toothbrush, bristles' (Figure 5.9) showed an *unconnected core* with *radials*. In Figure 5.42, Pete has *connected* plant with pot.

Advances in schematic development are frequently lost temporarily. This obscures developmental advances. Usually the first drawings in a sequence have the poorest forms as though the act of drawing needs to 'get into gear'. For instance, Pete (3:2:20) drew Figures 5.43 and 5.44 on the same day. The first was named 'Elephant' and the two small *enclosures* were named 'Eye ... eye'. He seemed quite happy about one eye being *inside* and the other *outside* the main *enclosure*. He went straight on to Figure 5.44, which he first named 'Elephant' and then 'Tortoise' – another example of fitting different but appropriate content on to a particular form. On two criteria, either skilled action or resemblance between mark and depicted content, the second drawing is the most advanced. Advances are developmental but not within a narrow time interval. Alistair's (3:10:1) drawing of 'Tortoise' (Figure 5.45) is similar in form to Pete's.

Clare (4:7:17) focused on a life-belt during a project visit to a lock. She had a long discussion with her mother about a true incident when a little girl, having fallen into a canal, was rescued by a man with a life-belt. This discussion included *functional dependency* relationships based on belt and rope. On returning from the visit, Clare drew 'Life-belt and the rope. A big rope, another rope' (Figure 5.46). Many children could not resist the impulse to add extra *radials* long after they knew how many appendages there were on the object being depicted.

Figures 5.47 and 5.48 show how *radials* gradually become more specific to the content being depicted. In these drawings children were careful to point out individual features, such as 'trunk', 'tail' and 'horns'. *Radials* also became increasingly organized within a *horizontal* and *vertical co-ordinate system*.

Figure 5.49, drawn when Saima was 4:6:12, shows that a complete *core and radial* form has been used for the representation of 'tambourine' but 'tambourine' is now just one object in the picture. Saima had been dancing, and tapping her fingers against one. The fingers (the *grid connected* with the right arm of the figure) are an important part of her representation.

Figures 5.50 and 5.51 show an interesting differentiation, mentioned earlier. Saima (4:7:5) and (4:7:8) began to draw *radials inside* and *outside enclosures* and to name with content that fitted the configurations. Figure 5.50 was named 'Clock and apple'. The *inside radial* was named 'hand' (the hand of a clock) and the *radial outside* the *enclosure* 'stalk'. Figure 5.51, drawn three days later, was named 'Saima is going to make a clock'. The *grid* shapes are 'numbers' and the *radials* are 'hands'. Within the general form of a schema, young children are able to make many, minute differentiations.

OPEN AND CLOSED ARCS

The use of the *arc* in project drawings appeared after the forms discussed so far. Similarly in early perception, during the first year, infants respond to simpler configurations before they begin to respond to *upward curves* (smiles). This again suggests a developmental link between early perception and later representation.

In common with all the marks discussed so far, the *arc* was frequently used for representing *trajectories*. Stephen's (3:7:17) 'Aeroplane landing on the runway' (Figure 5.52) is an instance of this. Stephen had painted several similar *trajectories* with expansive motor actions. One was called 'A cloud going down into a path'. The invention (rather than discovery) of content that can be expressed by a schema (in this case, a particular *trajectory*) is called by Piaget 'distorting assimilation' (Piaget, 1962, p. 102).

One of the most familiar and common uses for the *upward arc* is as an equivalent for a smile. Less frequently, a *downward curve* is used to represent a sad expression. Many investigators have observed this but have floundered on interpretations. For instance, Eng (1959) linked her niece, Margaret's, drawings of 'smiles' with Sully's theory of the emotions. She interpreted content. This is easy to understand because the figurative features of the drawings and Margaret's speech reflect content. For instance, after drawing an *upward arc* for 'mouth' Margaret said, 'That's cheerful isn't it?' (*ibid.* p. 51).

Researchers are constrained by the richness (or otherwise) of theories. Eng was not informed by theories concerned with commonalities. The theories of her time illuminated individual differences. This is probably why she focused mainly on content. When Margaret (4:9:7) represented 'Man' (Figure 5.53), Eng wondered why she represented a man in a frock-coat. What she is actually doing is trying out a wide range of content with her new form – the *arc*. With this new form she represented 'cheerfulness', 'fingers', 'frock-coat', 'letters' (Figure 5.54), 'trees' (Figures 5.55 and 5.56). She also drew a group of men skiing down a slope. The skiers have curved skis.

Eng categorized individual drawings into groups but again based on content. This failed because the content defied useful categorization. For instance, when Margaret drew 'tulip' and used a *zig-zag* form, this was categorized as the 'tulip formula'. When she drew 'button' using her *circle* schema, Eng called this the 'button formula'. Unfortunately, this led to almost as many categories as the content being represented.

It is doubtful whether 'content' has a developmental sequence because it is subject to individual first-hand experiences. There are, of course, common experiences – being smiled at and smiling are instances. Experience of skiing is not shared by all.

The Use of the Arc in Letter Formations

Before Figure 5.54, Margaret had drawn only *straight line* or *circular* letters as in 'O', 'H', 'L' and 'T'. In other words, she had used earlier graphic schemas. The formation of upper case 'B', 'D' and 'R' in Figure 5.54 is a manifestation of the use of the *arc*.

The relatively late use of the *arc* in letter formations requires a re-think about blaming parents for teaching children upper-case letters. An analysis of project children's drawings shows that there is a direct correspondence between the marks they use in drawing and marks they use for 'writing'. In environments where 'writing' goes on, early writing is as spontaneous as early drawing. Adults do not 'teach' as much as 'validate' with interest and approval.

When project child, Shanaz, was using a *grid* schema for the representation of 'aeroplane', 'dishcloth', 'sieve', 'net curtains', 'window', 'ladders', and so on, she signed her name with marks that had no relationship to letters in her name. She used a small *circle*, a back-to-front letter 'E' and a small *right angle*. These marks were identical to the marks used by Eng's niece at a similar age. However, when Shanaz began to use an *arc* in her drawing, like other project children whose names began with letter 'S', she produced letter 'S' with two distinct *arcs*, one below the other (Figure 5.57). She also modified her *grid* letter 'H' into a lower-case letter 'h'.

The earliest attempts to co-ordinate *lines* and *arcs* in letter formations consisted of placing *arcs next to* lines but not quite *connected*. For instance, Clare (4:7:17) (Figure 5.58) attempted to write her name from memory. The 'C' and the 'l' present little difficulty. The 'a' requires that the *line* and the *arc* should be the same height and that the *line* and *arc* should be in a particular right and left order. Clare has not managed this but the sources of both error and achievement are clear.

The project children found it easier to construct 'b' than 'a' because the *vertical line* was drawn first. In letter 'b' the *arc* is easier to place on the right. Having to place the arc on the left of the line in letter 'a' requires a directional back-tracking.

Letter 'e' presents a similar problem. Clare makes the *arc* and *next* to it draws a small horizontal line. The *line* is not tucked inside the *arc*. The letter 'r' does not present this problem because the *arc* follows on directionally from the *vertical line*.

Figure 5.59 shows one of Clare's drawings produced two days before she tried to write her name. The drawing was named 'Lesley's baby Deborah'. Like Figure 5.60 drawn by Shanaz (4:2:8) 'Chicken with eggs in the middle', it is an interesting example of the representation of *enveloping space*, but it also shows both mother and baby smiling with the aid of the *arc*. There are also *arc* 'fingers' and 'arms'.

At this stage many project children *divided circles* into two halves for various representations. Susan used a whole *circle* of clay to represent 'cake'. She cut this in two and called each piece 'half a cake'. At 4:1:5 she drew a face (Figure 5.61) and represented both 'lips' and 'eyes' with her new schema of *circles divided into halves*. However, she did not manage to use the new schema within a *horizontal* orientation.

Figure 5.20 shows the representation of 'umbrella' with a *grid* schema. With the *arc* appeared the more conventional *semi-circular* representation of umbrella (Figure 5.63). A similar shift took place from a *grid* 'horse' (Figure 3.1) to a *semi-circular* 'back of a horse' (Figure 3.2).

By 4:4:10, Shanaz could almost write her name but some letters were still being modified by her existing schemas. In figure 5.62, 's' and 'h' are still being constructed by *juxtaposing* separate forms. She cannot yet draw letter 'a' by drawing an *arc* on its side and then adding *a stroke* on the right, and yet she virtually managed this form four months earlier when she drew 'Basket' (Figure 5.64). Also, although she has the form for the representation of 'Z' she has not managed to combine this with the correct orientation. Her attempt resembles an upper-case 'N'.

The following observation illustrates, once again, how schemas lead to *functional dependency* relations. Shanaz (4:0:11) had been using the real but unheated steam iron in the home area. She pointed to the *arc* of small holes round the bottom front of the iron and wanted to know what they were for. Mrs B demonstrated the *function* of the holes by heating and using the iron. She had a rapt audience. Shanaz's mother (who spoke very little English) communicated excitedly in Urdu with another Asian mother.

In order to help both child and parent, Mrs B was particularly clear in her descriptions of what was going on with parents who spoke English as a second language. Another Asian mother had observed her son changing *balls* of clay into *cylindrical* shapes before bending them into *arcs*. Salam had organized the *three arcs* in order of *size* and had expressed great satisfaction. Mrs B wrote about this as follows: 'Salam made balls of clay in different sizes. He rolled out the balls and made them into arcs'. His mother drew a two-dimensional representation of the model.

Salam was so taken with this that it was used to start a book. Each page had a drawing with what he had said about it. The content of the book was very much influenced by his prevailing schema, the *arc*. The content was as follows:

Roads curve. Petals curve. When people smile their mouths curl up. When people cry their mouths curl down. When we bounce a ball the curves in the air get smaller and smaller [note that the decreasing height of the ball bouncing has been observed as clearly as has the *decreasing size of spheres* in his model]. The humps on a camel curve. Curly hair has curves, straight hair does not. A tortoise has a curved shell. The scales on a fish curve.

Salam became devoted to his book. Having identified the schema, some content seemed predictable, such as 'arches'. Other content, such as the bouncing ball, took the project adults by surprise.

During a visit to the zoo, Salam talked a great deal about the elephant and resisted leaving the enclosure. The next day he painted 'Elephant' (Figure 5.65). The drawing is an exercise in form (*the arc*) – the content is the experienced 'elephant', the marks are spatially organized within an internalized *grid* and the drawing is correctly named.

Shanaz, the Asian child who was so interested in the holes at the front of the iron, discussed with her mother the way in which dolphins and seals leap out of the water. She was interested in elephants' tusks, antelopes' horns and the rhinoceros's horns. On the bus on the way home from the zoo, she conveyed to Mrs B her latest bit of knowledge. She said, 'Do you know the monkey uses its tail for swinging?' (another *functional dependency* relation).

Many drawings amalgamated schemas in ways that seemed almost inevitable. For instance, Stephen (3:6:13), mainly exercising the *arc*, drew 'Man, nose, smile, arch' (Figure 5.66). He then said: 'That's a man going through the arch'. A wide range of content, such as arches and tunnels, also include the more dynamic notion of '*going through*'.

Randolph (3:11:20) reached a peak of assimilation in relation to the *open* and *closed arc* in Figure 5.67. He named his drawing 'People on the boat and the captain smiling and waving'. There was a discussion about the boat (*a bisected circle*) and captain's peaked cap (*a small arc connected* to a *rectangle*). Each of the 'people' has a 'beard' (*small arcs*). The people are 'smiling' (*small arcs*). The 'bridge' that surrounds the drawing is a *large arc*.

The use of the arc in representation comes towards the end of the basic graphic schemas. This position corresponds with the ontogenesis of perception in infants in that signification attached to *arc-like* configuration appears late in infants. Fantz (1961) expresses this evolution in relation to 'face' configurations. Perception culminates in recognition of (p. 72) 'happy or sad, pleased or displeased, friendly or unfriendly'.

This growing differentiation can be observed in representations other than the face. For instance, in Randolph's drawing: 'Boy's skipping. He's happy, he's sad' (Figure 5.5) the facial expressions represent 'happy and sad' with the aid of the *arc*. However, the skipping activity is represented by *arc* skipping-ropes.

Randolph first attempted to draw spectacles when he was 4:5:9 (Figure 5.68). The drawing is mainly an exercise in *core and radials* but he has discovered the *arc* and uses one for each side of the spectacles. When he drew 'Mr and Mrs Braham', six months later, there is not only a clear differentiation between the male and female figure but there are also other refinements, such as Mrs Braham wearing spectacles (Figure 5.13). This has been made possible by the co-ordination of schemas, in this case, *circles*, *arcs* and *projective space*.

Two months later, after a visit from the doctor and a quarrel with another boy for the much-desired stethoscope, he represented the full figure of the doctor together with his stethoscope (Figure 5.69).

OPEN CONTINUOUS TRIANGLE (THE ZIG-ZAG)

It was not easy to see continuity between sensorimotor actions and later *zig-zag* mark-making. The most likely precursor is sensorimotor experience of stairs. Crawling up and down stairs takes place at about 13–14 months (Sheridan, 1975, p. 36). Certainly, 'steps' and 'stairs' are often among the first representations expressed with this schema. Salam (4:6:21) drew 'The boat in Teddington Lock' (Figure 5.70). The 'boat' was the small scribble inside the *enclosure*. The *zig-zag* part of the enclosure was described as 'Steps going down into the lock. The gate goes *up and down*'. The language illuminated the drawing and included a dynamic component.

Salam (3:9:14) placed bricks in a *horizontal zig-zig* formation he called 'Steps'. Mrs B asked him if he could make the steps go in an upward direction but he showed no interest in this. Many children represented 'steps' following visits to the swimming baths.

Clare (4:7:17) used *zig-zag* lines to represent 'water' (Figure 5.71) and a different schema to represent 'smoke'. Her drawing and speech contained two 'proximity' relations: 'Mrs Bruce watching the water. House near the river'.

Within psycho-analytic theory, the *zig-zag* in drawing has been interpreted as a sign of aggression although this interpretation has been challenged (Sundberg and Ballinger, 1968, p. 983). Eng (1959), applying this theory, reported that Margaret had represented two rows of terrifying canine teeth with *zig-zag* lines. However, an examination of Margaret's other drawings show that her use of the *zig-zag* covers a variety of content difficult to link to aggression.

The schema appeared at 3:8:17 with eight *zig-zag* lines underneath each other. At 4:8:22 she drew *zig-zag* stairs with a figure climbing down (Figure 5.72). She named this 'A little girl climbing up to heaven. Her legs are like that because she's tired'. She followed this with an even longer flight of stairs and called it 'God carrying a soul up to heaven'. It was only at this point that she drew *zig-zag* teeth as well as 'writing' an upper-case letter 'M' for the first time.

A project child, Stephen (3:4:30), after a visit to the Natural History Museum, drew a *zig-zag* line above seven *vertical lines* and named it 'Stegosaurus' (Figure 5.73). From the age of 4 he always picked out the letter 'W' although it was not in his name. His drawings and models became increasingly refined. Figure 5.74 shows a clay model he made of 'stegosaurus' when he was 4:9:25. His advanced representations had a history in earlier ones.

As with other schemas, representation of the figurative did not preclude an 'action' component. For instance, Adrian (3:7:23), after using a saw, represented 'A saw sawing' (Figure 5.75). The saw blade was signified by the *zig-zag* but the action was represented by a *vertical scribble*. Some time later, on a visit to the Science Museum, he was absorbed by a working model of cog-wheels and said to Mrs B, 'Look, it's got teeth'.

The following observation generated a great deal of excitement among project adults. Salam, as early as 3:6:9, had used the *zig-zag* to signify 'king'. When he was 3:11:23, Mrs B found him in the home area placing knives into two heaps. When she expressed great interest in this he showed her the serrated edges on one set of knives. The other set had non-serrated blades. When Salam's mother had this categorization pointed out to her she laughed and said that now she realized why she could never get her pinking shears away from him (she was a home garment-maker).

Discussions on possible curriculum extensions led to the realization that many of the project children had the perceptual ability to identify leaves by three criteria.

1. The arrangement of leaves on a stem (*core and radial* schemas).
2. The edge pattern of leaves (*zig-zag* and other line schemas, such as *continuous curve*).
3. The general shape of leaves (*enclosures*).

The children were not 'operational' in that they could not 'hold on to' the three criteria simultaneously, but they could observe and represent each criterion sequentially. Presumably the ability to hold on to a multiplicity of relations at the late concrete-operational stage of development depends on being able to consider significant criteria separately at an earlier stage.

As with all the other schemas, naming (if viewed from a content point of view) could be taken as instances of 'flitting'. Randolph (3:6:27), for instance, cut out a *zig-zag* pattern to which he attached three different names: 'a bird's wing', 'a fish tail' and 'a fan'. He was 'fitting' different but appropriate content into his latest 'form'.

ANGLES, TRIANGLES AND QUADRILATERALS

There is confusion in the literature between form perception, form-copying and spontaneous form production and the ages at which each is said to appear. Mussen, Conger and Kagan (1969), for instance, referring to Stanford–Binet norms, state that 4-year-old children can discriminate between *squares*, *circles* and *triangles*. As most 6-month-old infants can discriminate between these shapes (Lovell, 1959, p. 104), they probably mean that 4-year-olds can copy test items of these geometric forms. If so this would not correspond to Gesell's (1971) norms where no 4-year-old could copy a triangle. Forty per cent of 5-year-olds and 95 per cent of 6-year-olds could (*ibid.* p. 165). Researchers who have studied children's spontaneous drawings have found that these forms are mastered long before they can be copied in laboratory conditions.[6] Copying should not be confused with recognition because 70 per cent of 2-year-olds can place a *circle*, *square* and *triangle* in a three-hole form board while doing the Stanford–Binet intelligence test.

Piaget and Inhelder (1956) have suggested reasons why there should be this lag between the production of spontaneous and copied shapes. If, as they suggest, the first abstractions of shape arise from co-ordinated sensorimotor behaviours, then copying the mere percept of an object involves a different process from the production of a drawing as abstraction (*ibid.* p. 25).

McCandless (1970) discusses the experiental origin of the spontaneously drawn *rectangle* and *triangle*. By 10 or 11 months, infants typically *pull themselves up into the upright position and step sideways*, hanging on to the edge of a table. As a 'feedback' from this *trajectory* they have a tactile experience of *edge* and *corner*. If this explanation is valid then the typical form-copying test is testing something other than drawing as reconstruction of action.

Although the route of constructing form from early action is by no means clear, development seems to follow a general route as follows. Infants can track objects moving in *straight-line trajectories* before they can follow objects that change and move in various directions. Similarly, when toddling, the child moves in a *straight-line direction* before he or she can *turn corners* (Sheridan, 1975). Internal images (of action) evolve that become co-ordinated with each other into clusters.

Where a change of direction is made in toddling or running, or as a change of direction at the corner of a table, a sensorimotor *right angle* is experienced. These experiences become clusters of differentiated movement images that, when applied in the activity of drawing, produce a figurative correspondence in different graphic forms.

Inner forms are always in advance of children's abilities to produce forms for the purposes of representation. Therefore, drawing lags behind recognition, which indicates internal images. Leaving aside this time lag, drawing takes a route similar to the route from action to image (Piaget and Inhelder, 1956, p. 46). Children try first of all to reconstruct a *rectangular* form in drawing by employing a *continous line*. This is probably an effort to preserve the unity of the shape as a whole (*ibid.* pp. 52–68). These early attempts fail because success does not depend initially on how objects look but on a set of co-ordinated actions.

Where co-ordinated actions are not sufficiently skilled, the figurative effects show 'poor' form. A new strategy is, therefore, adopted. Good form is sought and achieved by the use of *horizontal* and *vertical movements*. Of 4-year-old's who managed to copy a *square*, 10 per cent did so by drawing *horizontal and vertical lines* that met at the corners (Gesell, 1971). Eng (1959) recorded that her niece wanted her to draw a flag over and over. Although she was interested in the figurative effects she was mainly interested in how the flag (a rectangle) was produced.

Piaget and Inhelder (1956) give an interesting example of a $3\frac{1}{2}$-year-old child who, having drawn a *triangular* house, explained that she was really trying to produce a *rectangle*. She was able to describe the four movements necessary for success without being able to manage the co-ordination in drawing. There were many similar instances in project children.

Linda (3:4:27) made many attempts to paint *rectangles* but, at first, managed only one good *right angle*. She represented objects such as 'doctor's cabinet', 'house', 'letterbox', 'bed' and 'pillow', while simultaneously paying close attention to *rectangular* objects in the environment.

By 3:11:24, Linda had mastered the *rectangle* and was representing *subdivisions*. Her names for these products reflected her schematic concerns: 'a house with two doors', 'these are the slide steps' (here *'grid'* has evolved into small, *connected rectangles*), 'the top of the slide is to stand on' (this uses *rectangle* and expresses a *functional dependency relationship*), 'the door is open, its a cube' (*rectangle*) and 'a door frame, the door is open, a doorstep' (*three rectangles*).

Susan (3:1:6) became excited when she made a *quadrilateral* shape by pulling an elastic band around 3×4 nails. She said, 'Look, that's a bed'. Later she drew a man with one *rectangular* 'foot'. The other 'foot' was a failed *rectangle*. She scribbled over this and said, 'It's a broken foot'. There was a four-month gap before she drew another *rectangle*, following a visit, which she named 'The hothouse at Kew'. From then on she began to represent 'legs' with right angles. In most cases her figures looked as though they were running but Susan did not comment on this. She named Figure 5.76 'Two people, smile'.

At 3:9:22 she *connected four* small *squares* that she called 'Seats on the boat'; she cut out a *triangular* 'flag' and stuck it on to a 'flag-pole' she *connected* to the boat. Figure 5.77 (3:11:13) shows how far she has reached in drawing *rectangles*. She named it 'Mrs Bruce house and door'. She discovered the strategy of using an edge of the paper as one side of the *rectangle*.

Two months later, Susan (4:1:5) produced a series of drawings representing actions and ingredients involved in cooking. The *rectangle* was used for representing 'a cooker', 'butter', 'flour' and 'sugar'. 'Sugar' was represented by lots of small *dots* inside the rectangle, and the action of pouring was represented by an *oblique scribble*. 'Eggs' and 'dried fruit' were represented by *circles*. 'Cake in the oven' consisted of a *circle* inside a *rectangle*.

Susan tried to copy the word 'cooker' but failed with the letter 'k' because she could draw a *triangular* shape only in a 'pyramid' orientation, as in the *triangular* skirt in Figure 5.77.

Amanda made many three-dimensional models, using earlier schemas but always incorporating a *rectangle* as in the model 'These are the cigarettes' (Figure 5.78). When she was 4:0:25, after trying unsuccessfully to draw a *rectangle* with *a continuous line*, she folded the edges of a *rectangle* of paper but the last edge defeated her (Figure 5.79). She then tried to draw a *rectangle* with a continuous line but the effect was too rounded. She used *'grid'* for the inside and named it 'A crate for milk' (Figure 5.80). The next day she drew her first successful form with four separate strokes, named 'Mouse in a cage' (Figure 5.81).

Amanda began to turn corners without lifting her pencil at 4:3:26 (Figure

5.82). This produced a single *right-angle* 'mouth'. At 4:7:29 she was drawing *rectangles* with *one continuous line*. Figure 5.83 is named 'Lips are for talking'. By 4:7:23 she was drawing 'good' *triangles* and this followed an interest in all things *triangular*. She watched Shanaz cutting a round 'chapatti' into a *grid*. She intervened and said, 'No, you should cut it this way', demonstrating by cutting her 'cake' into quarters.

When she was given a sandwich in a local workers' cafe she announced loudly that she wanted her sandwich cut into *triangles*. In the social circumstances this could have been viewed as annoyingly precocious or as funny. However Amanda's mother was pleased rather than embarrassed.

FROM TOPOLOGICAL TO PROJECTIVE SPACE

We end this chapter with a brief consideration of the shift from *topological* to *projective* space notions used by project children. Project children used projective space mainly in:

1. the representation of one object in front of another (44 instances); and
2. objects or figures represented from different points of view (45 instances).

Piaget and Inhelder (1956, p. 467) describe the shift as follows: 'From the psychological point of view the essential feature of the shift from topological to projective representation is the introduction of the observer or, the "point of view", in relation to which the figures are projected'.

Randolph (3:11:28) did a rather messy painting but his description indicated that he might have been trying to represent objects relative to each other. He said, 'It's a helicopter and a plane and they are passing each other at the same time'. Four months later he drew himself in bed and in the bath. In both cases he covered up his legs with scribble and explained, 'because you can't see them in the bath or bed'. Randolph (4:10:11) told a story where the theme was the mobility of a mouse in relation to a cat. The idea being explored was that you cannot be seen if you hide (see p. 163 for the full story). Randolph (4:10:14) drew people watching a picture show and represented the backs of the audience. He explained, 'The pictures showing them what it is. It's the backs of their heads' (Figure 5.84).

Randolph (4:10:25) invented a game he played with Mrs B. He asked the question, 'Do you see this?' He showed the object to Mrs B and then placed it somewhere within view. He would then lead Mrs B to a position where the object was out of sight and say, with triumph, 'Now you can't see it, it's disappeared. I'm going to make it come back'. He would go and get the object and say, 'It's here again'. Lois invested a game so similar that it was virtually identical.

It would seem that these children were inventing a version of 'hide-and-seek' evolving from *permanence of the object* acquired during the first year. At the later level it is as if the child were saying, 'I not only know that an object is permanent but I can symbolically represent the hiding and finding of objects and this includes me'.

Lois (4:5:17) drew 'A cow being milked. You can't see its udder, it's inside the pail' (Figure 5.85). Lois (4:9:3) drew 'Man on a horse. You can't see his other leg because it's on the other side' (Figure 5.86). She followed this with 'Polly the cat. She's lying on her back so she can be tickled' (Figure 5.87).

Lois and Randolph are both able to *rotate* themselves mentally around an object as well as to *rotate* objects in the mind. They can represent the figurative effects of these *rotations* and explain actions and effects in speech.

The few examples given above suggest that, psychologically, the shift from topological to projective space in drawing, and in games, signifies a co-ordination of dynamic and configurational features of action and effect at a particular level of symbolic functioning. At this level, the static configurational aspects of objects can be represented as relative to the points of view of the moving observer.

NOTES

1. Britain also found that children work longer and produce work on a higher developmental level when they communicate with adults (cited in Mann and Taylor, 1973, p. 36-7). The Oxford research project echoes this finding (Bruner, 1980).

2. Clive Bell (1958), cited in Kellogg (1969), was crushing and dismissive. He wrote (*ibid.* p. 151) that to focus on the representative element in a work of art may or may not be harmful but it is always irrelevant.

3. See Matthews (1984) for a detailed account of the importance of early mark-making.

4. At around 10 months, Froebel project children also drew vertical lines. The line was a graphic effect of making the same gesture with which they threw objects out of their perambulators. The throwing also produced various visual effects.

5. See Rudel and Teuber, 1963; Olson, 1970; Berman, Cunningham and Harkulich, 1974.

6. Deutch, 1960, cited in Beadle, 1971, p. 154; Kellogg, 1969, p. 178.

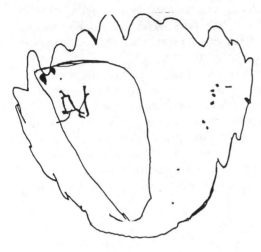

Figure 5.1 'Two bears. The polar bear in the water has a sad face'

Figure 5.2 'This bear has a happy face'

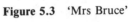

Figure 5.3 'Mrs Bruce'

Figure 5.4 'Oh! His hair is on top of his hat'

Figure 5.5 'Boy's skipping. He's happy. He's sad'

Figure 5.6 'Two eyes and a mouth'

Figure 5.7 'Face'

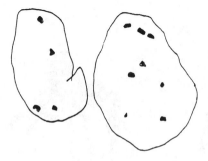

Figure 5.8 'Stone'

Figure 5.9 'Toothbrush, bristles'

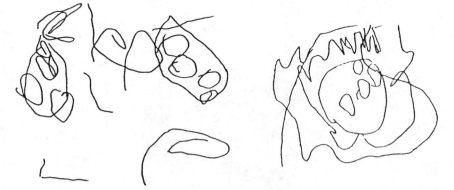

Figure 5.10

Figure 5.11 'Face'

Figure 5.12 'Humpty'

Figure 5.13 'Mr and Mrs Braham and dog'

Figure 5.14 'Draw-a-man' test

Figure 5.15 'Pakistani aeroplane, broken'

Figure 5.16 'Tiger, stripes'

Figure 5.17 'Draw-a-man' comparisons

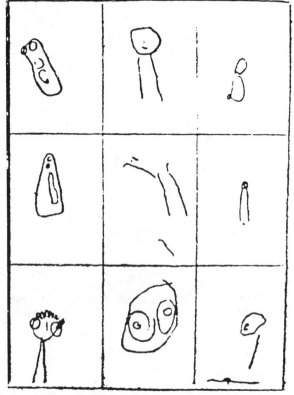

Figure 5.18 'My name'

Figure 5.19 'Lips, hairs, legs, letter "A", my name'

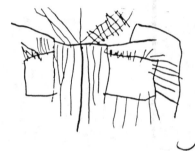

Figure 5.20 'Umbrella'

Figure 5.21 'Look … a leaf'

Figure 5.22 'Mum, dad, Nichola and me'

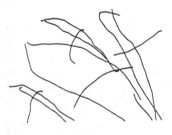

Figure 5.23 'Amanda's slide, Mum's slide', Nick's slide

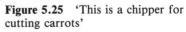

Figure 5.24 'Railway line'

Figure 5.25 'This is a chipper for cutting carrots'

Figure 5.26 'A man and a ladder for climbing up'

Figure 5.27 'Noughts and crossed'

Figure 5.28 'Rabbit ... long ears'

Figure 5.29 'Police dog, leg, leg, leg, leg, head'

Figure 5.30 'Elephant, trunk, eyes, four legs, tail'

Figure 5.31 'Button'

Figure 5.32 'My house'

Figure 5.33 'Conker'

Figure 5.34 'Hat. ... That's the rim'

Figure 5.35 'Deer with antlers'

Figure 5.36 'Spider on the grass'

Figure 5.37 'It's an animal, it has four legs'

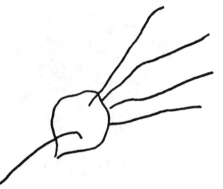

Figure 5.38

Figure 5.39 'Flower'

Figure 5.40 'Humpty-Dumpty'

Figure 5.41 'Animal ... one leg'

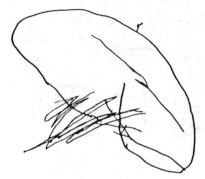

Figure 5.42 'Plant in a pot ... a bean plant'

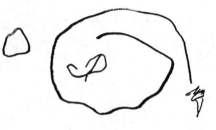

Figure 5.43 'Elephant, eye ... eye'

Figure 5.44 'Elephant ... tortoise'

Figure 5.45 'Tortoise'

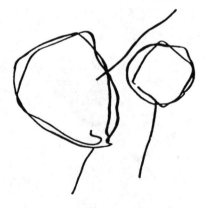

Figure 5.46 'Life-belt and the rope. A big one, another rope'

Figure 5.47 'Elephant, trunk, tail'

Figure 5.48 'Rhino, one, two, three, four legs and horns'

Figure 5.49 'Tambourine, man with one leg'

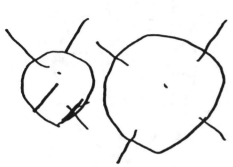

Figure 5.50 'Clock and apple, hand, stalk'

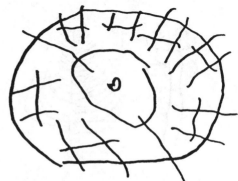

Figure 5.51 'Saima is going to make a clock, numbers, hands'

Figure 5.52 'Aeroplane landing on the runway'

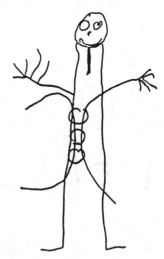

Figure 5.53 'Man'

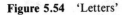

Figure 5.54 'Letters'

Figure 5.55 'Tree'

Figure 5.56 'Tree, Christmas tree'

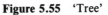

Figure 5.57

Figure 5.58 'My name'

Figure 5.59 'Lesley's baby Deborah'

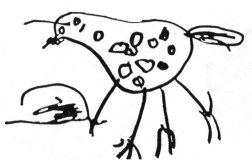

Figure 5.60 'Chicken with eggs in the middle'

Figure 5.61 'Lips, eyes'

Figure 5.62 'My name'

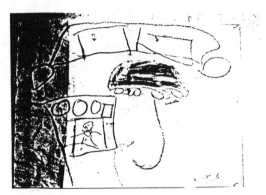

Figure 5.63 'Umbrella'

Figure 5.64 'Basket, a ladder'

Figure 5.65 'Elephant'

Figure 5.66 'Man, nose, smile, arch. That's a man going through the arch'

Figure 5.67 'People on the boat and the captain smiling and waving'

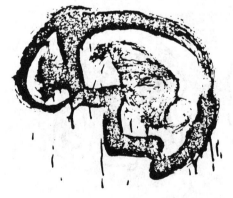

Figure 5.68 'The glasses'

Figure 5.69 'The doctor and that'

Figure 5.70 'The boat in Teddington Lock'

Figure 5.71 'Mrs Bruce watching the water. House near the river'

Figure 5.72   'A little girl climbing up to heaven. I've made her legs like that because she's tired'

Figure 5.73   'Stegosaurus'

Figure 5.74   'Stegosaurus'

Figure 5.75   'A saw sawing'

Figure 5.76   'Two people, smile'

Figure 5.77

Figure 5.78 'These are the cigarettes'

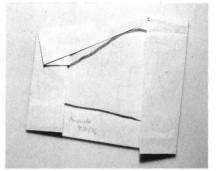

Figure 5.79

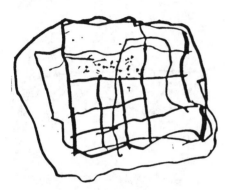

Figure 5.80 'A crate for milk'

Figure 5.81 'Mouse in a cage'

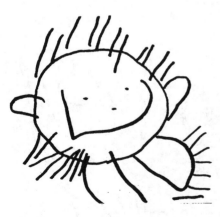

Figure 5.82 'It's my mum'

Figure 5.83 'Lips are for talking'

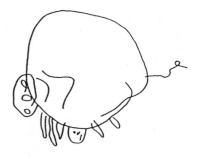

Figure 5.84 'The pictures showing them what it is. It's the backs of their heads'

Figure 5.85 'A cow being milked. You can't see its udder, it's inside the pail'

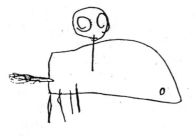

Figure 5.86 'Man on a horse. You can't see his other leg because it's on the other side'

Figure 5.87 'Polly the cat. She's lying on her back so she can be tickled'

6

FROM ACTION TO THOUGHT

The first aim of the Froebel project was to search for commonalities and continuities ('cognitive constants') in spontaneous thought and behaviour; in other words, to 'search for schemas'. A related aim was to provide developmental sequences of these continuities, or schemas, from early motor behaviour to 'thought'. The project findings show continuity from sensorimotor behaviours, through symbolic representations and functional dependencies, to 'thought'. General findings are given in Chapter 4.

In Chapter 5 the focus was on figural representation and its relationship with early perception. In this chapter the focus is on representation that stems from action. Eight schemas are illustrated and discussed separately at each level, moving from action to thought. Sufficient examples are given to allow the reader to evaluate the categorization of the observations and to consider their usefulness to teachers and parents.

At the end of the chapter, detailed examples of 'thought' illustrate the Piagetian notion that 'thought consists of internalized and co-ordinated action schemas' (Piaget 1959, pp. 357–386). Co-ordination is a feature of operative schemes. Furth (1969, p. 56) has described development itself as 'co-ordinations of co-ordinations of co-ordinations and so on'.

Developmental features of 'knowing' and co-ordinations involved in 'coming to know' have been widely hypothesized but examples are usually developmentally far apart. For instance, the scheme of *the permanent object* is said to be the forerunner of *conservation* (Piaget, 1969, p. 326). Evidence of more detailed increments in development is in short supply.

As discussed in Chapter 2, the gathering of evidence on early learning has not been helped by ambiguity of terms. Rather late in his writings, Piaget began to differentiate between the terms 'scheme' and 'schema'. So far in this book the term 'schema' has been used to describe all patterns of early repeatable behaviours. The illustrated categories in this chapter, 'From action to thought' may be nearer to what Piaget meant by 'scheme' rather than 'schema'. Piaget makes it clear that 'schemes' refer to 'real' operational systems of knowledge and 'schemas' refer to mere 'figurative' knowledge. 'Scheme' is conceptual and 'schema' is mainly configurational. At a 3-year-old level, for example, the figurative aspect of a toy car will be its external appearance. The operative aspect of the toy will reflect 'knowing' rather than perception. The following abstractions signify 'knowing':

1. The car continues to exist when it is not perceived.
2. The toy can be *displaced* from A to B and back to A.
3. Such *displacements* lead to *equivalence of distance between points*.
4. The toy belongs to a *class* of toys.

Although there are conceptual differences between 'operative' and 'figurative', they occur simultaneously in representation just as in infancy knowledge of location and state is built up simultaneously. Many drawings, paintings and models represent both configuration and movement, as in Figure 5.52 where the figurative *grid* schema is used to represent aeroplane and the dynamic *semi-circle* represents 'The plane landing on the runway'.

Another example of the difference between the operational and the figural can be taken from the activity of cooking. It is operational thinking that enables the cook to estimate the *quantity* of ingredients, the *sequence of procedure*, the *length* of cooking time, *degrees of temperature*, and so on. Glancing into the oven after a certain time in order to see whether the cake is brown is simply a figurative check on operational accuracy.

If the differences between 'scheme' and 'schema' reflect fundamental differences between operative and figurative thinking, they are worthy of further study. However, because of the exploratory nature of the Froebel project and the difficulty of clearly differentiating between observations of 'scheme' and 'schema', we will continue to use the word 'schema'. If more were known about the build-up of co-ordinated schemas and concepts, more would be known about how best to teach some of the key concepts of the curriculum right through schooling.

The practical *displacements* that enable a toddler to find his or her way round a garden become the spatial representations that enable him or her to find his or her way to school and later to represent such journeys in the form of a map (Piaget and Inhelder, 1969, pp. 93-4). These early behaviours may well be the precursors of mapping and aspects of mathematics and science. In environmental studies, street furniture might provide figurative cues on where to change direction but it is mainly the *displacements* that develop into internalized cognitive maps. These issues are developed in Chapter 9. In this chapter the developmental route of dynamic and internalized displacements is illustrated. The sequences illustrate various aspects of 'spatial thought'.

Hayes (1979), in dealing with computer technology, writes about the way science is to do with concepts and clusters of concepts (by which he means 'co-ordinations') and the way relationships have to be built up in development by observing the minute particulars of events and happenings. He writes about superclusters of concepts, such as systems of measurement of space and time, and notes that these are arrived at via earlier and simpler conceptual clusters, and that these important clusters are built up around such notions as *inside, outside, containment* and *ways through* from one place to another (*ibid.* pp. 242–70).

These concepts are illustrated in this chapter under the headings of *enveloping, containing, going through a boundary*, and so on. Each of these can be found in baby behaviour and each obviously has a healthy future in the primary-school curriculum even though 'matching' developing forms of thought with a progression from an early to a later curriculum has not yet been charted.

Piaget has said that at an elementary level 'form' and 'content' are indissociable because it is acts of assimilation that construct the forms of schemas. This is a difficult concept because, although 'form' can be detected under the surface of content (as is shown in this book) it is not known how much experience is required for a new form to be constructed. If schemas are constructed during the assimilation of content, it is the process of construction that needs to be studied. With existing research tools this is easier said than done.

The project findings, in this and the previous chapter, show clearly that, in symbolic representations, the 'form' of schemes, or schemas, can be distinguished from 'content'. After project visits, for instance, new content was represented within existing schemas. Schemas were thus extended by experience.

Each schema is illustrated at four different stage levels: motor, symbolic representation, functional dependency and 'thought'. This sequence shows differences of stage levels as well as continuity from stage to stage.

SCHEMAS AND STAGES

Of the observations analysed, 2,152 are described as 'action schemas'. These fell into eight clearly distinguishable categories. Each category below is given with the frequency of occurrence. Examples to follow will make the meaning of the labelling clear.

1. Dynamic vertical: no. 403.
2. Dynamic back and forth, or side to side: no. 357.
3. Dynamic circular: no. 280.
4. Going over or under: no. 204
5. Going round a boundary: no. 133
6. Enveloping and containing: no. 351.
7. Going through a boundary: no. 259.
8. 'Thought': no. 163.

Each of the above categories is discussed in this chapter within the following six sub-divisions:

1. Introduction.
2. Motor level.

3. Symbolic representational level.
4. Functional dependency level.
5. Thought level.
6. Discussion.

It became clear during the analysis of these observations that actions used instrumentally at a motor level were used as signifiers at the level of symbolic representation. The 'thought' level examples include earlier levels that have been internalized.

DYNAMIC VERTICAL SCHEMAS

Introduction

From six months, when toys fall from the infant's hand, he or she will watch the fall to the *point of arrival* providing all the action is within the visual field (Sheridan, 1975, p. 30). Infants of 8–11 months are able to monitor *vertical movements* of an object if a stable background is given as a visual frame of reference (Butterworth and Jarret, 1982).

The perceptual effects of objects thrown from 'pram' to ground are closely studied by the infant. Piaget (1969) suggests that, at first, each effect is separate and different, like still pictures. Gradually the child learns that his or her teddy bear retains its identity even though it is *upside-down*. More formally expressed, the child's knowledge of identity results from the co-ordination of changes of states of objects. In the last chapter the shift from topological to projective representation is shown. It is possible that this shift in representation is related to earlier perceptual co-ordinations.

At one year, infants are acquiring more advanced motor experiences of *verticality* when, for instance, they pull themselves upright with the aid of furniture. When 2-year-olds experience a *vertical ascent*, such as climbing, followed by a *vertical descent*, such as jumping, sliding or rolling, they experience asymmetry of effort that is probably why *equivalence* of *vertical distance*, as in the *upward and downward trajectory* of a cable car, is understood quite late.

The young children's judgements are influenced by their own internalized muscle effort and these will prevail until an Euclidean framework of fixed end-points of reference will free them from the error of personal perception (Piaget, 1970, p. 78). Apart from being repeatable, *trajectory* behaviour shows continuity. Motor-level examples are antecedent to symbolic representations that, in turn, are antecedent to later co-ordinations of schemas at a 'thought' level.

Motor Level

Jim (0:10:26) spent a lot of time throwing toys out of the 'pram'. Older children returned them with playful attitude. Salam (3:2:2) kept climbing up the ladder and sliding down the slide, His mother pinned appropriate speech on to his movements, such as 'You are climbing right up to the top of the ladder. What can you see from the top? Now you are climbing down. You are coming down backwards, aren't you?'

Kamal (2:1:3) came down the slide several times, his mother encouraging him with speech accompaniment. Kamal collected a brick from the classroom, put the brick on to the slide and made it slip down the slope. He repeated this several times (there was no verbal exchange in these examples).

Symbolic Representation Level

Brenda (3:1:23) dropped toy aeroplanes from a height, saying, 'The aeroplane has fallen down'. Later she played a *falling-down* game, shouting with enthusiasm, 'I've fallen down'. Jock (2:6:6), after visiting police stables where he had observed a policeman mounting and dismounting his horse, pretended to mount a horse by *climbing up and sitting astride* a climbing frame, saying, 'Me, policeman 'orsey'.

Stephen (4:3:25) drew 'Mother whale looking down. Little boy whale looking up' (Figure 6.1). Two different *vertical directions* are now made explicit with speech. Also, arrows signify in which directions the whales are looking. Randolph (4:4:1) drew an aeroplane. He described the drawing as 'The aeroplane over the water ... that's where you pull them down' (Figure 6.2). He was referring to the *vertical movement* of pulling down the blind.

Stephen (4:7:13) drew 'Submarine, periscope, water. The submarine is going up to the top' (Figure 6.3). Lois (4:6:3) sat inside the 'submarine' (a three-dimensional brick enclosure) asking, 'Are we near the top yet?' (symbolic representation of the *vertical trajectory* of the submarine).

Randolph (4:4:1) drew 'Bang, bang, this man is shooting him. The gun where you hold it' (Figure 6.4). For some time he had been able to represent *upright* and *prone* figures but now he was struggling to represent positions half-way between *vertical* and *horizontal*. He explained the *oblique angle* of the figure in his drawing by saying, 'I've done him like that because he's falling out of bed' (Figure 6.5).

Lois (4:7:15) drew an owl. She explained, 'Its wings are down because it's not flying'. After Brenda (4:4:7) had watched one of the gardeners chop down a dead elm, she ran into the classroom shouting, 'Mrs B, the tree is falling down'. Later that morning she made a model by sticking six-pipe cleaners upright into a piece of clay (*core and radial configuration*). She made one pipe-cleaner bend over so that it was at an *oblique angle*. She said, 'The tree has fallen down' (Figure 6.6).

Functional Dependency Relationship

The project teacher told an Aesop fable about a clever bird that, not being able to reach water in a dish, dropped stones into it. She demonstrated the story with a dish, water and stones. For several days after the story, Alistair (3:9:22) could not be parted from the materials. He became increasingly excited. When he dropped the stones his mother asked him what happened to the water. After some time he shouted, 'It goes up'.

Alistair (4:0:21) increased his height by standing on a chair in order to peg clothes onto a washing-line. Alistair (4:3:21) placed several blocks on top of each other in order to bring himself up to the equivalent height of the piano stool that was occupied.

Amanda (3:6:6) put water into a balloon. She told the teacher that the balloon filled with water was heavy. Mrs B asked how she knew. Amanda said, demonstrating, 'Look, I can't lift it. I can lift this' (lifting the one filled with air). Susan (4:1:8) attached objects to a hook on a crane. She hauled the objects up by pulling the string vertically.

Thought Level

Stephen (4:5:4) reported on the way home from the swimming baths, 'I jumped in the water from up'. Stephen (4:7:13) drew 'This is Teddington Lock. First level, gate, second level, gate, third level' (Figure 6.7). This was drawn several weeks after a visit but he had been using a simulated lock provided by the teacher.

Amanda (4:1:25) 'You know leaves? They fall off the tree on to the ground [pause] and acorns fall off the tree'. Amanda (4:4:6), after hearing a story, told the teacher, 'There was a mouse and it ran right up the inside of the clock'.

Discussion

When Jock threw things out of his 'pram' he used a *vertical arm movement*. Various objects were given to him, such as drums and cymbals, so that he could experience differential perceptual effects. What excited him most was being given a large brush with paint, with which he made short *vertical lines*. He was held steady by his mother. He was so excited by his marks that he jogged up and down with glee.

Some observations appeared to lie somewhere between motor and symbolic behaviour. In the absence of speech, these were coded at a motor level. However as 'emerging symbolism' is critically important in early development, they provided exciting topics to discuss with parents.

The example of Jock symbolically representing getting on and off a horse ('Me, policeman 'orsey') has already been given as an example of content experienced during a project visit. The example also illustrates the effect on both perception and representation of a prevailing schema. Out of all aspects of the visit, it was the *dynamic vertical aspect* (the policeman mounting) that Jock focused on and represented.

His sister, Lois (4:5:12), had just started to *represent objects from different points of view*. During the same visit she was observed staring at the behind of the horse. Later she painted an *arc* (Figure 3.2). She said, 'This is the back of a horse. He's carrying things on his back'. One year earlier, as already mentioned, following a previous visit to the stables she drew 'Horse with legs'. For this she used her prevailing '*grid*' schema (Figure 3.1).

The examples of the tree falling, the shot man falling and the person falling out of bed all represent objects in *intermediate positions between the horizontal and vertical*. The project children showed greater mobility of thought than much older children tested in the laboratory.

One of the main sources of evidence that children of 5 and under are 'pre-operational' (lacking mobility of thought) is from formal tests with a rotating rod where even 5-year-olds will represent only the *vertical* and *horizontal*. Piaget's explanation of this inadequacy is that young children cannot represent *intermediate positions* mentally and therefore they cannot on paper (Piaget and Inhelder, 1971, pp. 50–84). All the project representations of trees, people and objects falling, birds with wings down, and so on, do not support the theory that the thinking of children under 5 is 'static' and capable of registering only 'configurational' states rather than movement.

In the literature, the term 'operational' and 'pre-operational' are used to describe various levels of comprehension. Only at the age of 11 (in some experiments) do children fulfil the strictest requirements of *operational horizontality* and *verticality*. It is only then, for instance, that some children can draw the position of a 'mast' on a 'ship' at different inclinations when a jar holding the 'ship' and water is tipped (Piaget and Inhelder, 1956, pp. 381–411).

Piaget (1972b) also uses the term 'representation' in a broad and narrow sense. In a broad sense it means *seriation, classification, spatial metrics* and *projective transformations* (p. 81). Knot-tying involves spatial metrics and projective transformations (Piaget and Inhelder, 1956, pp. 467–8).

'Representation' in the narrow sense allows for the symbolic evocation of absent realities by way of the mental or memory image (Piaget, 1951, p. 67). Absent realities are movable and immovable. The motor *displacement* of objects leads to the internalized *displacement* of objects. This leads to the symbolic representation of those *displacements*. Examples given above indicate that the project children are able to represent symbolically *changes of position* of objects with *dynamic directional trajectories*.

When Alistair was $3\frac{1}{2}$ he had discovered how to lever weights (planks) upwards by hauling them over a wall with a rope. When he was 3:9:22, after much experiment, excitement and struggle, he talked about the water rising as a result of dropping stones into a dish. He cannot be said to have arrived at the concept of *displacement* but he has taken a large step in that direction via a *functional dependency relationship*. If he had been capable of static stage thinking only, he would not have been able to symbolize the *upward displacement* of water.

Stephen's *ordinal* description of the first, second and third levels of Teddington Lock is also more advanced than laboratory results would indicate. Children under 5 are said to think in *cardinal* terms only, such as one, two and three. As well as applying *ordination*, Stephen appears to have internalized the different levels of the lock in *ascending height*.

In order to show continuity of stages in relation to each schema, 'thought-level' examples given at the end of each section are short. Longer examples demonstrate co-ordinations of schemas and consequently would have obscured stage-level continuity. Long examples that demonstrate the complex co-ordinations of schemas are given at the end of this chapter.

BACK AND FORTH OR SIDE TO SIDE

Introduction

Infants pay a great deal of attention to *straight-line trajectories* and this has been well documented. Bower (1974) has shown that 1-week-old infants will show a defensive reaction to an object approaching them from straight ahead. Infants 20 weeks old will continue to track an object back and forth on a *horizontal trajectory* even though the object is made to change in size, shape or colour. Such experiments have shown that the movement aspects of objects are noted before their static configurations. Infants show surprise at movement incongruities before they notice configurational incongruities.

Bower (*ibid*. p. 201) found that *side-to-side* tracking precedes *circular* tracking. At an early motor level, *straight-line* toddling comes before *circular* toddling. In the Froebel project findings, *straight-line trajectory* representations came before *circular trajectory* representations.

Although *circular* and *semi-circular* tracking takes over from *straight-line* tracking, *straight-line* tracking does not disappear from behaviour – it re-appears in a new form at a higher level. Bower (*ibid*. p. 206) has pointed out the remarkable similarity between 3-month eye tracking and 9-month hand and eye tracking. At 3 months an infant will search with his or her eyes for an object where he or she last saw it. The 9-month-old will also search for the object where he or she last found it.

Piaget (1959) links the absorption of infants with trajectories with the later operational understanding of *lines*. He noted that Laurent, from 9 months, examined the route before and behind him as he was wheeled down a long hall (*ibid*. p. 203). He interprets this as establishing a *straight-line trajectory between two points*. Towards the end of the first year, Laurent was able to move himself from point A to point B. He was thus able to use himself as a moving object. He was able to toddle the trajectory.

When the youngest project children toddled they simply *displaced* themselves. Later they picked up objects and *displaced* those. At first they dropped the objects anywhere and later at the end of particular trajectories. At this stage the dropped objects formed *heaps*. It is not necessary to wait until objects can be defined logically, in class terms, before 'intensive' properties of those objects are defined. Each schema can lead to the definition of commonalities. If an adult talks to a toddler about what he or she is doing, 'Look, you brought all those things over here, didn't you?' he has a captivated audience. The question, 'What have these things got in common?' can be answered at many different levels: to the young child things can be *banged, thrown, transported, contained, gone through* and *gone round*.

Trajectory schemas have frequently been observed and described as norms without further developmental analysis. In the Stycar sequences, for instance, Sheridan (1975) describes typical absorptions of 1-year-olds just after they have learned to walk. In every case the infant pays prolonged and intent regard to objects that move in a *straight-line trajectory*. Examples are small toys being pulled along, rolling balls, people, animals and cars moving, and so on. The 1-year-old will create *trajectories* and *connection* by bringing two cubes together simultaneously.

When a 2-year-old establishes *starting-points* and *points of arrival* during *transporting* behaviour he or she is presumed, by Piaget, to be experiencing physically early *equivalence* of *distance, length* and *speed* by traversing A to B on a horizontal plane and then B to A on the same plane. This *displacement of objects* is used symbolically for the representation of events within the child's experience. A 2-year-old, for instance, imitated the coal-man carrying a sack of coal. He walked stiffly from side-to-side with a towel slung round one shoulder (a symbol for the *container* that, in this case, was a coal sack) (Werner and Kaplan, 1967). Both *trajectories* and *containers* had become signifiers for objects and events.

Motor Level

Jock (1:5:18) *transports* objects in a straight line from one position to another. He transports two of anything small and makes a *heap* in the telephone kiosk.

Jock (1:9:17) pointed his finger at a moving tractor and moving ducks at Kew Gardens.

Symbolic Representation Level

Jock (1:6:22) moved forward making a loud noise: 'Da da da da'. His mother said that whenever he hears an ambulance at home he begins to move forward, making this sound. Jock (2:4:29) transported a black bag around saying 'I'm Dr W' (his own doctor). The day before a doctor had visited the project in his white overall and had brought his black bag with him.

Adrian (3:7:17) lay facing downwards on the floor. He was pretending to swim in a *straight-ahead direction* to rescue his brother who was 'drowning in the water'. Adrian then pretended to climb aboard the ship and to haul his brother up.

Stephen (3:7:27) pushed and pulled a barrel in the garden. When he came inside he said he had made up a dance. He held Mrs B around the waist and moved *backwards and forwards* taking her with him in synchrony. The next day Stephen played 'tug of war' with Adrian. Each boy took hold of an end of a rope and tried to pull the other along. Following this, Stephen painted a *vertical line* with two filled in *circles* as *end-points* (Figure 6.8). He described the painting as 'This one is pulling that one along'. Randolph (4:3:14) painted 'A dog chased by a cat' (Figure 6.9).

Functional Dependency Relationship

Alistair (3:6:16) started a conversation with his father about a fishing-rod. He said, 'You know a fishing-rod? When you throw it [he made an enactive gesture of casting the line] the string goes right out'. His mother, who had been working with him the whole morning on wringing out clothes with a mangle, asked, 'What happens when you *reverse* the *rotation* of the handle?' Alistair said, 'The line gets shorter'.

Jock (4:9:3) and Kamal (4:1:14) each had a 'zoom-stick' (a rolled up tube that extends when blown into). This evolved into a game where they estimated how far away they would each have to stand in order for the end of each zoom-stick to just touch the other person.

Thought Level

Adrian (3:9:30) on the bus after visiting the baths: 'I put it over my head [the rubber ring] and I floated backwards and frontwards'.

Stephen (4:5:11), during a conversation with a student on the bus while going to the river, made the following statements:

Stephen: The bus is going fast ... we're nearly there ... the people could go over the bridge but not cars ... cars go on the road, but not on the bridge.
Student: How do trains get to the other side of the river?
Stephen: Railway track.
Student: Does that go over a bridge?
Stephen: No! [a pause] Yes it does.

Lois (4:7:7) had a long conversation with a student. During the conversation Lois showed that she was able to organize, on a thought level, familiar movements within three-dimensional space. She was able to talk about her cat moving back and forth and side to side as well as other trajectories. (The full conversation is given on pp. 71–2.)

Discussion

It is a norm of 2-year-old development that children can walk sideways and backwards (Cratty, 1973, p. 61). Children between 2 and 3 become aware of *front*, *back* and *side* and children can locate objects relative to these body reference points (*ibid.* p. 112). When the environment is supportive verbally, children become able to internalize successfully a range of actions. Tania (6:6:0) was able to give an articulate account of her 'bear' dance that contained 22 recalled events.

Jock (1:5:18) was demonstrating a transporting schema. When objects are perceived as equivalent in some way they form a primitive collection. The defining characteristic of the *heap* at the end of the trajectory is *transportability* or 'I brought it here'. The *trajectory* is the forerunner of higher-order notions, such as *distance*, *length* and *speed*. The *heap* is the forerunner of *classification* (Inhelder and Piaget, 1964; Piaget, 1968a).

When Jock pointed to the *trajectories* of ducks and a tractor he may have been half-way between the perception of moving objects and the representations of those movements. Ambiguous examples are difficult to classify but, as already stated, they generate a great deal of interest in communication with parents.

In the imitation of the ambulance, Jock uses his own movement as a signifier for the movement of the ambulance. Like most graphic representations, the '*chasing*' or action component in Randolph's (4:3:14) painting (Figure 6.9) can go unrecognized because the finished product necessarily takes the form of a static configuration. Adrian's 'rescue' play consisted of co-ordinated *straight-line trajectories*. Each trajectory had different dramatic content assimilated to it. Pushing and pulling can be extended by the provision of wheeled and non-wheeled boxes to be pulled on different types of surfaces. This extends the *moving of mass* into the concept of *friction* (Williams and Shuard, 1980, p. 280).

Although, in early education, children are usually allowed to transport objects about in outdoor space, inside the classroom the managerial interests of the teacher often prevail and the children are discouraged from moving materials. For instance, when children begin to represent the ubiquitous 'picnic', they remove crockery and cutlery from the 'home area' to the *end-point of their journey*. Many teachers scold them for doing so.

If viewed schematically, such behaviours would be extended rather than extinguished. Discussing the route taken on the picnic can lead to concepts of *distance*, *orienteering*, *cost* of journeys, and so on. Providing a carefully chosen picnic basket (*an enveloping space*) in which crockery and cutlery can be placed before being transported, is more likely to lead to notions of *volume* and *capacity* than insisting that the objects should remain in the home area.

In the fishing-rod example, Alistair (3:6:16) knew that the *distance* the line was cast was *functionally dependent* on the *rotation* of the handle. He was able to reverse this in his mind. If the *rotation* of the handle was *reversed*, the line would become *shorter*. Here *length* is a function of *rotation*. This example could be given equally under *rotation*. That day Alistair had learnt that water extraction from clothes was *functionally dependent* on the *rotation* of the handle of the mangle.

When children reach the 'thought level', the earlier motor and representational stages, with all the contents of past experience, are 'brought forward' to provide the 'form' and 'stuff' of thinking. As with all schemas, paucity or richness of experience becomes increasingly apparent with age.

CIRCULAR DIRECTION AND ROTATION

Introduction

Hubel (1971) discovered that where kittens are deprived of specific movement experience during 'critical periods' they are permanently damaged because their brain cells do not become sufficiently activated. After testing for the effects of horizontal and vertical stimulus deprivation, attention was turned to movement in a circular direction. The researcher points out that while thousands of brain cells are activated by the perception of stationary horizontal and vertical configurations, when objects are made to move, each orientation 'triggers' thousands of differentially activated cells. For every different movement there is a particular set of cortical cells that will respond (*ibid*. p. 131).

Hubel captures the dynamic activity of the brain when *rotation* is perceived. He comments that the number of cell populations responding to a slowly *rotating* propeller can scarcely be imagined.

In humans, where such movements have been widely experienced, simply thinking about them is sufficient to re-activate cells that were activated during initial perceptions. 'Representation', therefore, in the form of mental images, is literally a 're-presentation' of earlier experience. This evidence, and much more, indicates that movement schemas are both activated and nourished by matched stimuli in the environment and that one of the functions of symbolic representation is to re-activate original experiences, thus leading to stability of knowledge. The educational implications of this is that children should have many experiences of the '*movingness*' of objects and they should be given ample opportunities to represent these experiences through symbolic play, creative materials and speech.

The following observations show a developmental sequence from early action and perceptions of circular movement through to action and speech representations. These, in turn, lead to 'functional dependency' relations and 'thought'.

Motor Level

Jock (1:10:14) was fascinated by the record going round. After some time he drew a *circular scribble*. Jock (1:10:17) playfully walked round and round in a *circular direction*. Jock (1:10:23) spent a considerable time pulling a big car in a *circular direction*. Jock (1:10:29) connected an engine with a carriage. He then *swivelled round* on his bottom. As a result of this the train moved in a *circular direction*. Jock (1:11:5) ran, with delight, round the Pagoda at Kew Gardens.

Alistair (3:9:8), on a visit to the Science Museum, could not be moved from a mechanical model of a man *rotating* a handle, which turned a large wooden screw in order to winch water up from a well.

Symbolic Representation

Jock (2:3:30) went on a project visit to a windmill that, unfortunately, was not working. The adults demonstrated the movement of the sail with speech and arm movements. The teacher introduced a working water wheel into the classroom in order to extend the thinking of children who had a powerful *rotation* schema. Jock's mother, after working with him on the wheel for some time, asked Jock what he had seen when he visited the windmill. Jock echoes, 'Imwul [windmill] round and round'. He made his arms go round. The next day he drew a *circle scribble* and described it as 'round and round'.

Jock (2:4:3) drew a *circular scribble* connected with a *grid*. He named it 'Helicopter'. His mother pointed to the *grid* and asked what it was. Jock made an arm go round and replied 'round and round'.

Linda (3:6:28) walked round a fenced enclosure in the park. When she returned to her mother she said, 'The ducks can't get out'. At the project she made a *circular* railway track and made the train go round the track. Thirteen days later she made 'an island' with clay and said, 'Boats go all round an island'.

Shanaz (3:5:13) employed *rotation* movements in making up a dance. She climbed inside a large box and made a lorry and car move in a *circular direction* around the hole in which she was standing. She made her hands *rotate* round each other. She made her whole self *rotate*. She was able to change her *height level* while she *rotated*.

Alistair (3:9:8) made a scrap-material model of 'A train on a track'. He pointed to a bit of the model and said, 'That's where you wait and it goes round'. His mother said teasingly, 'I've never seen a platform go round'. Alistair said firmly, 'Well this one does!'

Alistair followed this by making 'A car with wheels'. He made the wheels go round and said, 'Look, they go round'. He then pointed to square shapes on top (seats) and said, 'And they go round.' He had been absorbed by the typist's chair.

Gary (4:2:16) asked the teacher if he could 'read' to her. After they settled he said, 'Look!' and swivelled a pencil. The teacher expressed interest and said, 'You made that turn round, didn't you? You made it *'rotate'*. Much later Gary showed the teacher a picture of a cement-mixer in a book. The teacher said, 'That's interesting, you have found something else that goes round, that rotates. Can you think of anything else that *rotates*?' After a pause Gary replied, 'Yes, a candy-floss maker'.

Functional Dependency Relationships

Brenda (4:7:14) was dancing round the maypole holding one of the ribbons. She kept reversing her direction. After doing this for some time she ran into the classroom and pulled the teacher outside. She was very excited and said, 'When I go round the string gets shorter'. She demonstrated this. She then reversed her direction and shouted, 'It gets longer'.

Jack (4:3:25) pretended to be the captain of a submarine. The children pretended that the enveloping space they had built with bricks was a submarine. Jack put a 'periscope' on top of the 'submarine' and pretended to wind it up and down by rotating an imaginary handle forwards and backwards. The height of the periscope was known to be functionally dependent on rotation.

Alistair (4:9:21), following a visit to the railway, worked with Jack (4:9:21). They made a 'level crossing'. They set up the railway track, intersected with a road (a *grid configuration*). They closed the level-crossing gates by rotating them so that they closed off the road. They formed a queue (*a straight line*) of waiting cars. They made the train go along the tracks. They *rotated* the gates back again and made the cars move across the railway line.

Jock (4:9:13) drew a circle scribble. He said, 'It's a spinner'. Two days later he pushed a short pencil through the hole in a milk bottle top and spun it. His mother made him a spinning-top with variously coloured segments that, when spun, appeared to be white. Although Jock was interested in the transformation of colour his speech indicated that he was more interested in his action of spinning. He kept saying, 'Look, you do it like this'.

Lois (4:9:8) painted over a doily and described the result as 'This is a fan to cool you down' (Figure 6.10). Clare (4:11:19) put one straw through the centre of six other straws and twirled it. She said, 'The wind makes it go round really'.

Thought Level

Jack (4:2:18), when asked what he had done the day before, replied, 'I went round and round on the helter-skelter, it was a spiral'. A few days earlier he had drawn a spiral and called it 'A cowboy ring' (a lasso) (Figure 6.11).

Alistair (3:6:13) noted the effect on wet clothes of turning the handle of a mangle. His mother encouraged him by suggesting he reversed his direction. Alistair's later conversation with his father about the relationship between casting out the line of a fishing-rod and reversing the rotation in order to make the line shorter has already been given.

Nicky (4:4:3) showed the teacher his watch, who said, 'What do you find most interesting about your watch?'

Nicky: You can turn the handle.
Teacher: What does that do?
Nicky: It turns the hands.
Teacher: Can you think of anything else that goes round?
Nicky: Yes, you can put this round your wrist [*going round a boundary*]. Look ... you can turn this round [he discovered that the glass cover could move round. He pointed to a small stud on his jeans and said]: That's round and you can turn it round. [He then detached himself from things that were present and said]: A merry-go-round goes round [pause] a ball goes round [pause] a wheel goes round. [He then pointed to a sand wheel and said]: When you pour sand on that it goes round.

Discussion

As with dynamic straight-line schemas, it would appear that objects that move in a circular manner, analogous to a behaviour pattern possessed by a child, have a particular fascination for that child. It is not clear whether Jock's circular scribble was an action representation of the revolving record but it is suggestive in that this was his first circular scribble. As mentioned earlier, these situations excited the parents because they found schematic explanations more interesting and reassuring than thinking of such behaviours as random. Such discussions sharpened adult perceptions in that related examples were then observed. When Stephen (4:2:6), for instance, made a swirl with paint, it might have been considered a mere scribble. His description, however ('That's like water going down a plug hole'), showed his ability to make an analogy between his *rotational* action and the dynamic features of water going down the plug.

It might be said that Jock's action representation of 'windmill' is also ambiguous in that it is not a direct imitation of the sails going round. However, his later action and speech representations, and his representations of the helicopter blades rotating, would indicate that he is sufficiently 'tuned in' to *rotators* to be able to learn from second-hand adult demonstration.

Linda (3:6:28) is showing a simultaneous interest in static configurations (a fenced enclosure and an island) and *circular trajectories* (the action of going round enclosures). This may illustrate Piaget and Inhelder's (1956, p. 25) claim that shape is constructed from action displacements performed on objects. When, for instance, the toddler steps sideways, hanging onto a circular table, he or she is acquiring motor images of circularity. This has more than just academic interest because, at the present time, young children are expected to construct shapes from the static configurations of shapes. Ponds and puddles are common content in young children's drawings and these emerge from active, not simply perceptual, explorations. Linda is also starting to inquire into the function of enclosures. They are: 'to stop ducks getting out'.

The *rotation* dance made up by Shanaz (3:5:13) was followed up by another activity that seemed unconnected with the dance unless viewed schematically. The teacher, in support of rotation schemas, had introduced nuts, bolts, screws of various sizes and tools to go with them. When Shanaz left her dance, she started to use this material. She was so eager to start that she took a screwdriver away from another Asian child, a boy. Her mother, who had been thoroughly approving and proud of the dancing to Asian music, so disapproved that she put this activity permanently 'out of bounds' for Shanaz.

It must be admitted that, as far as parents are concerned, to recognize a schema is not necessarily to embrace it. The *rotation* schema may have been behind Shanaz's enthusiasm for the dance and the use of the screwdriver but the dance was viewed as desirable and the other activity as un-ladylike. Pushing an Asian boy was the last straw. There are ethnic constraints against the extension of some schematic behaviours.

There were also sex constraints. An example has been given of Alistair's mother helping to extend functional dependency relationships with the mangle. Although the teacher expediently tried to transform 'mangling' clothes into principles of 'levers, pulleys and cog-wheels', fathers did not fall for it. They simply 'hung about' outside the home area not wanting to get involved in 'sissy' activities.

Ethnic and sex constraints were discussed openly and with good humour in the project. Male-sex stereotypes created quite a bond between mothers from different backgrounds.

The example of Alistair's (3:9:8) revolving train platform is interesting as it seems to illustrate Piaget's theoretical construct of 'distorting assimilation'. He was applying his *'rotation'* schema with abandon. His mother was trying to wean him away from the idea of a *rotating* platform because she viewed it as a wrong idea and, as far as Alistair's intentions were concerned, she was right. When Mrs B and the present writer pointed out that such things existed (the Round House in London used in the past for reversing trains), Alistair was not only absorbed, he was triumphant.

In the level-crossing example, Alistair and Jack were using *rotation* at a *functional dependency* level in that the *forward trajectory* of the cars was *functionally dependent* on the gates being *opened* and the *forward trajectory* of the train *functionally dependent* on the gates being *closed*.

In order to extend *rotation* and *sprirality* schemas, it was arranged that all the families would visit a helter-skelter on a very small fairground under a London motorway. (It is worth noting, while these schemas are being discussed, the kindness and complete acceptance of the owner of the helter-skelter to what must have seemed a bizarre-looking and bizarre-acting group of people.) After the visit there was an abundance of representations stemming from the visit. The teacher and parents made three-dimensional curves from plane spirals. The result resembled the helter-skelter. A three-dimensional model of a helter-skelter led to the discovery that marbles moved more easily down the slope than cubes.

GOING OVER, UNDER OR 'ON-TOP-OF'

Introduction

Bower (1974, p. 117) has established that 10-month-old-infants can discriminate between an object with a boundary resting *on-top-of* something else for instance, a book on a table or a box of matches on a book. R. Brown (1973) pointed out that the three young children he studied for speech development seemed to have an absorption with the spatial relationship, *on-top-of*.

In the analysis of project observations, it was not easy to differentiate between dynamic representations of *going-over* and *going-under* and figurative representations of *on-top-of* and *underneath*. Some examples of speech accompanied by actions were clearly dynamic when, for instance, cars were moved over and under bridges. Also, some representations were clearly representing the static states of objects when, for instance, cars were described as being *on-top-of* or *underneath* a bridge.

There were, however, some examples where a child seemed to be aiming for a correct static configuration but that also involved an internalized displacement. Examples involving 'placing hats on heads' may make this clearer.

Motor Level

Jim (1:7:2) had an obsession for placing one thing *on top of* another. As a result of his mother giving him the correct language, by the time he was 1:10:0, whenever he performed any kind of 'stacking' action he would say clearly: 'on-top'. He developed quite a ritual. He would put on a hat from the dressing-up box and then go round placing objects on top of other things. For instance, he would place a row of toy animals along the top of the painting easel.

Symbolic Representation

Pete (3:4:6) made a model with clay and named it 'People on top of the boat'. Lois (3:2:10) named her model 'A cake with two candles. That's the flame on top' (Figure 6.12).

Lois (3:4:0) made a model of a slide from a wedge of wood. She placed a circular metal disc at the top of the slope and said, 'It's a slide, me on the slide' (Figure 6.13). Lois (4:4:14) made a model described as 'A house with a chimney on top'. This was followed by another model called 'Snow on a boat'.

Randolph (3:7:22) was shown two rectangular table mats identical in every respect except that one was smaller than the other. He was asked, 'Are these two the same?' He said, 'Yes'. 'In what way?' 'They both go on top of the table.' Randolph (3:8:21) drew 'A man, a hat and a hammer' (Figure 6.14). Randolph (3:10:11) drew 'Me, hat and boots' (Figure 6.15).

Brenda (4:4:2) made lots of hats, each one worn. At 4:4:20 she drew 'Lady' (Figure 6.16), followed by 'People, they've got hats on' (Figure 6.17). Kamal (3:9:20) drew 'This is a mouse on top of the window'. Adrian (4:8:2) drew 'The hill has a lid on top. It's a funny hill with a roof on top. It's a dustbin with a lid on top with all the rubbish inside'.

Stephen (3:5:15) stuck a cake-paper on to a cardboard lid and put a yoghourt carton *on-top-of* the cake-paper. He then placed a cardboard tube *on-top-of* that. He described the model as 'That's the baking tray, that's the cake-paper, that's the cake and that's the chocolate on top'. Jack (5:1:2), having built a brick construction said, 'They live on top and we live underneath'.

Functional Dependencies

Randolph (3:11:14) drew 'A boat is going under the bridge' (Figure 6.18). Jack (3:11:2) pretended to be 'A captain on a boat'. The 'bridge' under which he was moving consisted of planks placed across the bars of a pyramid.

Randolph (3:6:19) hammered three nails into a wooden brick. He then hammered three nails on the other side. He called his model 'Three roots and three shoots'.

Thought Level

Stephen (4:9:1), while playing a game with Alistair, pointed to an empty space and said, 'The soldiers always sleep on that thin bit there' (he was referring to an imaginary bunk bed).

Salam (4:9:13), after returning from Kew Gardens, said, 'On the map you could see the trees, the road and the pagoda'.

Discussion

The representation of *on-top-of* was aided in three dimensions in that one object, standing for something else, could be physically picked up and placed on another object also used as a symbol. There were many three-dimensional representations, such as 'doll on bed', 'cup on table', 'me on the slide', and so on.

Stephen's (3:5:15) representation of the baking-tray, cake and chocolate followed a cake-making activity. The selection of the lid for the 'baking-tray' did not include the Euclidean notion of relative size, only the topological space notion of *on-top-of*.

Before Lois (3:3:22) drew 'Mrs Bruce' (Figure 5.3), she had been able to paint hair *on-top-of* heads in other paintings. However, her two-dimensional space order *on-top-of* was not quite stable. In Figure 5.3, instead of putting the 'hair' '*on-top-of*' the face enclosure she put it underneath. She noticed her mistake while describing the painting and she laughed.

In Figure 6.14, Randolph (3:8:21) has not managed to place the hat *on-top-of* the head. He is confined to the topological notion of *juxtaposition* or *next to*. By 3:10:11 (Figure 6.15), he is able to place a hat *on-top-of* a head in a drawing. Comparing these two figures (Figures 6.14 and 6.15), it can be seen that there are many more parts of a person represented and the parts are organized within a more complex set of *horizontal and vertical co-ordinates*.

Brenda (4:4:20) had a similar struggle. First of all she drew 'Lady' (Figure 6.16). She drew the figure first and then the hat to the side (*next to*). She then began to draw a face *underneath* the hat. She then placed another hat *above* the head *connected* to the figure. Brenda immediately did another drawing (Figure 6.17) she named 'People, they've got hats on'. Note the way in which Randolph's and Brenda's speech matches their stage of spatial ordering.

Opie and Opie (1959, p. 77) give examples of 'playfulness' with the notion that what is under is relative to what is over: 'Riddle me, riddle me, what is that, over the head and under the hat' (from a 12-year-old). Kamal (3:9:20) and Adrian (4:8:2) are determined to use their *on-top-of* schema in as many circumstances as possible.

It was difficult to be certain about *functional dependency relationships* in connection with this schema. There were examples such as 'cooking' *functionally dependent* on pots being *on-top-of* stoves and staying dry *functionally dependent* on having an umbrella above the head. (A 4-year-old intelligence test item asks, 'Show me what we carry when its raining' – Terman and Merrill, 1976, p. 100.

Trains having to be *on-top-of* tracks, boats going under bridges and cars going over bridges appear to involve functional dependencies in that 'keeping moving' depends on what vehicles are on and whether they are going over or under. Randolph (3:11:14) painted 'A boat is going under the bridge' (Figure 6.18). Previously he had been talking about the visit, during which he said, 'We went on a boat underneath the bridge'. In speech he is referring to location and state in the same sentence – if, that is, the spatial relationship 'on' can be described as state.

Similarly, Jack (3:11:2) represented 'on' and 'going underneath' in his action and speech representation. These, and many others, seem to be straightforward co-ordinations of *location* (going somewhere) and the state of being *on-top-of* (the boat). Randolph's (3:6:19) representation of 'Three roots, three shoots' is more than the representation of *on-top-of* and *underneath*: it includes *one-to-one correspondence*, *going through a boundary* and the fact that shoots and roots are *connected*.

There is a future for this schema in concepts of *area* and *volume*. *Conservation of area* is achieved when it is understood that the amount of area covered by objects is constant whether the objects are scattered or placed in a cluster. Curriculum objectives designed to bridge the schema of *on-top-of* with later 'concrete-operational' concepts still need to be worked out.

GOING ROUND A BOUNDARY

Introduction

Piaget and Inhelder (1956) have described three types of *enclosure*, each defined by a different kind of boundary. In a *three-dimensional enclosure*, such as a hollow cube, each surface is a boundary. *Two-dimensional enclosures*, as in *circles*, *rectangles* or *'hopscotch' outlines*, have lines as boundaries. *A one-dimensional enclosure* has boundaries defined by points, for instance, dots of ink on a piece of thread. In the Froebel project all three types of enclosure were used in symbolic representation. One- and two-dimensional enclosures are discussed in the last chapter, enveloping and containing space in this.

Matthews (1984) has investigated the notion of *going round a boundary* in relation to drawing, painting and symbolic play. He gives some interesting examples from his own children. Ben, at 2 years of age, made a *circular movement* with his brush. He said, 'It's going round the corner, it's going round the corner'. In his symbolic play Ben was absorbed with revolving toy cars in elliptical paths while 'bonding descriptive speech onto their trajectories' (*ibid.* p. 5). Matthews (*ibid.* pp. 17–18) notes that 'the outcome of rotational movement is the closed shape. This is followed by placing dots "inside" and "outside". Once this happens children have started to construct a pictorial space. Lines attain new meanings, new denotational values. The children can now create configurations'.

The notion of *going round* and *going through* are most often discussed in the literature in relation to children learning to tie knots. *Surrounding*, as in the case of putting beads around the neck, an elastic band around nails on a pin-board or placing quoits over a stick, is simpler than co-ordinating the three topological space schemas: *surrounding, enclosure* and *going through* (or going between), necessary for tying a knot (Piaget and Inhelder, 1956, p. 106).

Of 5-year-olds, 69 per cent reach this level of competence in that they can tie a single knot round an adult's finger that will not come undone when the ends of the laces are dropped (Terman and Merrill, 1961, p. 106). Before children can perform the topological feat of tying a knot, which involves making a three-dimensional inter-twinement from a one-dimensional string (Brearley and Hitchfield, 1966), they must be able to move the end-point of the string *in a straight line* (schema two), *in a circular direction* (schema three) and put it *through a boundary* (schema seven).

Motor Level

Jim (1:9:18) placed all the toy animals around the bottom of the toy helter-skelter. Jim (1:9:20) covered a plate with aluminium foil (*going round* or *enveloping*). Jim (2:5:3) picked up a watch and said, 'Put it there', holding out his wrist.

Kamal (2:11:3) made a line of toy cars, which he surrounded with his two arms and brought them forward into a heap. Lois (3:8:4) spent most of the morning putting a collar on a toy dog and dragging it along as though taking it for a walk.

Symbolic Representation Level

Stephen (3:1:14) pretended to peel potatoes (balls of clay). Clare (3:2:6) would not be parted from her book called 'The Snake that got Tied Up in Knots'. She insisted, like other children with this schema, on tying her cardigan round her waist by the sleeves. Clare (3:2:8) made a 'parcel'. She used a pipe-cleaner as 'string'.

Stephen (3:7:28) put a rope around Alistair. Alistair shouted, 'Look, I'm wrapping it round me, you hold on to it like this'. Alistair ran along in front of Stephen, they were playing 'horse and driver'. Stephen (4:1:4) on a visit to the zoo, looked at an owl and said, 'It has fur [feathers] right round its face'. Stephen (4:2:11) placed a long cylinder of clay around the boundary of a sphere of clay, which he called, 'A face smiling' (*going-round* and *connection*). Stephen (4:3:27) drew 'It's a house. The garden is at the back' (Figure 6.19).

Lois (4:7:24) drew 'Daddy [later changed to Dick] he's got a belt on' (Figure 6.20).

Functional Dependency Relationship

Stephen (4:2:11) made 'A basket with a handle'. He put his arm through the handle and carried it about. Stephen (4:3:27) drew 'My sausage dog on a lead' (Figure 6.21). He immediately followed this with 'Sausage dog tied to a post'

(Figure 6.22).

Jack (3:9:2) and Adrian (3:6:20) rolled out clay, which they put round their necks and wrists called the products 'a necklace' and 'a watch'. The teacher asked them what they did in order to get the clay that shape. Jack demonstrated by rolling out some clay. With questioning Jack arrived at the *functional dependency relationship* between *rolling-out action* and *length*.

Thought Level

Alistair (4:4:11), chatting to the teacher, said, 'I tied a rope round a brick and I pulled it along'.

Stephen (4:7:18) initiated a conversation with the teacher. He said 'I've got a new football shirt at home and it's got blue stripes round here'. He placed his two index fingers where a belt buckle would be and traced round his trunk to the centre point on his back. He continued, 'and its got a blue stripe round my arm like this'. He traced an imaginary line round his upper arm.

Discussion

The day after Stephen (3:1:14) had 'peeled potatoes', one of the youngest Asian girls came to the project with her hair shaved off (in order to increase the growth). Stephen rushed to his mother and said with some distress, 'Her hair came off'. Several times during the morning he was observed feeling his own hair and examining the short, tight ringlets of an African baby. He seemed to have made a frightening and false analogy between hair and potato skin.

Early attempts at *surrounding* were facilitated by pipe-cleaners, milk straws and cardigan sleeves. These allowed the children to perform a kind of slow-motion knot. After a doctor and nurse visited the project, where they demonstrated bandaging, all the dolls and teddy bears were bandaged from head to toe.

Going round, as with *on-top-of*, was easier with three-dimensional material, as in the 'basket', the 'smiling face' and actually putting a collar round the neck of a toy dog. The difficulty of representing *going round* in two dimensions is illustrated in Figures 6.21 and 6.22. Stephen did not seem to be able to make the collar *go round* the neck of the dog and the lead *go round* the post in the same drawing. Graphically representing *going round* seemed to require a conceptual struggle as did placing hats *on-top-of* heads. Project children made considerable accommodatory effort while doing these drawings. Again there is a close relationship between speech and schema. In spite of the difficulty of representing the relationship in two dimensions it was understood that *connecting* a dog to a post, or a dog to a lead, is *functionally dependent* on *going round* neck and post.

In Figure 6.19, Stephen represented a house. His description, 'It's a house. The garden is at the back' implies that he is able to make an internalized *trajectory* around to the back of the house. Perception alone can not reproduce the other side of objects. This example of *going round* suggests *projective* rather than *topological* space. Some children represented the front of a house on one side of the paper and the back on the other side. Mathematically this schema is extended in the primary school in activities such as *measuring* around wrist, waist, ankle and various kinds of perimeters.

Children's comics often contain 'maze' type puzzles where there are *open* and *closed* regions. *Open* regions can be *gone through* in order to reach *inside* regions. *Closed regions* have to be *gone round*. Linda was observing this while walking round the enclosure in the park.

Some games, such as 'rounders', consist of having to *go round boundaries* within a certain time limit determined by how long it takes one side to stop the ball. Many dances, such as 'square' dances, consist of variations on *going round* boundaries.

The notion of *going round*, when co-ordinated with *multiplication*, provides fertile soil for playfulness. When Pooh bear hunts the Woozle, he is, in fact, tracking his own increasing number of footsteps in a circular direction in the snow.

CONTAINING AND ENVELOPING

Introduction

Young children are clearly fascinated by spaces that *contain* or *envelop*, and these schemas have received more attention in the literature than the other schemas discussed so far. However, except for research on infants, even this powerful schema is most often noticed by researchers exploring some other issue. Donaldson (1978), for instance, while investigating children's concepts of *all* and *some*, found that her young subjects had such a strong bias towards perceiving the *fullness* or *emptiness* of garages that it interfered with their comprehension of her test questions. The powerfully salient point for the children was whether the garage had a car in it or whether it was empty (*ibid*. p. 67).

Bower (1974) has identified the origin of the notion *inside* as beginning at sensorimotor-stage four (from 6 to 12 months). At 5 months affective reactions indicate the dawning notion that one object can be *inside* another. If an infant picks up a cup and sees a toy underneath he or she is so surprised that he or she will gaze steadily at the two objects indicating that, although the event is discrepant with his or her expectations, it is noticeable. Exploration of *envelopment* comes later than the exploration of *trajectories*. In the project children's symbolic representations, *containing* and *enveloping* also came later than the representations of *trajectories*.

Harris (1975) has reviewed the literature on the evolution of the notion of *envelopment* during the first year and reports that it is only at approximately 12 months that an infant knows that object *a* can occupy the same space as object *b* if *a* is *inside b*. The realization that one object can be inside another is linked to the whole area of object permanence. Although these problems are solved at a practical level during the first year, the notion *in* or *inside* is not expressed in speech until around 2 years (R. Brown, 1973, p. 263).

Brown noted the frequency of the words *in* and *on* in the speech of the three children he studied. He also listed words that were used most often by the children when they were exploring the notion of *inside*. He found that the most frequently used words were related to the schema. They wanted to discuss topics to do with waste-baskets, boxes, pots, and so on.

Motor Level

All project observations consisted of children either putting objects into containers or getting inside enveloping spaces – climbing in and out of enveloping spaces by various means, by steps and ladders, by crawling through, by levering themselves downwards into holes, and so on. These behaviours appeared to be extensions of earlier locomotion skills. They also provided the experental basis for later symbolic representation.

Meryl (1:6:9) began to put small pieces of stone inside a narrow-necked container. Meryl (1:9:4) spent a long time putting toy animals inside and outside a cage. Meryl (2:1:25) placed all the toy cars and then all the toy animals into two enclosures. The teacher asked, 'Where is the horse?' 'Where is the elephant?' and so on. Meryl would pick up the named animal with a great show of pleasure. Her mother continued with this game.

Symbolic Representation Level

Brenda (3:1:2) made a model of a car. She placed a small *circle inside*, which she named 'A steering wheel'. Brenda (3:1:14) was dressing her doll. She said, 'This is a big dress to go on the big doll. My baby is dressed'. This example illustrates the way *envelopment* can lead to higher-order concepts, such as *size* and *one-to-one correspondence*.

Brenda (3:1:14) was cooking. The teacher asked her if she knew what an oven was for. Brenda said, 'Yes, it's to put things in'. After a little thought, she said, 'And it's to cook things'. Brenda (3:2:11) was telling her father about the visit of the deaf children to the project. She said, 'They can't hear'. Her father expressed interest. Brenda continued, 'They have plugs in their ears'.

Brenda (3:4:5) made a model called 'The crockery ready to be washed up' (Figure 6.23). This was followed by a drawing of 'Mummy's handbag', which was similar to Shanaz's (4:4:3) painting, 'Handbag' (Figure 6.24). Brenda and Shanaz played together in the home area. The play consisted of 'washing-up', 'drying-up' and 'putting the crockery away in the cupboard'.

Lois (3:5:15) made 'sausages' with clay and wrapped them in tin foil to cook them. Brenda (4:4:12) made 'a house' by placing two shoe boxes on top of each other (Figure 6.25). She described this as 'A house, it's got two storeys. That's upstairs and that's downstairs'.

Alistair (3:9:6) said to Meryl, who was playing with the dolls, 'Look, I'm putting this dolly to bed'. Meryl's reaction was of absorbed interest. Alistair (3:10:14) and Jack (4:7:0) played for most of the morning on the outside climbing frame. Their game consisted of one of them climbing to the top platform, or the bottom, making accompanying remarks, such as, 'I'm just going to pop upstairs now, Jack' or, 'I'm just coming downstairs now, okay?'

Saima (4:7:8) made a brick model of 'My house'. Her mother talked with her about the various rooms in their house. Randolph (4:6:19) drew 'Inside and outside my wardrobe' (Figure 6.26). He explained how the doors opened (the doors are sub-divided) and he discussed the drawers inside the wardrobe.

Shanaz (3:1:15) drew 'Eyes and mouth' (Figure 6.27). Shanaz (4:2:8) drew 'A chicken with eggs in the middle' (Figure 5.60). Randolph (4:9:25) drew 'Chair and house' (Figure 6.28). Randolph (4:9:25) drew 'Chair in a house' (Figure 6.29). Lois (4:2:20) drew 'It's a fruit bowl with a peach, a banana and an apple'.

Functional Dependency Relations

Lois (3:5:13) made a pancake with clay and carefully wrapped it up. She said, 'I've wrapped it up so the children wont burn their hands'. Lois (3:5:14) made a model house. When she finished she stuck sticky paper over the windows and said, 'Now it's dark inside'. Lois (3:5:14) found a worm. She covered it with sand saying, 'You know they live under the sand. At night he'll be asleep'.

Stephen (3:4:13) scribbled over a picture of 'a lady' and said, 'Now I've put her in a dark room' (Figure 6.30). Alistair (4:6:19) drew 'Alistair inside with two legs. I can't do any more children, there's not enough room inside the tent' (Figure 6.31).

Jack (4:3:1) made each toy animal 'walk' into a shed saying, 'It's going in there 'cos' it's cold outside'. He drew a rough rectangle and said, 'It's a box of chocolates'. He drew an enclosure round the rectangle and said, 'It's a big, big bag, that's a heavy bag'. A student asked what made it heavy. ''Cos' it's got all those things in it'.

Thought Level

Lois (3:5:15) drew her brother, Jock, in his cot. She covered her whole drawing with a blanket (a square of sticky paper) and said, 'I've covered him up with a blanket'. She then said, 'And I'll put the cot in a cupboard [pause] and I'll put the cupboard in a cave'.

Lois (4:1:9) on the bus on the way back from the Natural History Museum said, 'Tortoises live in cages. I don't think it was real ... was it? It was stuffed. A hippopotamus lives in the water. Sea-lions like dolphins sea-lions do. Sea-lions go in the water like dolphins'.

Brenda (4:5:23) initiated a conversation with the teacher about her nanny (grandmother). She explained, 'Not my nanny F, my nanny S. She's got two front rooms. David [her elder brother] says she's only got one, but she hasn't, she's got two front rooms. We've got one front room and it's the one with the record player in it'.

Discussion

As far as the project findings are concerned, it is clear that early hand and eye investigations of *enveloping* and *containing* reported by Harris (1975) are 're-worked' at a later level when the whole body is used for climbing in and out of enveloping spaces. The sensory and motor knowledge acquired is then translated into symbolic forms, such as symbolic play, model-making, drawing and speech.

When Brenda was 3:7:15, 10 months before her thought-level conversation with the teacher about her nanny's two front rooms, she played a game at home with her mother for as long as her mother was prepared to participate. In this play, Brenda *divided* their sitting room into two parts. She called one part the kitchen and the other part the bedroom. Brenda pretended to knock on a door saying, 'Can I come in?' Her mother had to pretend to let her in. Brenda then *moved through* a pretend door. In other words, the game consisted of *symbolic action displacements within a symbolic sub-division of space*. Her speech reflects the partitioning of space, as does Alistair and Jack playing at 'upstairs-downstairs' on the climbing frame and Saima talking with her mother about the rooms in their house.

Almost all the children represented 'darkness', as well as *envelopment* by scribbling over or *covering over*, their drawings. Stephen (3:4:13) scribbled over a sticky paper 'lady' his mother had made for him because she knew he was noticing *triangles*. He said, with considerable satisfaction, 'Now I've put her in a dark room' (Figure 6.30). His mother's feelings were hurt even though she had joined in with discussions on the schema of *covering-over*. Teachers tend to disapprove of children scribbling over their drawings, particularly after the drawings have become recognizable equivalents of reality and, therefore, likely to be appreciated by parents. If *covering-over* is interpreted as destructive then adult disapproval will follow.

Lois (3:5:15), covering over the drawing of her brother and suggesting that the cot should be put in a cupboard and the cupboard in a cave suggests aggressive 'sibling rivalry' if interpreted within a Freudian framework. However, this explanation could not be applied to the dozens of similar examples that were observed around this time, including the wrapped pancake, the darkened house and the covered-over worm.

Two satisfactory aspects of schematic interpretations is that they embrace a wide range of behaviours, and interpretations are positive. A clear instance of a positive interpretation, instead of attributing naughtiness, is the explanation given by Lois's family when they were late arriving at the project. In spite of having had an inconvenient bus journey with her two children, Lois's mother looked pleased. She said, 'You know that enveloping thing you have been going on about? Well, the reason we are late is because I couldn't find my shoes'. In the end she did, wrapped up in newspaper, in the dustbin. Lois had parcelled them up and posted them. Although inconvenient, Lois's mother found explanations based on schemas more interesting and satisfying than those based on sin.

As with other schemas, it was difficult to diagnose observations that seemed to be to do with *enveloping* but that were accompanied by early telegraphic speech. For instance, Kamal (2:2:29) had been showing his mother how he could climb in and out of a large, hollow cube with five holes. After this he made a model out of an egg box, which he called, 'Two holes'. The egg box could have been a signifier of the cube. The holes in the model could have represented the holes in the cube (*the salience of the circle*). The representation of *two* was consistent with his prevailing *two* schema. It was not known whether he was representing his actions of climbing in and out, although earlier he had represented himself going down the slide. Many early representations appear to be static but it is likely that they signify action not expressed in speech. Symbolic play reveals action more directly than drawing or model-making.

When Meryl (1:6:9) began to put pieces of stone inside a plastic bottle she was imitating only one aspect of an activity. Some of the older children had discovered that the creation of different sounds was functionally dependent on putting different material *inside* different *containers* (shakers). The teacher was extending this discovery in various ways. Meryl was not interested in making sounds, only in putting stones in the container.

The relationship between schema and affect can be illustrated by Meryl reacting differently to two situations. Susan silently 'took over' her play, which involved putting the doll in and out of a bed. Meryl complained loudly. Alistair (3:9:6) observed this. Later, when she had calmed down, he approached her and said, 'Look, I'm putting this dolly in the bed'. Meryl was absorbed by this. She became very excited when the teacher, while dressing her, said, 'You go inside a coat, don't you?' Meryl shouted, 'Inside a coat'.

As Meryl put animals *inside* and *outside* an open-topped cage, following a visit to the zoo, it was tempting to think that she was representing her first-hand experience that animals move between the inside and outside of cages. However, as she tended to perform the same schema on a wide range of other objects, it would seem that this was simply a general application of a schema.

Alistair (2:9:1) was more than willing to help clear up by putting all the dolls in the dolls' house. When he had finished he said to his mother, 'Now lets take them all out again'.

When Meryl was 2:1:25, she *sorted* toys into two groups of cars and animals and placed those *inside* different *enclosures*. Although her motivation may have been simply to *surround* two groups of objects, the possibilities for extension were greater in that there are particular *containers* and *enclosures* – for animals on the one hand and cars on the other. The teacher made two charts to support this level of *sorting* and *surrounding*. One chart contained pictures of animals seen at the zoo and the other animals seen in Richmond Park.

As already explained, it was not possible to quantify co-ordinations of schemas although these are probably of critical importance in the build-up of systems of thought. The schemas *going through*, *enveloping*, *containing* and *going round* were closely related and it was sometimes difficult to differentiate between them.

For instance, Lois *wrapped-round* the pancake in order to *envelop* it. She understood that this *envelopment* had a *function*. Similarly, Lois (3:5:15) *wrapped-round* sausages in order to envelop. This envelopment had a function.

A stage in the concept of *size* and *one-to-one correspondence* can stem from *enveloping*, as when Brenda (3:1:9) followed 'dressing' her doll with the comment, 'This is the big dress to go on the big doll'. *Scribbling over* and *folding-over* both appear to be variations on the *enveloping* schema. Children frequently represented 'darkness' by scribbling over what they had drawn, as in Figure 6.30.

Brenda (3:5:14), in common with several other children, began to fold 'letters' and to fit them into 'envelopes'. As Brenda posted her letter she tapped the top of the post-box and said playfully, 'And that's a "toppy" '. Although schemas have the important function of enabling similarities between objects to be understood, discrimination is furthered by the naming of differences with similarities. The 'toppy' of a car is different from the 'toppy' of a post-box.

Brenda (3:1:14) 'knows' that an oven is to put things in and, after a slight hesitation, arrives at its function. However, she has not arrived at the function of hearing-aids, which is to magnify sound. She used an earlier level of understanding, to insert or to *'go through'* is to block. The concept that 'hearing' is functionally dependent on a hearing-aid is too much 'beyond the information given' for a 3-year-old (Bruner, 1974a).

She did, however, make other discriminations. When Brenda was 3:8:5 she informed her mother that 'Ovens cook things and fridges make things cold'. Brenda (4:0:20) painted thick vertical lines that looked like a return to an earlier schema. However, they represented 'The lines inside a bulb'. Most of the children represented bags of various kinds when they had *containing* or *enveloping* schemas. A great deal of time was given to putting things in and out of bags while using dressing-up clothes.

Before Alistair (4:6:19) drew the tent (Figure 6.31) and said that there wasn't enough room inside for more children, he had systematically explored the tent in order to extend the schema of *envelopment*. He would make the guy ropes taut by adjusting the toggle and then crawl into the tent, lie on his back and look at the inside; he would then make the ropes slack and repeat the inspection. His comment reveals a dawning awareness of the *volume* taken up by his own body in relation to the *capacity* of the tent. Also, he knows that the *capacity* of the tent is *functionally dependent* on the tension of the guy ropes. This example, and the example of Jock (4:3:1) bringing in *heaviness* as a function of lots of things in a big bag, again illustrates the way in which schemas, with appropriate experiences, are further differentiated into higher-order concepts.

Prior to the 'thought level' observation, where Lois (4:1:19) thought aloud about stuffed animals, she had spent a great deal of time stuffing nylon stockings with soft paper. She called each product 'A snake'. She later described a gerbil as 'It's an animal and it has fur all over him [pause] so has a mouse'. When Shanaz (4:4:3) painted 'Handbag' she co-ordinated four schemas in her representation. She *connected* a *rectangle* with a *semi-circle* in order to signify *an enveloping space*.

The representation of *enveloping* space evolves into the representation of *sub-divided* space, as with the model of the two-storey house, the *inside* and *outside* of the wardrobe and the outside play of pretending to go upstairs and downstairs. Alistair followed this by putting a willing friend 'Down below in the prison'.

When Stephen (4:0:27) saw half a car in the Science Museum he would not look at anything else. He was able to re-create mentally the fact that it had half missing. Soon afterwards he drew 'A boat, broken in half'. As *sub-divisions of space* became more precise they were described in the language of *fractions*.

Saima (4:7:8) *sub-divided* the enveloping space of 'her house' into the bedroom, kitchen, bathroom, and so on. When she was 6 years old and at primary school, she wrote a long account of the layout of a Roman bath and accompanied this with a two-dimensional plan of the various parts of the bath. It is important to note that the motor-level exploration of spaces is followed by symbolic representations of those spaces, which are then sub-divided. Higher-order representations in writing, maps and plans follow from earlier, more direct representations.

As with the notion *on top of* discussed in the last section, there were two levels of difficulty in representing *inside*. It was easier to *enclose* marks, in a face enclosure, than it was to represent a three-dimensional relationship of *inside* in two dimensions. Shanaz (3:1:15), for instance, managed to place marks inside a face enclosure at a very young age (Figure 6.27). She called this 'Eyes and mouth'. She did not manage to represent objects inside three-dimensional space, in two dimensions, until a year later. In Figure 5.60, when she was 4:2:8, she was able to represent 'A chicken with eggs in the middle'.

It is of interest that she did not use the word '*in*' when she talked about the face, perhaps because faces are representations of configurations. 'Eggs inside a chicken', on the other hand, represents the concept of '*inside*'. Similarly, when Randolph (4:9:25) drew 'Chair and house' (Figure 6.28), both drawing and speech represent the spatial notion of *juxtaposition*. Randolph struggled with the problem of how to represent *inside* and at last managed to draw and name 'Chair in house' (Figure 6.29).

On first consideration it seemed odd that the children could not use the same technique or convention for representing *inside* they used in representing *enclosure* (eyes within a face). However, although the figurative effect of 'chair in house' is perceptually equivalent to 'eyes in face', the conceptual processes necessary for the two representations are not equivalent. 'Eyes in face' seems to be the figurative representation of a percept. 'Chair in house' is the operative representation of a *displacement*.

This time lag between two levels of representation is consistent with Bower's (1977a) finding that, during the first year, an 'eye' configuration within a 'face' enclosure is perceived much earlier than is the understanding of the relationship *inside*. The example has been given of Lois *covering over* her brother and putting him into a cupboard and then putting the cupboard in a cave. Shanaz, similarly, followed 'A chicken with eggs in the middle' with a story of a little girl who was hiding in the cupboard. He (the boy chasing her) looked in the cupboard. He saw the cupboard in a cave. The assimilatory exercise that starts with *A* inside *B* and *B* inside *C*, and so on, leads to various play forms based on *inclusion*, such as 'In a dark, dark wood, there was a dark, dark house. And in that dark, dark house, there was a dark, dark room. And in that dark, dark room, there was a dark, dark cupboard', and so on (Opie and Opie, 1959, p. 36).

GOING THROUGH A BOUNDARY

Introduction

Surrounding and *going through a surround or boundary* are elementary topological space notions. If a person is in a room, they are surrounded by walls. If they want to move from inside to outside, they will move through a discontinuity in the boundary (such as a door). They will move from a point inside the boundary to a point outside. According to Piaget and Inhelder (1956, p. 104) the trajectory of *going through the boundary* defines the topological space notions of *boundary*, *discontinuity* and *between*.

Young children spend much time exploring these topological space notions, initially at a motor level when, for instance, they push their fingers through clay. Most young children are interested in events such as water going through the boundary of a hose pipe and funnel, trains and cars going through tunnels, and so on.

Piaget (1953) gives some interesting examples of young children discovering that one object can go through another. Lucienne (1:1:0), for instance, in attempting to replace a stick through a ring simply presses the stick against the ring. She behaves as though encirclement can be brought about by mere contact (*ibid*. p. 320).

From 1:2 to 1:3, Lucienne systematically puts grass, earth, pebbles, etc., into all the hollow objects within reach. At 1:3, her finger explores the surface of a space and discovers that the metal handle is hollow. She puts her finger inside and immediately looks for grass to put in the opening (Piaget, 1959, p. 193). By the time she is 1:3:0 she has learnt the relationship *going through* by way of the relationship between the *container* and the *contained*.

In an earlier observation, Lucienne has passed a hoop over her head down to her shoulders, which looked as though she had understood the notion of *going through*. However, she then tried to perform the same operation with a lid. She put that on top of her head and tried to pull it down. She was surprised when it would not. She obviously had no idea that the bottom of the lid stopped her head from going through (*ibid*. p. 200).

In *The Origins of Intelligence in the Child* (observations 162 to 166) Piaget (1953, p. 320) describes, in great detail, what he calls 'the long apprenticeship' needed before Jacqueline managed to get objects through the bars of her playpen. She finally found, by *rotating* objects, that she could get the narrow side of the toy through the narrow space of the bars. The project children systematically explored the notion of *going through* at four levels of increasing complexity.

Motor Level

Jim (2:1:22) laughed as he passed a hoop over his head. Jim (2:2:5) kept putting his finger in the dead whiting's mouth.

Many motor examples of *going-through* consisted of the children experimenting with pushing one thing through another, for instance, pushing nails through clay. This produced a core-and-radial configuration that, from an early age, was given symbolic significance. For instance, Jim at 2:2:20 was absorbed by nails and screws pushed into a ball of clay. He asked, 'What's this, mummy?' When he was 2:4:11 he pushed four nails into a ball of clay and named it 'Spider, that's his legs'.

Symbolic Representation

Lois (4:1:25) painted 'A Lady sunbathing and the tree and the sun. The sun is shining through the trees'. Lois (4:2:16) cut a tin-foil cake container in two. In doing so she accidentally made a small hole in one half. She called the result 'A sofa with a hole in it'.

Just after this, Lois carefully made a small hole right through her 'home book'. Her mother found her looking through the hole, examining things.

The project teacher saw Susan (4:1:8) struggling inside a box.

Teacher: What are you doing, Susan?
Susan: Going through.
Teacher: You're going through what?
Susan: This box.
Teacher: You are going through the hole in the box are you?
Susan: I can jump out again.
Teacher: Can you? How do you do it? What do you do with your feet?
Susan: I dropped in again.
Teacher: Are you going to get into the next hole?
Susan: That's another hole. That's downstairs. [struggling to get through the top hole again]: I can't get up.

Later in the day Susan was watching some children climbing through the home-area window. She said to Mrs B, 'Look, they're going through that window'.

Teacher: You are interested in holes, aren't you? A window is a hole isn't it? Do you know what windows are for?
Susan: I'm going to jump out [meaning that she was going to jump through the window like the other children].

Susan (4:2:27) spent a great deal of time blowing through a recorder, looking through a kaleidoscope and threading beads. She made clear statements about what she was doing, such as 'I'm looking through the kaleidoscope'. She frequently followed this kind of activity with drawings. One consisted of a flat rectangle with a line going through the middle. This was called 'Looking through the kaleidoscope'.

Functional Dependency Relationships

While painting or making houses, many children left a small gap they described as 'The way in' or 'That's the way you get into the house'. A more formal way of expressing this is to say *'Getting on the inside is functionally dependent on going through a boundary'*.

Amanda (4:1:14) drew 'A house'. She cut out two rectilinear holes, stood the drawing against a wall and said, 'Look, a house, these are windows'. She brought the drawing forward, looked behind it and said, 'That's inside'. Amanda (4:1:2) pushed her finger through the gill and out of the mouth of the whiting and said, 'That's where it breathes'.

Stephen (3:6:13), after pumping water out of a simulated lock, drew a picture which he called 'A pump with water going through' (Figure 6.32). Stephen (4:3:29) painted a kettle (Figure 6.33). He told his mother, 'This is a kettle and this is the spout. The water goes in the spout' (the kettle was filled via the spout). Stephen (4:4:1) pointed out a red pipe that ran round the wall of the kitchen. He told his mother, 'The hot water goes through there'.

Jock (3:9:2) drew two drawings. One was called 'A cage with a lot of birds inside'. The second was called 'These are doors where Princess Anne and Mark Phillips can come through'.

Thought Level

After members of the institute's Movement Department had been working with the parents and children in the movement hall, Amanda (3:6:16) made a model of the climbing frame from tooth-paste boxes. She told her mother about all the actions she had performed on the frame in the hall.

Joel (3:9:12) drew 'That's a cage and that's rain. The cage is for people to go into when it's raining' (Figure 6.34). The teacher said, 'I didn't quite hear what you said, Joel. Did you say "cage" or "cave"?' Nicky (3:6:28), who was standing by, said, 'But you can see it's a cage. Caves have got stalagmites and stalagtites, they go up and down. A cage has got bars over the front. That's got bars over the front, a cave hasn't got bars over the front'.

The teacher said, 'But, Joel, if it's a cage, and people go into it when it's raining, won't they get wet?' Joel looking very pleased: 'Yes'. Teacher: 'But if they get wet won't they catch cold and have to go to the doctor?' After a polite smile Joel walked away.

Discussion

Amanda's initial exploration of the gill and mouth of the whiting resembled the motor explorations of the 2-year-olds but her speech showed that she was investigating on a higher level. She knew that breathing, in a fish, is functionally dependent on gills. Amanda knew a great deal about animals because her father bought and sold animals and she often accompanied him to markets.

The reader will have observed that the teacher's conversation with Susan (4:1:8) about the motor actions involved in climbing through the holes in a box was less complex than the teacher's conversation with Nicky (3:6:28) about the differences between a cage and a cave. There are various reasons for this. Susan was accepted into the project because her family circumstances were not propitious. She had four older siblings, two of them young adults, all kept by an unsupported mother. The educational standards of the whole family were very low. Her sister, older by four years, had not spoken for the whole of her first year at primary school. The school staff were anxious for Susan to attend the project. At the end of Susan's first two years in primary school, at the age of 7, she was 33 IQ points ahead of her sister and 36 percentile points ahead on the English Picture Intelligence Test. On the Neale Analysis of Reading Ability, Susan was three months ahead of her chronological age while her sister was three years behind.

Nicky (3:6:28), on the other hand, was in the kindergarten comparison group and had an IQ of 146. His reasoning is approaching *transitivity* in that he is able to reason that if caves have x and cages have y and the drawing has y then the drawing must be of a cage.

Joel's description of his painting, on first hearing, sounds like nonsense – which is why the kindergarten teacher asked for clarification as to whether he said 'cage' or 'cave'. A cave would be a logical place for people to go into when it was raining. However, the ensuing discussion made it clear that Joel meant 'cage'. It also became clear that he was exploring the notion of *'a' going through 'b'*, in this case, rain going through the bars of a cage.

The two kindergarten children were well nourished with rich experiences and precise language as were all the kindergarten children. The teacher was therefore able to communicate at a level far above chronological age. Although her particular question in this case, about people catching cold, illustrates a lack of 'match', the organization of her classroom allowed the children to make polite departures. Most teachers in early education will admit that 'matching' questions and comments with diagnosed schemas is as yet relatively unexplored.

As with all the other schemas discussed in this chapter, the schema of *going through* evolved from simple early behaviour to more complex understandings that required co-ordination with other notions. Two examples are given to illustrate this progression. The first example suggests that *going through* (in this case *looking through*) develops from a fixed point of view to a decentred point of view.

Stephen (3:7:19), while in the bath, playfully put a clothes basket with a plastic weave over his head. He looked through the holes and told his mother, 'I'm in my house, looking out of my window'. A few days later he drew a rectangle within which he placed a line of dots. He named this 'This is a coach and these are people looking out'. Although he had had much experience of looking out of the project-bus window, it seems unlikely that he would have been able to represent this in two dimensions without the requisite cognitive ability to decentre. His ability to represent people on the *inside* of a bus, *looking out*, implies some degree of decentration. In other words, a shift to reversibility is implied. There were many drawings of people looking out of windows, particularly from children in the kindergarten group. Most children were able to say quite clearly what the person would be seeing from the window.

Six-year-olds frequently represent animals looking through the bars of cages or people looking out of buses, cars and trains. If these drawings do indicate decentration it could be an important indication to the teacher that the children are beginning to understand spatial relativity, in that objects that are seen are relative to the point of view of the observer. They are shifting from *topological* to *projective* viewpoints.

The second example shows an evolution from *going through* to *time* measured by *going through*. At one point Salam (4:4:15) was pouring water through a very narrow-necked funnel and began to count as a measure of how long water took to go through.

THOUGHT (INTERNALIZED ACTION)

In this chapter we have selected examples that illustrate different stages in the development of specific schemas. However, in everyday cognitive functioning, particularly as children become more mature and acquire more experience, 'thought' reflects clusters of schemas that contain a wide range of content. In brief, schemas become co-ordinated with each other and develop into systems of thought.

Unfortunately co-ordinations of schemas and richness and variety of content can only be illustrated and described rather than measured. Specific schemas have been used to show the sequential and systematic progression from motor behaviour to 'thought'. The 'thought' level examples have been detached from longer initial observations.

In Chapter 4 (pp. 71–2) a complete conversation between Lois (4:7:7) and Mariam, a student, illustrates co-ordinated schemas, all of which have been discussed individually in this chapter. Lois was talking about her cat. When 'thought' level observations are looked at in their entirety they show that the children are able to recall and anticipate in imagination the displacements of objects and people within a three-dimensional world. When this stage of internalization is reached, representation can consist of soldiers hiding from imaginary pursuers. The pursued move from point to point, sometimes from one covered position to another. Trees are climbed in imagination in order to escape from the dogs of the enemy. Imaginary submarines are boarded and then submerged. Imaginary aeroplanes are boarded and flown. The children pretend to parachute down, swim away from sinking ships, hide in caves while the enemy marches over the top, and so on.

Action, graphic and speech representations that convey dynamic space notions set within a three-dimensional world have their earlier equivalents at the sensorimotor stage. This route was predicted by Piaget (1959) but only the sensorimotor stage was documented in detail. After discussing the origins of *'space as a container'* and early *rotation* behaviour, Piaget (*ibid*. p. 196) describes and gives one complex illustration of what he calls 'the last essential acquisition' (by this he means internalized action or 'thought'). This is where the child establishes relations of positions and displacements among objects and simultaneously gains awareness of his or her own movements as displacements.

The example Piaget gives is of Laurent (1:2:0) who makes sufficiently complex trajectories to indicate that he has a *mental map*, albeit rudimentary, of his surroundings. He can, for instance, take a detour around a sofa in order to fetch a ball that has rolled under it. He has learnt that two different routes can have the same starting-point and the same finishing-point. He knows how to reach a gate by toddling in a straight line or by another route where he first passes some bushes. When he goes via the bushes he takes a right-angle route. He discovers this itinerary by chance. When he reaches the gate he can reverse his action back to his various starting-points. Piaget traces Laurent's displacements in relation to ten different points in the garden. He shows how a child forms a *group of displacements* and thus acquires a *cognitive map*.

Piaget describes (*ibid*. p. 199) the end of the sensorimotor stage as follows: 'The objective groups discovered during this stage [sensorimotor stage six] remain limited to the displacements directly perceived and do not yet include any displacement simply imagined'. Piaget did not follow through these *groups of displacements* to the symbolic or imaginary level.

The following observations from the Froebel project children show that they have some kind of *cognitive map* and they have assimilated sufficient environmental content to represent imagined situations. However, as will also be seen, Stephen's cognitive map is not sufficiently stable to share with more than one other child.

The 'game' or 'play', shared by Stephen (4:9:1) and Alistair (4:3:2) illustrates 'thought' in that certain spaces are given symbolic significance but the symbolism does not depend on concrete objects acting as signifiers. The two children are attempting to understand each other's point of view, that is, each other's construction of spaces that are purely imaginary.

When two other children joined the game it became too difficult and Stephen complained to Mrs B about their behaviour. The crux of the complaint is that the two who joined them were not playing the game that Stephen and, to a lesser extent, Alistair, had in mind. It was difficult enough for Stephen and Alistair to share their fragile thoughts with each other, without the well-intentioned intrusion of the other two.

Imagined Locations

A game started with Alistair and Stephen agreeing on an imaginary bed position for where soldiers sleep. The soldiers were making an imaginary tar road next to a river. When these locations became established with some difficulty, Pete joined in and lay down on what had been designated as a soldier's bed space. Alistair was the soldier.

> Alistair: Pete, you don't sit there. I sit there you sleep there [pointing to an empty space].
> Stephen [pointing to the same space]: They always sleep on that thin bit there [it was not clear who 'they' were].
> Alistair [checking with Stephen on one of their agreed upon locations]: This is the river, eh?

Amanda was doing something to what she called the road but that was a space demarcated by Stephen and Alistair as the river. After Stephen had expressed his annoyance with Amanda, he decided to change the location of the river.

> Stephen: The water's over here now. It's gonna be the water, Amanda was doing it and I told them off [Pete and Amanda]. I don't want them to do it.
> Mrs B: What is it that you are doing?
> Stephen: Alistair filled this up, this hole [an imaginary hole in the ground] so that Pete don't do it again [Pete doesn't need to do it again].
> Mrs B: You know you said you were road men. What are you putting on the road?
> Stephen: Tar.

Alistair (not realizing that Stephen had changed the location of the road to where the river used to be, in the light of Amanda digging there) said, 'It's a river'. Stephen got annoyed again: 'No, I want the tar over there'.

Mrs B, trying very hard to follow Stephen's changed cognitive map of the location of the river in relation to the road, asked: 'So this bit can be the river, can it?' Stephen: 'No! This is the tar, over there is the car. I've done the tar here. We're not playing with him any more' (meaning Pete).

Discussion

At this stage of social play, Stephen's affective response towards people who fail to follow his imagined locations is one of extreme annoyance. This could be dismissed as cognitive egocentricity but it is just as likely to be based on a cognitive ability to imagine without the requisite speech to convey the imaginings to others.

This example draws attention to the difficulties involved in communicating a subjective system of symbolic locations without the aid of socially shared public speech. Stephen's cognitive map is not private in the sense of being incommunicable because Alistair had already understood where things were located in their play. It was a cognitive achievement for Stephen and Alistair to be able to communicate sufficiently well for them to agree on imagined events taking place in imagined places.

The dissatisfaction and complaints expressed by Stephen indicate that he had the desire to be clear about features of the game but not yet the verbal capacity to negotiate his meanings with more than one friend.

'THOUGHT': TELLING A STORY

When Randolph was 4:10:11, he spontaneously told a story to the project teacher, Mrs B. The narrative aspect of the story is not particularly coherent but what is clear is that he is verbally expressing a set of dynamic space notions, each of which had been explored by him, at earlier levels, during the previous year. The story is as follows:

> Randolph: One day the lion went down seeing if the rabbit is here. So he was peeping and he was looking and he point to the cat. One night he was hiding near the cupboard, where we can't see him. The little mouse was peeping and he was turning round not looking. One night the cat was looking round and so one night he stuck his head in the clock. And one night he was rolling down and he couldn't hear what is making a noise and so he was behind the cat and the thing still on his head and so one night he was trying to take it off. The night he said he was going to help him and he said, 'I am not your friend' so he run away. I telling a story. Whew!
>
> Mrs B: Thank you, Randolph, I enjoyed that very much. It was a lovely story.

Discussion

Internalised trajectories, expressed in the story, are as follows: *lion went down, he point to the cat he ran away*. The *trajectories* are described in terms of *purpose*: *the lion went down to find a rabbit* (it could even be said that finding a rabbit was *functionally dependent on going down*). The sentence, 'He was near the cupboard', expresses a *proximity* relation. He makes his characters *rotate* for the purpose of looking round: 'the mouse was not looking round and the rat was looking round'. One of his characters is hiding therefore he cannot be seen *relative to the point of view of the observer*: 'the cat was hiding where we can't see him'. A character can put *part of himself inside an enveloping space*: 'a head in a clock'. A character can 'roll down the hill' (*dynamic rotation*). In speech he can express a projective space notion: 'he was *behind* the cat'. He expresses the spatial notion of *on-top-of*: 'he was trying to take off the thing on his head'.

It cannot be said that this story reflects thought that is static. Randolph is able to describe actions – to evoke the past in the absence of objects originally acted upon. His actions are replaced by words. This is the point of departure for thought (Piaget, 1968b, p. 22).

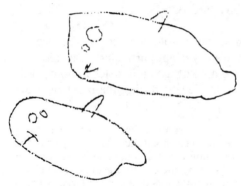

Figure 6.1 'Mother whale looking down. Little boy whale looking up'

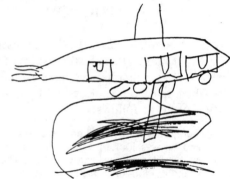

Figure 6.2 'The aeroplane over the water. That's where you pull them down'

Figure 6.3 'Submarine, periscope, water. The submarine is going up to the top'

Figure 6.4 'Bang, bang, this man is shooting him. The gun where you hold it'

Figure 6.5 'I've done him like that because he's falling out of bed'

Figure 6.6 'The tree has fallen down'

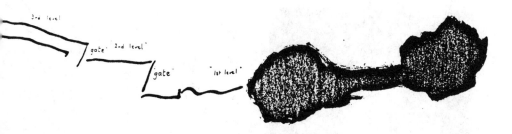

Figure 6.7 'This is Teddington Lock. First level, gate, second level, gate, third level'

Figure 6.8 'This one is pulling that one along'

Figure 6.9 'A dog chased by a cat'

Figure 6.10 'This is a fan to cool you down'

Figure 6.11 'A cowboy ring' (a lasso)

Figure 6.12 'A cake with two candles. That's the flame on top'

Figure 6.13 'It's a slide, me on the slide'

Figure 6.14 'A man, a hat and a hammer'

Figure 6.15 'Me, hat and boots'

Figure 6.16 'Lady'

Figure 6.17 'People, they've got hats on'

Figure 6.18 'A boat is going under the bridge'

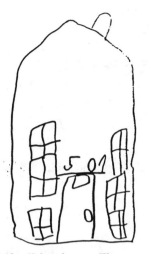

Figure 6.19 'It's a house. The garden is at the back'

Figure 6.20 'Daddy [later changed to Dick] he's got a belt on'

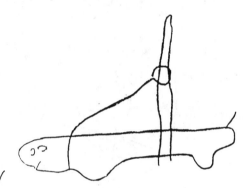

Figure 6.22 'Sausage dog tied to a post'

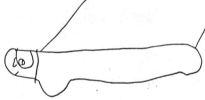

Figure 6.21 'My sausage dog on a lead'

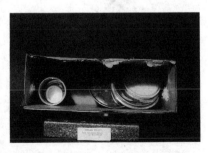

Figure 6.23 'The crockery ready to be washed up'

Figure 6.24 'Handbag'

Figure 6.25 'A house, it's got two storeys. That's upstairs and that's downstairs'

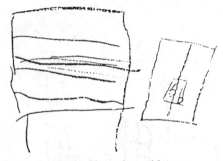

Figure 6.26 'Inside and outside my wardrobe'

Figure 6.27 'Eyes and mouth'

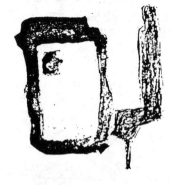

Figure 6.28 'Chair and house'

Figure 6.29 'Chair in a house'

Figure 6.30 'Now I've put her in a dark room'

Figure 6.31 'Alistair inside with two legs. I can't do any more children, there's not enough room inside the tent'

Figure 6.32 'A pump with water going through'

Figure 6.33 'This is a kettle and this is the spout. The water goes in the spout'

Figure 6.34 'That's a cage and that's rain. The cage is for people to go into when it's raining'

PART III

PART III

7

CONTINUITY IN THE CURRICULUM

INTRODUCTION

The central principle of the 1988 Education Reform Act (ERA) is that every pupil should have a balanced, relevant and broadly based curriculum. However, 'It is not enough for such a curriculum to be offered by the school: it must be fully taken up by each individual pupil' (DES, 1989a, para. 2.1). This introduces two, somewhat different, meanings of 'continuity in the curriculum'. One meaning describes what is to be offered to children as they proceed through school. Selection will be made by school staffs from publications on different areas of the curriculum such as those distributed by the DES. Schools can abstract pro-grammes of study for particular purposes, for instance, to delineate which teachers will tackle which topic and when. Also, sequences of what is on offer to children in different subject areas, at different stages, can be displayed for the illumination of, for instance, parents.

Before ERA many schools had implemented a more systematic and coherent organization of what was on offer to children of different ages and stages from the beginning to the end of schooling. A whole-school approach to the organiza-tion of curriculum content into concepts, topics or themes, now essential, is an improvement on individual teachers organizing and delivering their own curriculum.

In the literature, 'continuity' is mainly discussed in relation to what is on offer and what will be delivered. Under 'Better schools' (the DES (1985, para. 63)) states: 'The 5-16 curriculum needs to be constructed and delivered as a continuous and coherent whole, in which the primary phase prepares for the secondary phase and the latter builds on the former'.

This aspiration is commendable but it will take time before secondary teachers know what is being offered in their subject to children from 5 to 11 and before primary teachers know how the various concepts they are presenting have evolved from early education and how they will be developed at the secondary level. The detailed documentation of National Curriculum topics will probably assist this broad aim of achieving continuity of curriculum content over time.

The other meaning of 'continuity' is given importance in official publications but detailed discussion flounders because it is difficult to demonstrate. The DES (1985) states:

> To deal adequately with pupils within one phase of education requires a thorough understanding of the educational needs of children in that age range and a view of how a particular phase relates to the whole process [para. 5].
>
> There are limitations in a curriculum which is no more than a list of subjects ... it is too easy to define the content of each subject with no reference whatever to the learning processes to be used [para. 18].

Again, DES (1985, para. 124) states: 'Teaching and learning experiences should be ordered so as to facilitate pupils' progress, with each successive element making appropriate demands and leading to better performance'.

Perhaps the greatest difficulty in evaluating pupil progress is diagnosing successful 'match' between the learning of individual pupils and offered curriculum content. This requires a high degree of professional understanding of the processes of incremental learning. The more the teacher learns about the understanding of individuals, the more effective he or she will be able to select appropriate curriculum content for both individuals and groups.

Curriculum development in early education can best take place within early education. With the introduction of the National Curriculum there is a possibility that teachers will feel pressured to prepare young children for what is to come rather than validating existing cognitions and motivations. As discussed in Chapter 1, viewing early education retrospectively highlights cognitive deficits rather than competence. Continuity is more likely to be achieved by documenting the developmental links between successful early learning and later learning.

Curtis (1986) gives examples of 'discontinuity' between early and primary education that are immediately and distressingly recognizable. Children in early education may be learning about real fundamental notions while using sand and water. In the reception class the sand and water tray may be 'somewhere to go when "work" is finished' (*ibid*. p. 159). 'Fundamental notions' and explorations, as discussed throughout this book, are thus trivialized. As suggested in Chapter 4, the concepts of 'work' and 'play' need to be linked more clearly with fundamentals of the learning process.

One of the most pressing discontinuities, which generates widespread concern, is the mismatch between the cognitive concerns of 3- and 4-year-old children and what they are being offered in some reception classes. Highly trained teachers in early education must take over the teaching of 3- and 4-year-olds in primary schools.

To sum up this introduction, teachers are now being asked to study the nature of knowledge, as laid down in National Curriculum documents, the ways in which knowledge is acquired in children at different stages of understanding and to produce evidence that there has been a match between what is on offer and what has been assimilated. All teachers will know that this prescription for successful continuity is more easily declared than demonstrated.

In Chapters 5 and 6 of this book, continuity between cognition in infants and the Froebel project children from 2 to 5 is discussed and illustrated in relation to particular schemas. In this and the following chapters an attempt will be made to illustrate how children build conceptually on what has gone before. Examples from children are taken from the literature as well as from observations in primary schools. The areas of the curriculum vary. Some examples are taken from children's writing, from mathematics, design and technology, and so on. What links the examples is how schematic development and curriculum extensions before the age of 5 have direct links with concept development and curriculum extension in children between the ages of 5 and 11.

CONTINUITY IN LANGUAGE AND THOUGHT

Before discussing the findings of the Froebel project on language and thought with implications for the primary curriculum, it is necessary (because of the rapidly developing links between constructivism and the study of early language) to give a short summary of recent research.

For many years research into language development was dominated by linguists who had been influenced by Chomsky's theory that infants come into the world with an innate language acquisition device. Chomsky (1980) said, 'I consider that there is strong evidence that particular aspects of language are innately determined' (cited in Piattelli-Palmarini, 1980, p. 173). Even more controversially he said that ' "Human language" is a "mental organ" having an innate structure as specific as that of the eye or the heart' (*ibid.* p. 276).

In academic debate Chomsky's position has been contrasted with constructivist theory, Piaget being the main protagonist. Piaget's position on knowledge in general is that it can be constructed only through interaction between certain inborn modes of processing and the actual characteristics of physical objects and events. Although Piaget denies that infants are born with innate cognitive structures, he agrees that cognitive structures are present from birth. He maintains that functioning, assimilation and accommodation immediately create schemas or cognitive structures, and structuring is brought about through an organization of successive actions performed on objects (*ibid.* 1980, p. 23).

In debate both Piaget and Chomsky have shifted from their initial, rather extreme positions. Chomsky (1980) agreed that there were interactions between innate mechanisms and aspects of the external world and that, therefore, experience had some effect. However, he diminished the importance of environment by saying (*ibid.* p. 172) that 'Certain kinds of interactions with the external world serve a triggering function only for the acquisition of language'. There is a conceptual difference between Piaget's claim that 'assimilation' 'feeds' early cognitive structures and Chomsky's 'triggering' that merely actualizes what is already there.

For teachers, the middle ground between extreme innatism and extreme environmentalism provides the fertile soil for facilitating language and thought in children. Cognitive structures are clearly of importance in relation to children's understanding while environmental content provides 'food' for the thought structures.

Vygotsky maintained that thought and language have different genetic roots in that the two functions develop along different lines and independently of each other. However, he suggested (1962, p. 41) that there is a close correspondence between thought and speech. His views correspond to Chomsky's statement: 'I take it for granted that thinking is a domain that is quite different from language, even though language is used for the expression of thought' (Piattelli-Palmarini, 1980, p. 173).

Fodor (1980) illustrated the essential semantic relationship between language and thought when he pointed out that you can't learn a word that expresses a concept you don't have. 'Nobody would learn the word "cat" unless he knows what a cat is' (Piattelli-Palmarini, 1980, p. 173). Here, Fodor draws attention to the meaning, aspect of language as opposed to linguistic form. An important educational issue is to ascertain that a 'match' exists between existing forms of thought and appropriate speech.

FORM AND MEANING

Since Chomksy, linguists have sought clarification on the structures of language whereas psychologists and educationalists have been more interested in children and the processes by which they acquire language. Research findings on early language and thought can be separated into information on the 'form' of utterances and the 'meaning' of utterances. Studies edited by Snow and Ferguson (1977) have found that the main aim of mother–child dialogue is the construction of conversational meaning and that this aim over-rides syntactic considerations (reported in Lock and Fisher, 1984). Of particular interest is research on meanings intended by speakers.

Although Piaget has consistently maintained that sensorimotor actions are inextricably bound up with early speech, he has never produced evidence from children in support of this claim. Recently, however, there has been evidence that infants use early speech (verbal signs or signals) for expressing satisfaction or lack of satisfaction with the outcomes of intended schematic action. This will be discussed in detail as it coincides with some of the findings of the Froebel project.

Although debate on 'innate versus environmental' remains inconclusive, research (generated within the debate) has led to the realization, important to teachers, that all children, whatever their ethnic or cultural background, acquire 'forms of utterances' in broadly the same sequence. A few instances of 'form' will pave the way for a differentiation between 'form' and 'meaning' as well as a closer examination of the 'meaning' aspect of language.

There are nine known major periods of the forms of language acquisition starting with *cooing*. This includes *speech sound discriminations*, such as 'ba/pa', which lead eventually to an advanced concern with the 'graphic representations' of language, such as the alphabet, writing, signs and isolated words in texts. This sequence applies to children all over the world (Slobin, 1973, discussed in Lock and Fisher, 1984, p. 8).

'*Cooing*' precedes *babbling*, which leads to first words. First words include *discrimination of word pairs*, such as 'bat/pat'. Although it is accepted that two word utterances contain semantic relations, it is now becoming clear that one-word utterances such as *up*, *no* and *more* also include meaning.

Several researchers have recorded that most young children use words such as *gone*, *there*, *oh dear* and *no more* in their early language use. There is also general use of locative expressions such as *down*, *up*, *in*, *out*, *on* and *off*. The Froebel project findings show that location words are used in a very wide range of situations. These are discussed in detail in Chapter 6.

As mentioned earlier, it is not difficult to record children's behaviour or use of words. What is difficult is to conceptualize the meaning of the raw data of observation in ways that are useful for some purpose or other. Gopnic (1984) observed children's use of certain words within contexts and used constructivist theory to explain what children appeared to have in mind in their early use of speech. Her conclusions may help to illuminate what Piaget had in mind when he insisted that both knowledge and speech proceed from action.[1]

Gopnic recorded language in children from the age of 1 to 2 and observed that certain words were used within certain contexts. She hypothesized that early words were intended to encode perceptual features, sensorimotor schemes, actions, events or relationships (see Lock and Fisher, 1984). She assumed, as was assumed in the Froebel project, that if a child always says *down* when objects move downwards, the child has some general concept of *downward movement* and that this concept was being encoded by the use of the word *down*. All of the nine children she studied used *down*, *up*, *in*, *out*, *on*, and *off* 573 times in locative contexts. In some contexts the children commented on the movements of objects but in 401 (70 per cent) of contexts the children made or tried to make an object move in a particular direction.

Words, such as *no*, *oh dear*, *more* and *there*, used within contexts, signified success or failure and the criterion of success or failure, from the infant's point of view, is of particular interest. The words expressed satisfaction or lack of satisfaction with the effects of schematic activity. If children placed one brick *on-top-of* another successfully they would say *there* (240 instances). Alternatively, if the brick fell off they would say *oh dear* (320 instances). Similarly the word *no* was used to signify that an aim had not been achieved or that objects had not behaved as expected. The word *no* was used 149 times when the child could not achieve his or her aim because of the actions of other people. For example, one child said *no* when an adult closed the lid of a tape-recorder he was trying to open. Another child said *no* when the adult wanted to put a particular lid on a box and he wanted to put a different one on.

The general factor behind the *oh dear* and *no* responses is the mismatch between what was anticipated and the actual outcome (*ibid*. p. 89). Infants 'know' that schematic action performed on objects can bring about a desired state. Confirmation is expressed by *more*, which encodes the fact that a plan is to be repeated (*ibid*. pp. 91–2). Disconfirmation is expressed by *no* or *oh dear*. Later these expressions are applied to more general events that are not the result of direct action: *more*, for instance, was used to mark the fact that two objects were similar.

This work seems to support Piaget's claim that the first mental representations are the results of internalized actions. Enough schematic, sensorimotor actions have been performed to set up anticipations. The anticipations show a continuity with skilled action and the effect of action. Early speech does arise from sensorimotor schemas, as Piaget claims, but more as a commentary on the effects of action rather than directly from the actions themselves.

NOTE

1. Gopnic (1984, pp. 83–101) uses the term 'plan' rather than 'schema' but her definition of 'plan' is similar to that of schema: 'A plan is an action, or a series of actions, performed in order to bring about an outcome. In plans, as in schemas, actions produce effects'.

8
SPEECH AND WRITING IN RELATION TO SCHEMAS

'A word is only as good as the knowing structure which uses it' (Furth, 1969, p. 111). The Froebel project findings give support to the 'cognition hypothesis of language acquisition' in that speech used by project children reflected prominent schemas as well as the content assimilated to schemas.

'The cognition hypothesis for language acquisition' (Cromer, 1979, cited in Lee, 1979), corresponds to the constructivist position on the relationship between speech and cognition, the early stages of which have been illustrated through Gopnic's work in Chapter 7. The hypothesis is that speech is acquired in synchrony with acquired meanings. To the constructivist, speech is a necessary but not a sufficient condition for the construction of logical operations. Language is important but as part of a more general cognitive organization that has its roots in 'action'. 'Language is one of the elements of a cluster of signs resting on the semiotic function and in which symbolic play, deferred imitation and mental imagery participate' (Inhelder, 1980, p. 133). One implication of the 'cognition hypothesis' for teaching is that the language used by adults must be sufficiently elaborate to support and 'flesh out' advances in children's thinking.

The cognition hypothesis has been mainly supported by research on children over the age of 6 where speech forms alter to match increasingly complex concrete-operational thought structures. Before a child acquires *seriation* he or she will use speech that reflects *absolute size* notions, such as 'I am big, you are little'. As *seriation* proceeds towards greater differentiation, speech extends and *comparative terms* are used, such as 'I am bigger than you'. Similarly, when a child becomes able to think in *hierarchical categories* he or she will be able to make statements such as 'All sparrows are birds and all birds are animals and all animals are living beings' (Piaget, 1972a, pp. 78–81).

Sinclair-de-Zwart (1969) studied the relationship between speech and *conservation*. She found that 90 per cent of *non-conservers* used *absolute* rather than *comparative* terms to describe quantity. Conservers were able to *co-ordinate two sentences* when they were able to *co-ordinate two dimensions* cognitively. They would say, as well as understand, that 'This is short but it is also wide'.

Support for the natural order of thought preceding language comes also from attempts to train non-conservers into becoming conservers by the use of speech. Children were given *comparative terms* in order to accelerate *comparative thinking*. Even when children successfully learnt the verbal expressions they rarely advanced conceptually. Similar results were found when attempts were made to generate *seriation* structures through speech training (Inhelder, 1969, p. 232; Tamburrini, 1982).

Not only do children not advance conceptually through verbal means alone but they also actually transform test questions to fit in with their existing level. Piaget calls this 'distorting assimilation'. *Pre-ordination* children were asked to give more sweets to one doll rather than another. They were then asked to repeat the question. They transformed the question into absolute terms, such as 'You said I had to give a lot to that one and a little to that one' (Duckworth, cited in Schwebel and Raph, 1974, p. 144).

The general route of development is from early gross generalizations towards progressive separations and finer differentiations (Jakobson, 1941, cited in Cromer, 1974). Early babbling developing into speech has been compared with early scribbling developing into drawing and writing. Several strands require a more detailed examination. Even symbolic play (which is widely accepted as important in early childhood education) has remained elusive when attempts have been made to measure its occurrence in an educational setting (Sylva, Roy and Painter, 1980). The route 'from action to thought' has aroused interest but has not been studied systematically and longitudinally. It is illustrated and given substance in Chapter 6 of this book. Early scribbling developing into drawing and writing is illustrated in Chapter 5.

As already stated, Piaget considers sensorimotor intelligence rather than language to be the true foundation of operational thought, with mental representation being the culmination of sensorimotor intelligence. Few people would deny that speech is the major vehicle in 'carrying forward' sensorimotor developments and learnings to symbolic levels of functioning. The problem has been how to document this hypothesized route.

One problem is that early 'two-word' utterances are ambiguous. After climbing in and out of holes in hollow wooden boxes for some time, Kamal (2 years old and still in the main an Urdu speaker) made a construction from a part of a cardboard egg box. He described it as 'two holes'. Various schemas could be involved, such as *the salience of the circle* (the shape of the hole), *going through the boundary, two-ness,* and so on, but cognitive features are difficult to abstract from such short utterances. Because of this difficulty many project observations were coded at a motor level though they may have contained a symbolic component.

Intention and meaning were clearer when utterances were made in context. What young children say usually relates directly to what they do and see. As speech use and comprehension increased, ambiguities decreased. Support for the cognition hypothesis in the Froebel project findings is almost too obvious. A random inspection of any schema illustrated in Chapters 5 and 6 will show the close relationship between schema and speech use. Professionals and parents could work together in order to facilitate the necessary links between forms of thought, the content of thought and appropriate speech. As already mentioned in Chapter 4, there were relatively few symbolic representations of project children that did not involve speech – indicating that children like to talk about what they are doing.

FROM MARKS TO WRITING

There are different views on when writing begins. It is generally held that writing is writing when another person can read what is written without too much difficulty. Looking at writing from a developmental point of view, it could be said that the origins are to be found soon after birth when the infant distinguishes things that move from objects that are static. Both the perception and production of writing can be seen in these terms. Print as a product appears to be made up of *fixed patterns*. Writing as a process gives information on the *movingness of writing*: 'The moving finger writes and having writ moves on'.

The Froebel project children's early writing was consistent with early symbolic representations in general. The movingness of cars or planes was represented, as was the movingness of writing as a continuous movement of the pencil across paper. There were not many instances of this pretend, cursive writing but the few examples that were produced were usually called 'a letter' or 'a shopping list'. Several writers have drawn attention to the ubiquity of the 'shopping list' in early writing (Temple, Nathan and Burris, 1982, p. 33; Payton, 1984, p. 37; Sanderson, 1987, p. 3). Perhaps shopping lists and letters as instances of writing in action are produced mainly in homes. The few instances of this kind of imitation on the part of the project children may reflect a paucity of writing in the home.

As most print in the general environment is fixed and does not contain information on the writing process, the project teacher made a point of writing, in the presence of the children, about things that were happening. The intention was to convey the message that reading and writing are everyday activities. Parents soon joined in with this and 'home books', containing positive messages about matters of interest, were carried back and forth between home and school.

Several project children represented the *linear configuration* of writing with short *horizontal lines* or with strips of sticky paper. Most of the project children's highly specific representation of what they called 'writing', 'letters' and 'names' were consistent with the graphic schemas they used for drawing other objects that shared a figurative similarity.

Pretend writing started with rows of discrete marks, such as short *vertical lines*, *crosses* and *circles*. Therefore, the project children's early writing, in a general sense, reflected both action and figurative schemas. When the children became interested in *circular* things in the environment and they were able to reproduce *circular* things in their drawings, the letter 'O' was singled out for reproduction rather than, say, the letter 'Z'. Letter shapes, like other shapes in the environment, were consistently assimilated to existing levels of mark-making. When *grid-like* marks were made, *grid-like* letters appeared, as did other *grid-like* configurations, such as cages, cranes, scaffolding, hammocks, the Eiffel Tower, railings and train tracks. Teachers and parents tend to show enthusiasm when standard letter forms appear. When an adult admired, at some length, a 4-year-old's upper-case 'H' the boy said, somewhat annoyed, 'It's a clothes line with two props'.

When project children were able to co-ordinate *vertical lines* with the *open semi-circle* they made a major step forward in the production of letter formations. This was achieved after much time-taking effort. Figure 5.18 shows Randolph's attempts to copy his mother's writing of his name. 'R', 'P' and lower-case 'A' are tackled with co-ordinated *line* and *semi-circle*. The *oblique line* has hardly started to emerge from the earlier *core and parallel radials*. Figure 5.19 shows the striking similarity between the graphic schemas used for letters and the drawing of a man.

Almost a year later, Randolph is still working spontaneously on all the letter forms needed for his name. 'The glasses' show a connection between two *core and curved radials* (Figure 5.13). The *curved radials* (arcs) are used five times in the spontaneous writing of his name. He now connects an *oblique line* correctly for his upper-case 'R'. From this time onwards, Randolph had no difficulty in representing the upper-case letters, 'A', 'M', 'K', 'V' or 'W'.

The similarity between general graphic schemas and letter forms is apparent in developmental studies of children's drawing and yet the similarity has often escaped notice. Eng (1959) gave enough illustrations from her niece, Margaret, to show the obvious link between letter and drawing forms but, as already discussed in Chapter 4, seeing commonalities requires attention to form rather than content. When Margaret managed to draw the *triangular* form (Figure 5.54) she not only drew an upper-case 'A' and 'M' but she began to draw *triangular* houses, groups of people wearing *triangular* capes, a sitting figure, a *zig-zag trajectory* behind a sledge, a dog kennel with a *triangular roof*, and so on.

The *open continuous triangle* (the zig-zag) opened up opportunities for the representation of zig-zag phenomena, such as 'steps', 'teeth', 'waves', stegosaurus and so on. Letter forms represented at this time were 'W', 'M', 'Y' and 'Z'. Figure 5.62 shows that Shanaz is able to draw all the letter forms needed for her name but she is not yet able to orient the letter 'Z' on a horizontal plane.

However, particular enthusiasm for 'letter-like' forms need not preclude validation for other graphics, which also have a future. *Arrows pointing in different directions*, *spirals*, *helixes*, and many spatial orders are not related to the forms and directionality of reading and writing but they can be very important in science, mapping and mathematics, not to mention painting and drawing. As each graphic form emerged in the Froebel project each was admired and the various uses were discussed. The teacher would comment on the use of marks by pointing out that *a curve* had been used for drawing an arch, a boat, a cup and a 'c'. The children gave enthusiastic responses to these comments. Adults can over-emphasize early writing but they can also miss it. Shirley Payton asked her 3-year-old, 'Are you drawing a lovely picture?' The child replied, 'No, I'm writing "S" for Sally'.

As the project children acquired graphic forms they used them to represent known objects, which included letters and words. The children also combined marks and by so doing created new graphic forms that included letters. *Connecting* a *vertical line* with a *semi-circle* allowed '9', 'P', 'B', 'b', 'D' and 'd' to be constructed. Varying motor actions that leads to variability in mark-making are instances of accommodation. Clay (1975) has named this a 'flexibility principle'.

The spontaneous repetitions of each new form in drawing and writing are instances of assimilation. Assimilation, as repetition, has the main function of 'practice makes perfect'. Clay (*ibid.*) describes this as the 'recurring principle'. Of greater interest than repetition *per se* is the way in which instances of assimilation can be used as indications of cognitive level. There is, for instance, a great developmental difference between the repetition of circles and crosses and repeated words or repeated sentences. Knowledge of levels of assimilation is synonymous with knowledge of stage levels.

Progress from early to later learning is illustrated in Chapters 5 and 6. It seems likely that the advanced reading scores of the Froebel project children were related to the procedure adopted in the project of paying minute attention to each observed increment in each child's learning over two years. The significant differences between the project children's scores and those of their older siblings indicate that the early education received in the project facilitated later development in reading.

CONTINUITY BETWEEN DYNAMIC SCHEMAS AND EARLY WRITING

Thirty-seven examples of early writing were collected from Sarah over three years (from age 4 to 7) by her teacher, Margaret Palladino, at Eveline Lowe Primary School, London.[1] Her teacher selected examples in order to show developments in Sarah's writing as discussed in the literature on early writing.

Only one aspect of Sarah's writing will be considered here in order to show a continuity between the cognitive form and content of earlier schematic behaviours illustrated in Chapter 6 of this book and the cognitive form and content of much early writing. Of the 37 examples of Sarah's writing, 25 show this continuity.

Many of the examples consist of simple *forward trajectories* with *one or two end-points*, such as:

This is me going to the shops.

Mummy comes to tell Kelly's got to go home.

This is a lady getting married and the people watching and the car to take them home.

Penny and Paul take the baby for a walk.

Snow White went to a little house. She looks after them in the woods.

My name is Sarah. I've got blue eyes and blond hair. I go to school in my dad's car. Debbie picks me up. When I get home I play out. Then I go in I have my dinner. I get undressed. I watch the telly. Mummy says go to bed now Sarah.

One day it was a girl's birthday. She got a puppy dog. She named it Sibar. She took it out for a walk. Her mum said she had to come in. She went in. She was tired and went to bed with her puppy dog. The end of the story.

One day a girl said can I go out? Yes said the mum take the dog. Alright said the girl. When she got there she picked blackberries and strawberries. Time to go home the girl said to the dog, so they went.

The example just given shows a simple *trajectory* and *return* but *the end-point* of the *trajectory* includes *collecting* two types of berries. In other words, there is now a co-ordination between the *spatial trajectory* and a *logical classification* (two types of berries).

The following is a written sequence of nine events that is equivalent, but at a higher level of symbolic functioning, to the action and speech representations of earlier development.

One day daddy and mummy went out for the day. Let's have a picnic said mummy. I have brought some sandwiches so they had a picnic and then they went blackberry picking. Then they went home and had their dinner and watched telly and went to bed and they went fast asleep.

The next example contains co-ordinations of schemas of *inside/outside*, *enveloping space*, *rotation* and *trajectories*.

This is the story of the horse. His Name is Sandy. She is brown all over. Sandy belongs to a farmer and he lives in a stable. Sometimes the farmer lets him out in the field because he doesn't like being stuck in the stable all day. Out in the field Sandy runs about and rolls in the sand.

The following sequence of five cooking events consists of four actions of *'placing inside'*, one action of *'rotation'* and one action of placing *'on-top-of'*:

I made some pastry.
I put the flour into the bowl.
I put the water into the bowl.
I put the milk into the bowl and we stirred it. And we put the pastry onto the tray.

The functional dependency understandings of the following example are twofold: the figurative effects of ball and flat shapes are *functionally dependent* upon different kinds of *rotation* and cakes not sticking are *functionally dependent* on *greasing the surface* of the tin: 'I rolled the dough into a ball. I rolled it out then I cut out shapes. And then I greased the tray and put the cakes into the tray'. Cutting out shapes involves *going through* boundaries.

In the following, some of the processes of baking that were included in earlier written accounts are now left out. This may illustrate a 'speeding-up' of 'thought'. First written (and previously spoken) accounts include many actions in sequence but once the sequence is internalized, and thoroughly assimilated, some details become redundant.

We picked blackberries. We washed them. We made pastry. You need flour, margarine and water. I put it in a bowl and mixed it with a wooden spoon. I put it in the tray and put the blackberries on top and put the pastry on top of the blackberries and I put it in the oven for an hour.

NOTE

1. Margaret is now Headteacher of St Georges School in London.

9

SPACE – CONFIGURATIONS, DISPLACEMENTS AND CURRICULUM EXTENSIONS OF SCHEMAS

The study of space is usually referred to as geometry. The following two definitions give equal weight to the dynamics of space and to the configurations of objects in space:

> Geometry is concerned partly with the properties of space in which bodies are situated, in which they move and in which events happen and partly with the shapes and configurations of objects in space.
>
> (Land, 1960, p. 160)

> Space only has meaning when it contains objects which we can see in relation to one another, or can observe in motion as they change their position relative to ourselves or to one another.
>
> (Williams and Shuard, 1980, p. 108)

The Froebel project findings provide evidence of a continuity from early sensorimotor behaviours through symbolic behaviours that subsequently become internalized into 'thought'. Information from the literature on early perception, considered together with the sequences of the Froebel project representations in Chapters 5 and 6, suggest a continuity between the early perception of shapes and states and the later representation of those states.

The literature on early perception shows that infants respond positively and selectively to increasingly complex stimuli that 'match' an increasing complexity of perception (Bower 1974, 1977a). Bower's test stimuli start with vague 'eye' and 'face-like' configurations that approximate closely to the human face. The most complex level of stimulus consists of two clearly different faces. A similar sequence of complexity was found in project representations. The most complex level of representation differentiates between two different human figures (Figure 5.13).

Piaget (1959, pp. 357–86) has called the considerable time 'lag' between perceived stimulus complexity and representational complexity 'vertical décalage': 'Décalage in comprehension [is] due to the passage of one plane of activity to another (a higher plane), for example, from the plane of action to that of representation'. The idea of 'décalage' has not generated much research, which is a pity because achieving continuity in the curriculum would be assisted by such studies.

Infants gradually recognize that there is a correspondence between some states, such as the mother's face, and other states, such as other faces. The infant establishes *term-for-term topological correspondence within enclosed spaces*. Infants can be observed pulling at features of their mother's face until they learn that face features cannot be rearranged. A child learns to recognize familiar states in spite of changes of distance and in spite of differences in perspective.

In the primary school, the formal properties of topological features of objects are apparent (Sauvy and Sauvy, 1974). Two 6-year-old boys set up a model of a railway track, a brick road, cars, flats and two bridges. They were reluctant to clear it away so the next morning the teacher set up the model as she remembered it. The two boys pointed out the lack of equivalence between their model and the teacher's attempts at recreation. They decided to remake the model. It was clear that they had internalized their previous spatial constructions and that they had a stable set of topological relationships of *connection, separation, proximity* and *spatial order*. They hit on a useful notion. If you want to share an *equivalence* you had better make a map, which they did. The early learning of *term-for-term topological correspondence* is later symbolically represented in drawings that are 're-workings' of earlier perceptions. This is most clearly seen in drawings of faces.

Action representations (or symbolic play) in early education can be viewed similarly. In Chapter 6 an example, 'imagined locations', shows a certain stage in the *co-ordination of fixed positions and action displacements*. Stephen, at 4, can express his 'imagined locations' but his 'thoughts' are still too fragile to share easily.

It is known that early perception is assisted by speech and that a knowledge of the properties of objects evolves into the symbolic representation of those objects. Early perceptual experience precedes drawing and drawing usually precedes writing. Poor writers often show immaturity in their drawings and in their speech.

The aspect of intellectual functioning under discussion here is to do with the fixed properties of objects. Knowledge of fixed materials and their functions is an important aspect of environment. An intelligence-test question for $4\frac{1}{2}$-year-olds asks what a house or window is made of. Answers provide information on the conceptual and perceptual differentiations that have been made before school. Where experience and speech are lacking, a study of the local environment is indicated, preferably with the help of parents. The town environment contains (among other things) wood, board, bricks, cement, stucco, shingles, tile, stone, lumber, blocks and rocks – each with either different or similar properties and uses.

Children's answers to what things are made of and why we have them indicate both cognitive form and cognitive functioning. Correct answers to IQ tests are as follows: a house is to go in, to cook in, to make us warm, to sleep in, to keep off the rain, and so on. Summative test results are arrived at by answers marked either right or wrong. However, as Piaget found, test answers gave useful information on the genesis of knowledge in that they indicate which schemas are uppermost. A door is for *going through* to the *inside* of a house, and so on. Schemas suggest topics that can be pursued in depth in early education. Aspects of 'The Three Little Pigs' 'match' schemas. The houses *envelop* but their *strength* is *functionally dependent* on the materials used (*properties of objects*).

FROM TRACKING TO MAPPING

Throughout this book reference has been made to action patterns that lead to action representations (Chapter 6) and behaviours of looking or gazing, which lead to ikonic or figurative representations (Chapter 5). A map may suggest an ikonic picture of fixed points in space, and examples are given of early representations of fixed locations in Chapter 6. However, it would seem that early maps are primarily records of action.

Britton (1970) captures the configurational and the action basis of 'recalled space'. He and his brother would set out from their home on the outskirts of town. He writes (p. 11):

> I could walk into the country. On Saturdays we did, my brother and I. As we explored the area we drew a map of this precious bit of countryside, and I can recall one name on it ... there was a long winding lane called Hobbleythick Lane. With the name comes a picture of a tall, ragged hawthorn hedge: one only, though I suppose there may have been a hedge on the other side also. *THE MAP WAS A RECORD OF OUR WANDERINGS.* There were other representations ... my brother certainly used to stop occasionally and make a drawing of something he had seen. Neither the drawing nor the map was Hobbleythick Lane: each was a representation, and each representation was differently related to the thing itself. Each was in a different way a record of experience and each was capable, in a different way, of setting up or reviving expectations about the area. The map, we might say, was a more general representation, the drawing more particular [*my italics*].

The developmental route of mapping is from *tracking* and the *displacements* of toddlers to being able to find one's way about familiar neighbourhoods because of having developed a *mental map*. Actual maps are graphic representations of trajectories in relation to fixed points. These are sometimes drawn by children as young as 3.

There is a sound basis for studying the local environment in early education because children have been exploring location and states from birth spontaneously. School can provide continuity in that the study of space and place requires a co-ordination of motor action and the perception of things encountered at various points. Although the ikonic or figurative features of places helps to fix them in the mind, it would appear that the most important aspect of neighbourhood studies is action.

In an otherwise excellent book on curriculum development in 'the study of places', the importance of pictures in learning about the environment needs qualifying. It is suggested (ILEA, 1981, p. 6) that 'The teacher must encourage the children to extract the maximum information from each picture'. It is doubtful whether important information can be extracted from pictures unless they are figurative reminders of personal experience, as with Britton's brother. The difference in interest and information between other people's holiday snaps and one's own is well known: 'The figurative aspect of knowing does not have an intrinsic development but remains ever in close dependence on the operative developmental stages' (Furth, 1969, p. 58).

The close dependence of the figurative and operative in 'mapping' is found in an example of good nursery-school practice given by HMI (DES, 1989b, p. 13). Children under 5 were taken out walking in the locality. Buildings in the area were photographed, as well as children standing by their own front doors. A board game was devised by a group of children showing the various routes taken by different children from home to school. These were drawn by the children, and showed how routes passed well-known landmarks represented by the photographs. The children drew plans and pictures showing streets, shops and other features. The children's figures cut out from the photographs were used to represent the players.

DISPLACEMENTS AND INTELLIGENCE TESTS

As discussed in Chapter 2, cognitive gain in early childhood education is evaluated either by summative or formative procedures. Even though IQ scores may increase as a result of education it is not usual, except in the most general terms, to attribute IQ gain to either successful teaching or learning. This is because test items are judged by the percentage of children who pass or fail rather than on the match between the conceptual difficulty of test questions and the concept levels of testees. However, when the schematic or conceptual levels of test questions are considered, it becomes clear that concept formation, education and parental support can all contribute towards success. There are very few test questions that do not have a potential to 'tap' schemas or concepts.

One test item at a $4\frac{1}{2}$-year-old level, for instance, requires an ability to hold in the mind for a short time *three trajectories, three end-points* and *three actions* to perform at the end-points. In this test the child is instructed to put a pencil on a chair, open a door and fetch a box (Terman and Merrill, 1976, p. 164). Success requires a *mental map*, albeit temporary, *of three trajectories connected with three end-points*. The tasks to be performed at each end-point are related to earlier spontaneous behaviours, such as placing things *on-top-of* other things, opening doors (*going through boundaries*) and being intrigued by *enveloping spaces* such as boxes. Where the earlier transporting behaviours of toddlers have been supported by adult speech the children will be more proficient in carrying out such instructions.

If 'maps are about the space we use' and intelligence tests contain questions about space from the early years right through to the highest adult level, which they do, it is important to encourage consciousness of space, and the objects that define positions in space, from the earliest years (Gerhardt, 1973; Bailey and Burton, 1982).

THE MATHEMATICS OF MOVEMENT IN A STRAIGHT LINE

Williams and Shuard (1980, p. 106) write 'Mathematically, "motion in a straight line" without any change of direction is a *translation*. Various mathematical activities can be based on this early concern ... A child sees these movements every day on the roads and in his own actions'.

Three-year-olds like to thread beads, stack bricks and line up toys. This spontaneous behaviour of making horizontal and vertical linear patterns is there for all to see. The problem is to trace the origins, diagnose the potential in the present and predict the future of such behaviours all from the point of view of extending cognitive forms with worthwhile curriculum content. *Connecting bricks* into *lines* is an early stage of a *synthesis of displacement* and *additive partitioning*, which leads to a true concept of *measuring* (Inhelder, Sinclair and Bovet, 1974, Preface, p. ix).

One of the earliest space concepts is *connection*. When children connect squares they either describe their action ('I put these together') or they describe the figurative effects, as in 'this is a pavement'. These descriptions lead to functional dependency relationships when they observe that connecting more results in *getting bigger*. Early schemas have been co-ordinated into new, higher-order concepts and can lead, in turn, to *tessellation*.

In the following example, the mathematical actions of *connecting* with noted effects are clearly articulated (Schools Council, 1974, p. 23).

> A roadway of bricks was constructed by a group of boys:
> J: 'Look at how long it is.'
> P: 'We can make it much longer. There are lots more bricks yet.'
> A: 'Yes, let's make it longer and longer till it touches the wall' [Note that 'more' (the unconnected bricks) can be imagined as being connected and thus adding to the length of the road].
> J: 'It's too long we'll have to make it shorter.' They removed three blocks at the closed end. As he is using the operation of *subtraction* on length he could be shown an economical way of representing his subraction with symbols.

When *number* as *discrete elements* can be *combined* or *partitioned* in order to *vary length*, the teacher is in business for the development of linear measurement. Linear measurement requires the co-ordination of three earlier schemas, a given *space between two end-points*, the *connection* of standard units and *number*. Children can sometimes be observed *measuring*, with only two co-ordinated schemas, *the space between end-points and number*. Their answers will be different from children with three co-ordinated schemas because they have not *connected* their standard unit. *End-points connected by lines* are often represented graphically and figuratively with appropriate content, such as 'telephone' or 'vacuum cleaner' pinned on to the configuration. 'This one is pulling that one along' is a case in point (Figure 6.8).

DYNAMIC SCHEMAS AND DESIGN AND TECHNOLOGY

In Williams and Jinks (1985, p. 13) children are set a task, 'a specific design brief', as follows: 'Make an object which will travel across a table top and stop at the edge'. David and Steven, both 6 years old, make a car out of a light cardboard tissue box. They attach (*connect*) wheels that are wobbly but they do *rotate*. They attach (*connect*) a piece of string to the front of the car and attach a weight to the other end of the string (a piece of wood). They place the car near the far edge of the table top, let the string rest on the full length of the table top and allow the wood to make a '*downward trajectory*'. As the wood is heavier than the car, the weight of the wood draws the car across the length of the table (on a *horizontal trajectory*). As the *length* of the string is a fixed length, *the end of the trajectory* of the car *corresponds to the horizontal trajectory* of the car and the car stops at the edge of the table instead of toppling over. One of the children wrote 'The piece of string must be as long as the table is high. When the wood reaches the floor it stops the car'. He is expressing necessary *equivalence* between the *height* of the table and the *length* of the string.

The cluster of schemas or concepts required for this 6-year-old solution to the given problem in 'design and technology' includes several that can be acquired before the age of 5. These include *rotation*, *connection*, *vertical* and *horizontal trajectories*, *going through and round boundaries* (as in making knots) and *equivalence between three pairs of end-points* (height and length of table and string).

ORIENTEERING

Blomberg (1982) suggests that children under 5 are capable of orienteering using three or four fixed points. At each fixed point each child can perform a task such as stamping or punching a hole in a control card. Structurally, this curriculum extension is similar to the intelligence-test question given earlier.

After 'doing the course' the teacher can symbolically represent the fixed points and the spatial relationships between them. The points can be given a nominal description, such as red, white and blue. This allows number to be used for each trajectory or complete course. Blomberg's orienteering suggestion provides curriculum substance in that it extends on what children are doing spontaneously in their play. Four-year-olds like to hide at fixed points (called by different names) followed by chasing between points.

DISPLACEMENTS IN LITERATURE

Many analogies used in speech, poetry and prose have their roots in early trajectories. Trajectories are used metaphorically, as in 'sinking into despair' or 'rising to the height of our ambitions or emotions or powers'. *Displacement is the distance* and *direction an object moves between two points*, and each time an object in motion changes direction, it ends one displacement and begins another.

Rhyme and story material can nourish early trajectories by supplying simple variations on movements:

> Here is a crocodile crawling through the mud. Crawling, crawling, crawling through the mud. Here is a penguin waddling on the path, waddling on the path ... and so on.
>
> 'Hickory Dickory Dock
> The mouse ran up the clock'
>
> (Schools Council, 1974, p. 20)

In traditional nursery rhymes, 'The Grand Old Duke of York' marching up and down the hill is loved at many levels. Jack and Jill falling down the hill was much appreciated and imitated in the project.

Situations in stories where objects fall down usually receive a great deal of attention and laughter. Much slapstick comedy is based on dynamic trajectories with something unexpected happening at the end-points. Emma, a 4-year-old kindergarten child, heard the story about the tortoise who wanted to fly. The tortoise asked his wife to put out everything soft in case he didn't succeed. The birds organized his literal downfall. They changed the message from 'everything soft' to 'everything hard'. Emma thought that it was wrong to get his wife involved in his downfall.

Children who have discovered that hauling objects upwards is a function of vertical leverage find Paddington Bear's attempts to lever a bucket up on a rope very funny. The weight of the bucket pulled him up into the air (Bond, 1976).

The spatial structure of the story, *Sam Who Never Forgets* (Rice, 1977), is to do with trajectories with stopping-off points. Sam, the zookeeper, transports appropriate food to a whole range of animals in the zoo. The story suggests that he may have forgotten the poor old elephant. The listener accompanies Sam on his route around the zoo together with his stopping-off points. Co-ordinated with this spatial organization there is a logical classification of animal foods, a one-to-one mapping between food and animal and possibilities for extending 'enveloping spaces' by naming animal enclosures:

> He sets off transporting food in his wagon. He delivers:
> Green leaves to the giraffe
> Bananas to the monkeys
> Fish for the seal
> Red berries for the bear
> Food for the crocodile
> Food for the long-legged ostrich
> Fresh meat to the lion
> Oats for the zebra

At the end of his round the wagon was empty. All the animals were very concerned when a tear began to fall from the elephant's eye. Then Sam reappeared and he shouted, 'I never forget'. He produced a whole wagon full of hay. Sam and the elephant hugged each other. Here Sam's action at each stopping-off point had the effect of lessening the amount of food left (*subtraction*) until there was nothing left – or so it seemed.

Early trajectories develop into notions of *direction* (Figure 6.1). *Time* and *distance* also have their origins in early *trajectories*. Four-year-olds who race each other typically strive to be first at the point of arrival. The point of departure at this stage is hardly considered.

There is a speed question in the Stanford–Binet intelligence scale at the $4\frac{1}{2}$-year-old level under the heading of 'giving opposites'. The child must complete: 'The snail is slow; the rabbit is ???' Correct answers are quick, swift, speedy, fast, rapid, faster. A failed answer is 'Running faster'. The idea of how to generate speed is emerging but two speeds are not yet compared.

The story of the hare and the tortoise may 'flesh out' the cluster of concepts of 'cleverness' in relation to 'distance' and 'speed'. In a difficult version, the tortoise gets his wife to bob up at the end of the furrow while he bobs up at the other end. The cheating consists of moving sideways from furrow to furrow instead of running along each furrow as in a race. If a child laughs at these deceits it may indicate that he or she has a *dynamic model of horizontal and vertical co-ordinates in his or her mind* within which he or she can fit the complex movements in the story. It would indicate that he or she can 'play' with fixed locations and movements between these fixed locations. On the other hand, further questioning may reveal that the received curriculum content consists of someone slipping in the mud!

CURRICULUM EXTENSIONS OF SCHEMAS

Rotation

Wherever children have plenty of material and freedom of choice in early education, schematic behaviours will be obvious to the aware observer.[1] Teachers in Cleveland, for instance, found that their perception of children's behaviour was illuminated by some of the Froebel findings (see Nicholls *et al.* 1986). Although schematic behaviours are obvious, worthwhile curriculum extensions do not immediately suggest themselves. In some of the constructivist programmes examined by Forman and Fosnot (1982) teachers were able to observe children creating and inventing while using open-ended materials, such as sand, bricks, boards, rollers, levers, pulleys, and so on. The teachers frequently admitted to being 'stuck' for appropriate follow-up ideas. This means that there are great opportunities for teachers to work individually or together on curriculum extensions. What is needed particularly is evidence on whether 'offered' curriculum extensions have actually been 'received'.

The following few observations were selected from many collected by teachers in Sheffield (Sharp, 1987; Nutbrown, 1988). Carl (3:9) pointed out cement-mixers and wheels at the building site. When he returned to school he said he wanted the see-saw to go round and not up and down. Betty found that the bowl containing dough would spin. She tried to spin the dough without the dish. She placed the dish with dough on an old record-player and spun it round for about four minutes. She found a clock and rotated the hands. Outside she ran round the climbing frame five times before she climbed the ladder and slid down the slide.

Four boys took selected wheels from the wheel box and began to roll them down planks. Emma rolled the rings along the carpet. Mum joined in. Other shapes were tried out. Emma rolled the shapes to mum and laughed when she discovered only the cylinder worked. Emma jumped up and began to twirl round. Mum said, 'Stop it, you'll be dizzy'. Teacher sang, 'The wind blows high, the wind blows low, round and round the windmills go'.

There are many ways of extending *dynamic circular* or *rotation* schemas. All the 'ring' nursery rhymes with their actions can be taught, such as 'Here we go Round the Mulberry Bush' and 'Ring-a-Ring of Roses'.

In children's literature there is a wide range of situation comedy that depends on understanding functional dependency relationships. When Paddington Bear, for instance, decides to be an interior decorator, he uses an electric rotator to mix the paint. To the child with appropriate concepts, this has predictable, disastrous and hilarious results (Bond, 1976).

Informed adults notice different degrees of understanding in children and can extend these in various ways. An important starting-point is to validate ongoing knowledge by acceptance. Some kinds of extension require professional initiation but can involve non-professionals. For instance, a teacher observed children rolling out dough. She wanted to know whether the child had perceived any relationships between the action of rolling and the figural and transformational effect on the dough, so she asked a 'functional dependency' question. Knowledge of the correspondence between actions and the effects of action lie behind all Piaget's *conservation* experiments. Examples of this level of extension are not difficult to find in the literature because of the link with *conservation*. For instance, the Schools Council (1974, p. 23) gives the following example of diagnosis and extension.

Four-year-olds are making pastry for jam tarts. Ian (4:6) says, 'I have more than you'. Stuart (4:4): 'You've just rolled yours more' (has he noticed the effect of rolling?). Glen (4:3): 'But Ian can make more tarts so he must have more.' The teacher suggested that the children all rolled their pastry into balls again in order to compare the size. They did so and agreed on the initial equivalence of the balls of dough. Teacher: 'If they are the same, how could Ian make three tarts and you only two?'

Glen: 'Ian spread his thinner.' The teacher's intervention was in the direction of *conservation of quantity*. Glen, at 4:3, knows that the figural effects of extra rolling signifies differences in thickness and not differences in quantity.

There are many functional dependency relationships based on rotation in mathematical and scientific literature. For instance, in the Bullock Report (DES, 1975), an example is given of a mystery object that stimulated junior-aged children to use a great deal of language in the process of discovering that the object was a land-measuring tape. They arrived (*ibid.* p. 56) at the exciting conclusion that distance was functionally dependent on rotation. Trundle wheels of various sizes are useful in demonstrating that each *rotation has a specific distance that is functionally dependent on the rotation and diameter of the wheel.*

The example from Nicky (4:4:3) in Chapter 6 of this book (who lists rotating objects), makes it clear that there is no need to delay the introduction of cog-wheels, sand wheels, water wheels, food-mixers, land-measuring tapes, and so on, until statutary schooling.

When, at the end of the Froebel project, the writer began to visit primary schools, the schematic bases of speech, writing and all other kinds of representation stood out as it had not before the project. On the very first visit to a school in Richmond, a middle-class area on the outskirts of London, a video-tape was made of a 5-year-old boy, Tom, who began a conversation with his teacher as follows: 'Do you know that the earth goes round the sun in little balls?' The teacher made a fist and said: 'Suppose this is the sun, show me what you mean'. Tom made a *circular and rotational movement* with his finger around the fist. He proceeded to talk about night and day and the seasons with a high degree of accuracy.

This satisfactory situation can be compared with the research findings of Cohen (1985) on the nature of junior children's scientific misconceptions. Cohen found that at the age of 12 some children had the idea that the world was round like a plate. Many could not co-ordinate distance and rotation sufficiently well to arrive at the stage of knowledge reached by Tom. It would appear that in these cases schooling had not supported children's fundamental and spontaneous concerns.

Containing, Enveloping and Covering-Up

The possibilities for extending the notions of containing and enveloping are particularly rich. Different kinds of dwellings, seeds, fruit and animal coverings can all be explored. The purposes of different kinds of enveloping spaces on the street can be studied, and so on.

One of the earliest indications of the schema is where children put objects into containers and then take them out again. The following story is a perfect accompaniment to the *putting in* and *taking out* schema.

There is a cupboard in our kitchen.
It is full of pots and pans.
I like to take them all out
and play with them.
Mummy says why don't I think of something else to do
because I am in the way.
So I think of something else to do.
But Mummy says will I please come back
and put all the things away.   (Burningham, 1975)

A nice aspect of one of the illustrations in the book is that he looks just as pleased to be putting things back as getting them out – because he is. A project child at this stage, having agreed to 'clear up' by putting furniture back in the dolls' house said with great enthusiasm, 'Now let's take them all out again'.

As with all schemas there is a social and affective dimension. A horse is placed 'safely' inside an enclosure. A doll is wrapped up and made 'warm and cosy'. As 'form' acquires a range of differentiated content children sometimes disagree over content. For instance, Brenda and Stephen co-operated while building an enclosure. Disagreement began after they covered over the top. Stephen wanted the enveloping space to be a cave and Brenda wanted it to be a bee-hive. Brenda was particularly determined because she had been learning a 'bear' dance and some of the dancers were bees coming out of a hive.

Enveloping and containing can be extended through cooking. Frugal cookery as well as many of the great cuisines of the world consists of wrapping up food in various ways as in pies, pasties and Chinese dumplings. When Lois (3:5:15) wrapped her model of a sausage in tin-foil, her mother explained that she had been including Lois in home-baking sessions that covered a wider range of cooking than hitherto. There are great opportunities in early education to introduce children to various foods *en croute* (French), lamb cooked in paper and stuffed cabbage leaves (Greek), samosas (Indian), dumplings, buns and pancakes (Chinese), eggs stuffed with various mixtures, stuffed fish, and so on. The possibilities are endless and yet in many schools rock cakes and jam tarts are regulars and the school helper performs most of the action.

Schools Council (1974, p. 13) suggests questions a teacher might ask in extending 'covering-over' using sand. Does a child know that sand, which covers, can be heaped into a mound and that the mound can be pushed back to cover objects such as the tray, the aeroplane or models of people? Has the child experimented to see whether it takes more sand to cover the people or the aeroplane? This extension could lead to the co-ordination of *quantity*, *covering-over* and *seriation* in that more is needed for covering-over different-sized objects.

It is suggested that the teacher can ask appropriate *time* and *size* questions, such as 'If I give you this little spoon and this big spade, which one will help you to cover the aeroplane most quickly?' If this level of extension is understood it could lead to a range of games with the theme, 'How long does it take?'

The following suggestions are from *Starters Science: Coverings* (1974).

Our bodies are covered by skin. Look at your hand with a magnifying glass. What do you see? Hands covered with dirt! What can we use to get the dirt off? If you fall and cut your knee what do we cover the cut with?

Think of different animals, what kinds of skin do they have? Do they have the same kind of skin all over? Animal skins are used for leather. How many things can we collect made of leather? Can we identify the different types of leather (some teachers may now avoid using such content for ethical reasons).

Different kinds of coverings have different names: hair, fur, wool, feathers, scales, shells. Trees are covered with bark. Take rubbings with wax crayons. How many different kinds of bark can we find?

What kinds of coverings do buildings have? Study the neighbourhood for different coverings on buildings. Why are they different? What kind of cover has a greenhouse, a lorry? What kind of coverings are you wearing and why? Do people who help us wear special coverings? What is inside the coverings of fruit? How many things in your house can you think of with coverings? What are those coverings called? Why is food covered? What is the most exciting kind of covering you can think of? Presents are covered by paper. Have you ever had a present in a parcel?

When the project teacher provided a tent in order to extend on the enveloping-space schema, it was anticipated that an exploration of the tent would lead somewhere in that most explorations do. What was not anticipated was the spontaneous extension from the exploration of enveloping space to higher-order notions such as volume and capacity. This conceptual advance was spontaneously generated by Alistair, who represented his explorations graphically and in speech (Figure 6.31).

When it was realized that *volume* and *capacity* could stem from an interest in *enveloping*, a picnic basket was introduced that had a *specific capacity* designed to take specific crockery and cutlery. This was an improvement on existing containers in which the children *heaped* objects. Toddlers *heap* objects but so do older children if more appropriate materials are not available.

Another advance from enveloping space was an interest in *sub-divided space*, as in the sub-division of houses into rooms and cupboards into sections.

Inside: Play Form

The schema that starts with a simple exploration of *in* and *out* reaches a peak of complexity and playfulness with the following playful form of *inclusion*. The route is from city to 'flowers in a basket'. Not only can the order and inclusion be followed one way but the *order* can be *reversed* (Piaget, 1965). A similar form is used by junior-aged children on the first page of a new exercise book where the name is followed by the address and ends with 'The Universe'.

> This is the key of the kingdom.
> In that kingdom there is a city
> In that city there is a town
> In that town there is a street
> In that street there is a lane
> In that lane there is a yard
> In that yard there is a house
> In that house there is a room
> In that room there is a bed
> In that bed there is a basket
> Flowers in a basket

Basket in the bed
Bed in the room
Room in the house
House in the yard
Yard in the lane
Lane in the street
Street in the town
Town in the city
City in the kingdom
Of the kingdom ... this is the key.

Going Through and Round Boundaries

In the Froebel project, Randolph hammered three nails into the top and the bottom of a block of wood. This represented three plants and three roots. An obvious extension is to plant fast-growing plants that break through the boundary of soil. This is an extension of content and form. The form is '*going through*', from underneath to above the earth. The main property of plants is to grow. This is not as easily understood as the effects of hammering nails into wood.

Creatures can be studied that go through soil, fruit, flowers, leaves, vegetables and clothes. Eric Carle's (1969) much-loved story of the very hungry caterpillar is illustrated by actual holes through the pages left by the caterpillar as he eats his way relentlessly through many things. Four-year-old children were digging the garden with a spade and a garden fork. Richard, a student on third-year teaching practice, talked about the different effects of the two tools from the point of view of worms: 'Look at the way the soil goes through the prongs of the fork. Which do you think is better for worms, the spade or the fork?' Child: 'The worm can go through the prongs. It wont get hurt.'

Richard read a story called *The King's Flower* by Anno (1981). The children showed particular interest in the section where the king builds an enormous bird cage to keep the birds in. The birds discovered they could fly through the bars, which they did. A great eagle threatened the smaller birds. They flew back into the cage and were safe because the eagle was too big to pursue them into the cage. There was rapt attention from the children. What is obvious but remains difficult to measure is the way in which schemas become clustered and evolve into higher-order concepts. '*Going through*' leads into *equivalence* and *differences in size and width*. In the story the width of spaces between the bars allowed the little birds to fly through but not the big eagle.

Joan (7:2) was making a cage for her zoo. Her first plan was to cut out a whole face of the box. Then she said, 'It would be easier if I cut out strips and the bits that are left can be the bars'. She did this by opening the box into a *net*. Having cut the bars she stuck the box together again and then realized she couldn't get the animals in. She quickly unstuck the back face and cut out a door. Most enveloping spaces must have an opening for going through.

Going through

There are various extensions that are obvious because the concepts being developed already have a wide currency. A comparison between the thickness of wood and the length of nails is one. Children are interested because, in real life, nails too easily drop out of wood.

Some new furniture was delivered and difficulty was experienced in trying to move some of the tables into the classroom:

N: (4:11) Alan and me will carry this table.
A: (4:10): We have to change it round. It's too wide to get through the door.
Teacher: What about the round table?
N: Oh, we'll never get it out. We'll have to smash the windows.
Teacher: I don't think I'd like that.
N: Well, we can't get the table out. It will get stuck.
M: (4:9) We can turn it on its side, then the door will be wide enough.
N: No, we'll have to cut the legs off.
M: No, we'll be able to get it through.
N: I don't believe it.
Teacher: Well, let's see if it will go through.
N: It has gone right through. It fits exactly.

(Schools Council, 1974, p. 23)

In this entertaining example, '*going through*' is co-ordinated with *length* and *width*. The children are speculating on the *equivalence* between the *size* of the table and *the space it has to go through*. The teacher says just enough to allow M. to have his wonderful idea of turning the table round. Although the solution of cutting the legs off leaves much to be desired it shows that N. is able to subtract length.

Margaret (6:4) has two straws in her milk bottle. Amanda: 'Why have you got two straws?' Margaret: 'Because I drink slowly.' The *multiplication* concept being expressed is that twice the quantity of milk can be sucked through two straws as one.

Going through co-ordinated with a property of objects (sharpness)

Fiona was having difficulty in using her knife. The teacher said: 'Turn it round and use the sharp edge'. M.: 'The thick side isn't sharp, is it? The thin side is.' The teacher explained how knives were made sharp. M.: 'Wood can be made sharp, can't it?' [Pause] 'Corners are sharp, aren't they?' Teacher: 'Can you think of anything else that's sharp?' M.: 'That round light isn't sharp, is it?' The next day M. was pushing nails through a cotton reel. 'Look ... the ends are sharp.' He used this as a bomber diving onto paper and then onto wood. He pointed out the different effects.

Two days later he asked the teacher to write his name on his clay model. Teacher: 'How can I do that?' M.: 'With something sharp.' He found a nail. The next day he made a man by pushing nails and pins into a cork. When he showed it to the teacher he laughed and said, 'Do you know what? I tried to stick nails into that plastic bottle.'

Going through mazes

Almost all intelligence tests include items on '*going through*' and '*going round*' maze boundaries. Six-year-olds are tested on three mazes (*parallel lines representing pavements*). The instructions are that the little boy wants to go to school the *shortest* way without getting off the pavement. What is required is a demonstration of the *shortest trajectory* between A and B within the boundary of the parallel lines (Terman and Merrill, 1976, p. 108).

Children's comics usually contain 'maze' type puzzles where there are open and closed regions. *Open regions can be gone through in order to reach 'inside' regions. Closed regions have to be gone round.* A project child, Linda, discovered this while walking round an enclosure in the park.

Zoo, by Dienes and Holt (1972), contains many suggestions on how the teacher can develop ideas on open and closed boundaries in relation to 'inside and outside'. Most schools have tunnels in the playground. Going through tunnels leads to the idea of linear order – the first in is the first out the other end (see Piaget and Inhelder, 1956, Chapter 3).

Mark (4:2) made a hole with his finger half-way through a ball of clay. He said it was a hole for a rabbit to go into. Teacher: 'What if it is chased by an enemy, how would it get out?' No comment. Half an hour later he was sitting with a book open at a rabbit warren and he had made a rabbit's hole with six entrances or exits (Eveline Lowe Primary School).

Children show a persistent interest in water going through taps, hoses and pumps and in air going through open and closed objects. Questions pursued in the project were as follows: Where do firemen get water from if there is a fire? Where are the hydrants? How long is the fireman's hose that the water has to go through? Where does the water come from when it comes through the tap? Where does it go to when it goes down the drain? What happens to the level of water if you plunge your arms into the bowl? What happens if you blow air into an open-ended object such as a hose? What happens if you blow into a balloon? Can you pump water into a balloon or into a paper bag? (See Schools Council (1974) on the use of water.)

Play with 'going through'

Five-year-olds laughed at Simple Simon sieving water. Joke: a sieve is not a container: water goes through it (Athey, 1977). Libby told a very funny story about an elephant getting stuck in a hole. She ended with, 'Just like Winnie the Pooh!'

The 'Kitchen Sink Opera' (Bainbridge, Stockdale and Wastnedge, 1970) is a story that starts with a serious paragraph about a sink. When all the washing-up was done it used to have a little sing, such as 'There's a hole in my bucket, dear Lisa, dear Lisa'. The old kitchen chairs got furious: 'Pipe down ... that's enough, they're singing Noah's Flood on TV we want to watch'.

Going through and going round: art extension

Eight-year-old children were introduced to tie-dyeing. They were told that they had to tie the string very tight. One girl asked, 'What would happen if you didn't tie it tight enough?'

> Friend: It wouldn't come out, it would be all one colour.
> Why would it be all one colour?
> Because the knots would come undone.
> What do we tie the string for?
> To keep the dye out. You have to tie it tightly. The string has to be tight and the knots have to be tight. Yes, that's it, if you tie it tightly the dye can't get in under the string but if you don't tie it tightly the dye gets underneath and then it doesn't work and you get all one colour.

(Keeping dye from parts of fabric is *functionally dependent* on *going round boundaries of fabric in the form of tight knots*.) The transformation is able to be anticipated in the mind with some difficulty.

Going through boundaries in literature

In children's literature, *going through* is often linked with the *size of the diameter of a hole*. Pooh Bear gets stuck in the hole because he has overeaten. In *The Tale of Mrs Tittlemouse*, by Beatrix Potter, she makes the door smaller so that Mr Jackson can't get in. Then she passes food to Mr Jackson through a small window.

One of the most dramatic manifestations of 'going through' in our society is the vacuum cleaner. Gunilla Wolde (1975) has written a wonderful book about this. It is firmly established that Emma is not allowed to switch it on herself. When daddy uses it (!) Emma has fun watching all the puffy balls of fluff roll into tiny little sausages (transformation due to suction) just as the cleaner gobbles them up.

Tiny specks of sand that Emma can hardly see make a scratchy sound as they disappear. With a rattle and a clatter a button and a lego brick are sucked inside the cleaner. Teddy has a hard time but he is too fat to get gobbled up. When teddy's tummy gets stuck in the hole they decide it isn't a good idea to vacuum teddy.

There is a tricky moment when Emma assesses the vacuumability of baby brother and he shouts for daddy. Emma vacuumed his sock instead and it is sucked into the hole with a loud 'glump'. Daddy switches off the electricity and takes out the plug. Emma shakes the bag hard and everything comes out. In the story there is a happy end with Emma doing it all again but, naturally, she has learnt not to put certain things through the vacuum.

NOTE

1. Teachers in Cleveland carried out a project, involving parents, building on some of the findings of the Froebel project. Nicholls, working with Beryl McDougall, Adviser for the Education of Young Children, observes, 'Both teachers and parents in Cleveland are becoming keen schema-spotters; strong links are being formed between them as they pool their observations of children's learning patterns' (Nicholls, 1986).

10
EXPERIENCE FROM EDUCATIONAL VISITS

One of the most important findings of the Froebel project highlights the importance of early experience. An analysis of the content of symbolic representations showed that 60 per cent consisted of objects and events experienced in connection with visits. This high figure shows the degree to which first-hand experience provides the content or 'stuff' of thought. Schemas and concepts are 'forms' of thought and experience 'feeds' those forms with content – worthwhile content, it is hoped.

Following a visit to an airport there were representations of stationary and mobile planes. Following a visit to Westminster Abbey there were representations of features of the abbey including horizontal and vertical sculptures, arches and rectangular paving-stones. Widening children's experience beyond school walls is widely thought to be desirable. Many HMI reports of the past few years have spelt out the features of good teaching. Examples abound in these reports of teachers taking children out into the local and wider environment.

School visits do not automatically enrich the mind in that 'minds that have nothing to confer, find little to perceive' (Wordsworth, cited in Hutchinson, 1969, p. 88). All project visits were meticulously prepared for and followed up by staff who involved parents as much as possible.

The quality of teaching involves continuity of learning in pupils throughout the seven or nine years of primary education. A whole-school approach aims at avoiding gaps in the curriculum as well as too many repetitions. From frog spawn, through tadpoles to frogs, is a favourite topic frequently offered yearly. Repeated content, however, if sufficiently rich in possibilities, can generate new learning in that content offered is not synonymous with content received. Different thought structures construct similar content differently at different times. Examples were given earlier of Lois representing 'horse' with an early '*grid*' schema (Figure 3.1) and, one year later, representing 'horse' within a *projective space* schema (Figure 3.2).

'Experience' itself can be defined as 'that which is being assimilated by the child' and not 'that which is presented to the child'. Such a difference requires professional knowledge of the structures of thought, curriculum content that is likely to be assimilated to those structures and evidence that the offered curriculum has been received. These issues provide growing points for parent and professional co-operation.

In the project, aspects of early learning were illuminated by studying children from very different socio-economic backgrounds concurrently. It gradually became clear during the project that schematic behaviours were common to both groups, as was some 'everyday' content. Some content, however, reflected different experiences. Examples will make the schematic similarity and the content difference clear.

In a single morning children in the different groups were observed representing *trajectories* with a *starting-point, several stopping-off points and an end-point*. This is a common form of representation that probably has its motor roots in early toddling behaviours and before that in early tracking behaviours. The project children were pretending to be dustmen collecting rubbish. Their starting-point was a depot, their stopping-off points were individual houses. They pretended to lift each bin and emptied the rubbish into the lorry. They deposited the rubbish at the dump and took the lorry back to the depot. The kindergarten children were collecting skiiers from various hotels in order to transport them to the ski lift.

It is difficult to evaluate such differences educationally. The differences in content simply illustrate different cultural specifics that are assimilated to common forms of thought. In a culturally diverse society, different interpretations of apparently common events amount to different experiences. The dear little pink pig of European literature (more harmfully included in intelligence tests) is experienced somewhat differently by Muslims.

Anti-racist and anti-sexist policies pursued in British schools might be furthered by exploring aspects of being human that are shared – in that shared experiences create bonds. Many experiences that were associated initially with very different cultures have become generally adopted when seen to be desirable and to extend choice, such as adopting different ways of cooking food.

Visits increase the 'stuff' of mind in project children but an important question remains unanswered: Does increasing the quantity of experience speed up the genesis of forms of thought? It is unlikely that content differences in themselves produce differences of form. What is likely is that where schemas have been well nourished by wide experiences, consistently accompanied by articulate speech, development has been accelerated in some way as yet unknown.

It is worth repeating an example given in Chapter 6 from a kindergarten 3-year-old, where rich content is accompanied by an advanced cognitive form. In relation to Figure 6.34, Nicky (3:6:28) said, 'But you can see it's a cage. Caves have got stalagmites and stalactites: they go up and down. A cage has got bars over the front. That's got bars over the front, a cave hasn't got bars over the front'. As already mentioned, the basic schema is grid but Nicky's form of reasoning is approaching *transitivity* applied to *grid*: If A = B and B = C then A = C. Stephen, a project child, also applied higher-level thought to a *grid* configuration when he described the levels of Teddington Lock in *ordinal* terms.

By the age of 3, many of the kindergarten children were so widely experienced that it was difficult to detect the cognitive structures under an abundance of content. As the project children gained wider experiences as well as the symbolic tools with which to represent those experiences, the gap between the two groups narrowed – if standardized test scores can be taken as a measure. The differences narrowed in other ways that can only be described. For instance, everyone became more talkative. Project parents, and increasingly the children, hardly drew breath during project visits.

In infants there appears to be a fairly fixed order of 'unfolding' of cognitive structures that, over time, can be impeded or enhanced to a marked degree by conditions of poverty or privilege. Some variation stems from differences in nourishment, from food for the body right through to food for the mind. Rats, for instance, deprived of suitable early experience retain 'hard-wire' mechanisms in the brain (invariants) but they have a lack of 'soft-wire' mechanisms (dendritic connections built up by experience). Photographs of brain structures in deprived rats resemble photographs of a tree in winter with bare branches. Photographs of dendritic connections of well-nourished rats resemble a tree in full leaf and flower (Rose, 1978).

Early learning is critical learning because this is when the brain is most susceptible to environmental modification. Increased experience and increased possibilities for symbolic functioning bring measurable improvements in under-functioning children. Early education provides young children with 'food for thought'. Common knowledge of the cognitive capacities of privileged and under-privileged children strongly suggests that early enrichment has a cumulative effect in that subsequent experiences are amplified by enriched minds.

Widespread testing on entry to school would provide more accurate information on the efficacy of schooling than testing at the age of 7. Such testing would probably reveal significant correlations between test scores and social and economic inequalities.

11

PARENT AND PROFESSIONAL PARTNERSHIP IN EARLY EDUCATION

Not all parents wish to be involved in play, care, or educational projects. For various reasons many parents with young children continue to work. In the 1990s there will be an increased demand for mothers to have paid employment as well as to raise families. Research shows that a large number of parents want to be involved in their children's early school experience but with more explanation and discussion than is usually given (Smith, 1980). The involvement of parents in the Froebel project is evidence of how deeply committed parents can become if they are included in professional concerns rather than with peripheral issues.

Professionals necessarily have more specific knowledge in their particular sphere than the non-professional. Where professional 'expertise' is applied in an hierarchical manner it has been found to have a negative effect on parents. However, where professionals give clear information without undue structuring, 'professionalism' (in the positive sense of sharing skills and expertise) is enhanced rather than eroded (Pugh and De'Ath, 1984, p. 178).

In the 1980s educational projects involving parents have produced evidence of educational gain as in the reading progress achieved within the PACT scheme in London (Hewison, 1982). Reading is an area of the curriculum where it is possible to measure gains by standardized as well as other criteria.

In the Froebel project, shared illumination was related to the structures, the content and the processes of the children's learning. There is no shortage of good practice in early education or in primary education. Neither is there a shortage of excellent parent–professional partnerships in nursery schools, classes and early-childhood centres. There is, however, a shortage of reports that contain explanations on the nature of excellence. Teachers of young children could make a revolutionary move forward in developing a pedagogy of the early years if they recorded how they have conceptualized and shared their professional concepts with parents together with subsequent gains made by children.

The lack of knowledge of children's thinking from 2 to 5 was openly discussed with Froebel project parents and formed the basis for a shared search. This gave parents a position of considerable importance in the project right from the start.

This particular approach could be adopted elsewhere. The project professionals worked with the parents with the main aim of extending the children's learning through experience and the representation of those experiences. Representation provides evidence of 'received' curriculum content. These issues provided the material for ongoing communication between parent and professional.

The professionals identified schemas but, once identified, parents were able to give examples, some of which have been given in Chapters 4, 5 and 6. Professionals have useful knowledge but it is not always shared with parents. For instance, many project parents did not realize (what most professionals take for granted) that children's behaviour is orderly and predictable. As mentioned earlier, 'naughtiness' was dreaded by parents. Predictability was increased because the main aim of the project was to search for regularities. This, in turn, generated increased feelings of security and changed attitudes.

The search for regularities provided fertile soil for a successful partnership, which is discussed in Chapter 4. The many examples illustrated and analysed in Chapters 5 and 6 provided material for daily discussion. Because the search was for fundamental patterns of thought, parents became increasingly involved, to the point of fascination, in educational issues that, in the past, might have been thought to be the sole province of professionals.

As knowledge increased, the capacity of parents and professionals to extend the children's learning also increased. It was by this process that involvement increased. Not only did the children's symbolic life flourish but the parents attributed new significance to much of their children's behaviour. This process began during early home visits. Parents were well briefed not to show feelings in test situations but it became clear from later conversations that the testing led parents to buy educational materials. The parents had no difficulty in broadening their concept of parenthood to include knowledge of their children's cognitive functioning as this functioning became illuminated during the project.

Many parents of the kindergarten children also wanted detailed communication during home visits and tried to keep the writer much longer than practicable. During one visit Piaget was mentioned to an architect mother. Her child had a large room full of low-cost building materials. By the next visit the parent had read Piaget's book on 'space' (Piaget and Inhelder, 1956) and wanted to discuss her child's concepts in the light of this. Many parents, irrespective of social, cultural and economic circumstances, would like a support system while they have young children. Parents have a great deal to give to each other as well as to the children.

Because of the critical importance of the early years (Bloom, 1964), the availability and willingness of parents to join in with early school experiences (Smith, 1980; Tizard, Mortimore and Burchell, 1981), the decrease in time spent on child bearing and rearing and the time gained by the use of modern appliances in the home (Shipman, 1972), parents could now be in a position to acquire more knowledge and increase their interest in children's thinking. By the end of the century there will be many more old people than primary-age children. The time is right for parents, grandparents and professionals to work together in order to increase quality of mind in young children.

APPENDICES

APPENDIX I
ANALYSES OF PROJECT OBSERVATIONS

Aims one and three of the Froebel project (see p. 49) required the collection and analysis of instances of children's spontaneous behaviour. Research procedures developed through the following stages.

Initially, observers recorded the behaviour and speech of children, either individually or interacting with others. Speech was recorded in as much detail as possible and permanent products, such as paintings or models, were collected, dated and analysed. Observations ranged from a couple of sentences to several pages. Video- and audio-recordings lasted as long as the episode being observed. Some recordings were as long as half an hour, the length of the tape or a few minutes.

Speech from video- and audio-tape was transcribed verbatim by the project secretary. An example of a long observation is given in Chapter 5. It consists of a discussion between a project child and a student. An instance of a short observation is as follows: Salam (2:11:26) drew a vertical line and a circle. He named the circle: 'Conker' (Figure 5.33). Such observations, gathered daily, provided the raw data for 'ongoing' analyses. Video-recordings were particularly useful as every detail was preserved. This enabled the same material to be reviewed at subsequent levels of analysis.

The first level of analysis consisted of entries on to forms that were placed into long file drawers. This facilitated alternative groupings of examples. One basic grouping, for instance, consisted of analysed observations arranged longitudinally for each child. This gave information on the development of individuals. Another grouping consisted of examples of space concepts from all children classified by age, which gave information on stages of space concepts. Initial observations were dissected and organized within variables discussed in Chapters 4, 5 and 6.

The following four factual variables remained throughout subsequent stages of analysis: name, sex, chronological age and date of recording (tutorial time unit – TTU):

1. *Name of child* Twenty children were each assigned a number (from 1 to 20). Substitute names have been used throughout the text for anonymity.
2. *Sex of child* (2).
3. *Chronological age* (14) (ages were grouped into fourteen chronological age units). The earliest observation was from a child at 9 months, 8 days. Observations from the oldest child were made when he was 5 years, 1 month old.
4. *Tutorial time unit (TTU)* (6 terms) Each day of the project (three hours per morning) was counted as a 'tutorial time unit'. Two academic years amounted to 340 TTUs. For

computer analysis these time units were grouped into six terms.

The following conceptual variables were entered into the specially prepared forms:

5. Form of a schema.
6. Type of functioning.
7. Parent participation (PP).
8. Content.
9. Material used.

These five variables were used in the earliest attempts to detect underlying patterns in the raw data. The method adopted was as follows.

Each initial observation was studied and entries were made under variables. It became clear, almost immediately, that many of the most simple observations contained more than one schema and some contained more than one type of functioning. Also, regarding parental participation, a parent might intervene during only part of an observation. For instance, during the first week of the project, Clare (3:0:26) was sorting objects collected during a visit to the park. When she sorted on her own she put the following materials into separate lines: conkers, acorns, leaves and twigs. A student helper pointed out that an acorn had a little 'cup'. Clare said nothing but looked carefully at the acorn. Clare's mother subsequently joined her, held out a box and said, 'What shall we put in here?' Clare put four acorns in the box and then continued to put objects into lines.

This observation had two entries under 'Form of Schema':

1. Clare is assimilating like objects into line-formations.
2. Helped by an adult she appeared to be 'pushed-over' into a different form of grouping but soon returned to 'lines'.

At this point it was thought (but only on a 'hunch' basis) that *grouping objects into a container* appeared later in development than *grouping in lines*. This was subsequently supported by computer analysis of schemas in relation to age.

On the day following the above observation, Clare (3:0:36) was presented with trays with an acorn in one, a chestnut in another and a stone in a third. It was intended to see whether she would *classify* by grouping similar objects within the containers. What she did, in fact, was to *line up* all the boxes in a neat row. She looked very satisfied with this and changed activity. Help given by Clare's mother was entered under the variable, 'parent participation' (PP). Help was attributed to the mother for *putting like objects into a container* but not for *putting objects into lines*.

More refined classifications of 'schemas' began to emerge. Some schemas were mainly 'graphic' or 'figurative' (see Chapter 5), some were mainly 'action' based (see Chapter 6). As analysis proceeded it became apparent that schemas could be further sub-divided into 'different levels of cognitive functioning'. Eventual computer analysis showed a significant age difference between the following levels of cognitive functioning:

1. Motor.
2. Symbolic.
3. Functional dependencies and thought.

(See pp. 68–165 for examples of these different levels.)

Further sub-divisions of categories were arrived at after examining professional literature on speech, space concepts and other areas of concept formation. As professional concepts became clearer, the children's current behaviours, and past observations, were illuminated. As communication between staff and parents improved, and as the significance of behaviours became clearer, the quality of initial observations improved and more detail was recorded.

The number of observations analysed amounted to 5,333. Each of these was sub-divided into ten conceptual variables and each variable contained categories. For instance, the variable 'parental participation' had four categories ranging from 'No parental participation' (category one) to 'Parent trying to extend the child's learning with knowledge of the child's prevailing schemas' (category four). (See Chapter 3 for details and results.)

It is difficult to convey the excitement that accompanied the continuing analyses of observations. Many sequences of related observations were gathered over days or weeks. These were particularly absorbing and informative. Chapters 5 and 6 contain many such sequences.

The analysis of observations showed that cognitive development does not consist of sequential and permanent increments. Stability of new concepts and schemas is finally achieved but the process of gain resembles a graph of a bank statement of a person who saves. The curve of gain is clear over time but there are oscillations of gain and loss around the trend. These oscillations are noticeable on a day-to-day basis but can be 'ironed out' in a longitudinal analysis.

The final count of analysed observations, as mentioned above, was 5,333. A computer card was punched for each observation with variables and categories. After entering data on to a computer tape it was analysed by the writer at London University Computer Centre. The analysis of the data prior to entering into computer cards took almost one year because of the constant search in the literature for illumination on aspects of cognitive development. It is important to mention this because researchers are seldom given sufficient time to carry out detailed analysis of data. Once the information was stored, various sortings could be carried out relatively quickly.

The chronological-age sequences of schemas, as presented in Chapters 5 and 6, were arrived at via computer analysis but the computer sorting was simply a speeded up counting of instances that had been categorized conceptually and entered manually onto cards.

Some 'hunches' were supported by computer analyses and some were not. Only positive findings considered to be useful to teachers, and others working with young children, are presented in this book.

It is worth repeating what has been stated in the main text – the sequences presented and illustrated in Chapters 5 and 6 should not be considered as general scales of development. The experimental nature of the project mitigates against such a conclusion. They can be considered to be scales of the particular group of children studied, but even here a qualification is needed. As explained above, both initial and subsequent observations were influenced by the conceptual awareness of the professionals involved in the project. As awareness increased, schemas were 'spotted' in younger children.

Throughout the book it is hoped that enough examples have been given to enable professionals to judge the usefulness of the categorizations applied to the raw data of initial observations.

APPENDIX II
INFORMATION ON PROJECT FAMILIES

PLACE AND COUNTRY OF ORIGIN

The four Asian families came from Pakistan and all spoke Urdu. One black family came from Guyana. One black, unsupported mother was born and brought up in Jamaica. One father and one mother (brother and sister) had Armenian parents who became immigrants to the UK. They were born and began their education in Alexandria, Egypt.

Four parents came from towns in England other than London. Seventeen parents were born in the area where they now live. One mother had relatives and friends living on a gypsy site in the local area.

HOUSING CONDITIONS

A home is classified as overcrowded where there are more than one-and-a-half persons to a room (1961 census). Kellmer-Pringle, Butler and Davie (1966, p. 87) point out that this official definition employs quite a severe standard many people in the community would not accept. Altogether there were 82 people in the project families. The total number of rooms, excluding kitchens, amounted to 51. There were, on average, 1.6 persons per room. Only two children in the whole group had their own room. Eleven children had their own bed but shared a room. Nine children shared a bed. Taken as a group, the families lived in overcrowded conditions. Over half the project families were rehoused within two years following the project.

SIZE OF FAMILIES

The average number of children in the families at the start of the project was three, range: one to six. There were 48 children in total.

EDUCATION OF PARENTS

Two Asian parents had not attended school. Three mothers and two fathers left school at the age of 14. Ten mothers and seven fathers left at 15. One mother and four fathers left at 16. One mother and one father left at 17.

Fifteen mothers and eleven fathers left school without a qualification of any kind. Two fathers took one ordinary-level certificate. One Asian mother and father had degrees from a university in Pakistan.

After leaving school, one father had studied building construction and two mothers had taken courses in shorthand and typing. One father had served an apprenticeship at Mercedes-Benz. One mother was a State registered nurse.

EMPLOYMENT OF FATHERS

Unemployed (4), drivers (4), bus conductor (1), railway-track worker (1), museum attendant (1), electrician (1), Post Office engineer (1), small pet-shop owner (1), postman (1). There is no information on the employment of fathers of unsupported mothers.

EMPLOYMENT OF MOTHERS

Housewives (14), several had cleaning jobs, garment work at home (2) (both Asian), ward-orderly in a hospital (1), nurse (1).

PARENTAL ATTENDANCE DURING THE PROJECT

During initial home visits, parents were invited and encouraged to attend the project as often as possible. The following figures give each parent's attendance at the project as a percentage of the child's attendance. Each family is identified by a letter, from 'a' to 'q'. The first figure after the letter is the parent's attendance during the first year of the project. The figure in brackets is the attendance during the second year of the project. Where a family had more than one child attending the project the parent's attendance is linked with the oldest child.

a, 23 (79).	b, 24 (70).	c, 33 (5).
d, 43 (44).	e, 50 (11).	f, 53 (56).
g, 55 (43).	h, 62 (22).	i, 64 (42).
j, 64 (56).	k, 78 (38).	l, 88 (66).
m, 91 (71).	n, 92 (33).	o, 95 (24).
p, 95 (40).	q, 98 (90).	

The low attendance of 'a' during the first year is because the mother was employed full time and her sister-in-law brought 'a's child as well as her own. 'a' subsequently gave up her job, which accounts for the high attendance during the second year.

The low attendance of 'b' was due to a different concept of 'mother' in an extended Asian family – 'm' took over the role of caretaker of 'b's' child.

Both 'c' and 'e' had low attendances while they were pregnant. They both had large families and other members brought project children during these times. After both births, attendance increased and the new babies were brought to the project regularly.

The attendance of 'h' went down in the second year because, due to financial constraints, she had to increase her cleaning jobs. Both 'n' and 'o' also took employment in a residential nursery during the second year of the project.

During the first year of the project, only three mothers attended less than 40 per cent of the time. Six mothers attended over 80 per cent of the time, which amounts to four days out of every five.

During the second year only six parents attended less than 40 per cent of the time. 'q', whose attendance was outstanding, was the oldest mother in the group. She had been a child bride in Pakistan, had a large family, including several grown-up children, could speak very little English and clearly loved working in the project with her daughter. When her youngest daughter was 7-years-old she had a higher reading age than an older sibling aged 13 years. Neither mother nor father could read English. Father could read Urdu.

The attendance of the project children's older siblings during their primary-school holidays is as follows. The same letter signifies the family. The first number gives the number of siblings and the second number gives the total number of attendances over the two years of the project.

a, 0 (0).	b, 3 (57).	c, 3 (6).
d, 2 (20).	e, 2 (43).	f, 1 (31).
g, 0 (0).	h, 1 (19).	i, 1 (28).
j, 2 (42).	k, 1 (21).	l, 0 (0).
m, 2 (57).	n, 1 (7).	o, 1 (47).
p, 5 (100).	q, 4 (72).	

('c' brought her young infant, who was not counted as one of the project children, 47 times).

Attendance of fathers is as follows. The letter gives the family and the number in brackets gives the number of attendances. The two single-parent families have 's' in the bracket instead of a figure. In the case of 'p', the mother's own father came several times.

a, (7).	b, (0).	c, (0).	d, (0).
e, (1).	f, (5).	g, (0).	h, (11).
i, (1).	j, (s).	k, (5).	l, (15).
m, (1).	n, (2).	o, (23).	p, (s).

q, (0).

Of the five fathers who did not attend the project, two were Asian fathers who were very much to the fore during home visits but left their wives to attend the project. Several uncles, aunts and grandparents visited occasionally.

APPENDIX III

ACKNOWLEDGEMENTS FOR FUNDING FROEBEL EDUCATIONAL INSTITUTE (FEI) PROJECTS AND BACKGROUND TO THE PROJECTS

ACKNOWLEDGEMENTS

The Council of Management of FEI contributed £3,000 per annum for five years, as well as £700 for the purchase of a project bus.

The Leverhulme Trustees provided £23,000 over five years in the form of a research fellowship.

In 1972 the Calouste Gulbenkian Foundation contributed £1,520 followed by £1,899 in 1973.

The Ester Lawrence Association gave £1,700 shares and £700 cash.

The Drapers Company donated £250.

ILEA provided some project furniture under the Urban Aid Programme.

BACKGROUND TO THE PROJECTS

During the early 1970s, Miss Molly Brearley, CBE, Principal of the Froebel Educational Institute, formed a working party to initiate research into children's thinking and learning in the early years. A committee met termly from 1970 to 1979, during which time they 'steered' through two projects. Molly Brearley had served as a member of the Plowden Committee and both projects were influenced by the findings and recommendations of the Plowden Report (Central Advisory Council for Education, 1967).

Two particular recommendations determined the aims, funding and selection of children for the Froebel projects. The first concern was 'pedagogical', arising from how little was known about the cognitive development of children under 5. The second concern was 'sociological' with its focus on the effects of different socio-economic circumstances on groups of children. These two concerns are conceptually different. They have different motivations, aims and methods and they are informed by research findings from different disciplines. Lawton (1975) pointed out that discussions about knowledge, and how it is structured and organized, must not be confused with questions of a social nature.

The Plowden Committee (Central Advisory Council for Education, 1967, para. 1165/j) suggested that the paucity of knowledge about children's learning might be remedied by means of further research. It was suggested that investigations should be carried out on the effects of teaching and the school environment on children's concepts. Consequently, a general aim of both Froebel projects was to try to increase knowledge of cognitive functioning in young children. This entailed using methods and strategies appropriate to fundamental research on individual children.

The 'compensatory' recommendation of Plowden, arising from sociological research, was based on the disturbing associations between poor socio-economic circumstances, poor school achievement and low measured intelligence (Hindley, 1965). This situation continues and many children start school far behind others but there is less acceptance than hitherto of pejorative descriptions applied to groups.

THE FIRST FROEBEL PROJECT

The first project (1971–2) was for severely deprived children from a residential nursery. The children were brought by bus, with their nurses, to nursery school in the college grounds. A graduate teacher set up the nursery in an old but attractive building in the college grounds (Mrs M Walsh subsequently became headteacher in two London schools and is now Lecturer in Education in an institute of higher education).

This first project was deemed a success from the point of view of the particular children involved. However, the aim of finding out more about children's learning in general was not fulfilled. In spite of a great deal of effort, made by a large number of professionals, the progress of the children could not be documented in a form that could be conveyed to other professional people or generalized to other underfunctioning children. After four terms of nursery education, the children's advance was marked but no one involved in the project knew how to document or measure the psychological or educational improvement. The first project revealed a need for detailed research into the more minute units of psychological growth (incorporated FEI report, 1971–2).

With the widespread use of the birth-control pill the number of infants who were deprived because they were unwanted decreased. Many industrial societies turned their attention to the low educational qualifications of children living in poor neighbourhoods. Nationally funded schemes, such as the Headstart programmes in the USA, were launched. The Bernard van Leer Foundation published a selective bibliography on compensatory early childhood education in 1971, which give 4,000 references up to 1967, after which date they gave up the search as it was not possible to keep abreast of publications on the subject.

The Plowden recommendations on 'positive discrimination' were addressed to populations rather than persons. It was suggested, for instance, that there should be a national policy of favouring schools in neighbourhoods where children are most severely handicapped by home conditions (Central Advisory Council for Education, 1967, para. 1243/8). It was suggested that the DES should designate schools and areas in most need as 'educational priority areas'.

Attempts were made to identify a wide range of social and economic circumstances that were thought to mitigate against satisfactory achievement in school. However, definitions of 'social handicap', 'underprivileged' and 'deprivation' were very wide indeed. 'Underprivileged' could refer to children lacking companionship, poor and/or overcrowded homes or children living in flats lacking space.

It was suggested that early education should be given to those with high priority but 'priority' was not confined to the effects of shortage of money or dire poverty of low social class. Priority, for instance, was given to children of teachers who were in such short supply that help with child care was offered to get them back to work. 'Priority' could be on medical grounds following illness in the family or it could be given to mothers near the end of their tether (*ibid.* para. 295).

These background circumstances are given to explain the juxtaposition rather than a blending of Froebel project aims. In the second Froebel project, reported in this book, the 'compensatory' aim, for which funding had been received, determined the selection of families from an Educational Priority Area and the use of socio-economic criteria. It also led to the procedures of testing the children on standardized tests 'before' and 'after' the educational programme. These 'summative' results are given in Chapter 3.

The 'pedagogical' (as opposed to the 'compensatory' aim) demanded that the selected group of families should be stable because of the intention to study the children in depth over two years.

THE WHITE PAPER, EDUCATION: A FRAMEWORK FOR EXPANSION (DES, 1972)

The first project ended just as Mrs Thatcher's white paper was published. Recommendations indicated that there would be a large expansion of nursery education (DES, 1972, para. 309). From a position where only 5 per cent of 3-year-olds had full or part-time education within maintained schools, the Secretary of State for Education and Science promised places for all 3- and 4-year-olds whose parents wished them to attend school. The demand was anticipated to be for 90 per cent of 4-year-olds and 50 per cent of 3-year-olds. The proposed expansion determined, to a certain extent, the purpose, form and organization of the second Froebel Early Education Project, reported in this book.

In January 1973, the writer of this book was awarded an FEI Leverhulme Research Fellowship for two years (this was subsequently extended for a further three years at a Principal Lecturer level), and a second project was planned. Funding was given to investigate 'The nature of preschool programmes suitable for underprivileged children'. On this issue, the findings of the Froebel project are clear. All young children require rich experiences and the material and linguistic means for representing those experiences. Where such experiences, and the means for symbolic expression are lacking, extra resources are needed for remediation.

The National Curriculum does not focus on cultural differences but on knowledge that ought to be shared by all and to which every child has a right. Knowledge components laid down in National Curriculum documents are deemed 'classless'. It will, no doubt, continue to be more difficult to transmit successfully this necessary knowledge in some social and cultural circumstances than in others. Highly skilled teachers will be needed in the future, as they have been in the past, to teach children who are disadvantaged because of home circumstances.

BIBLIOGRAPHY AND REFERENCES

Ahrens, R. (1954) Beitrage zur Entvicklung des Physiognomie-und Mimikerkennes, *Zeitschrift fur experimentelle und angewardte Psychologie, 2*, in T. G. R. Bower (1977a), op. cit., p. 79.

Aitkenhead, A. M. and Slack, J. M. (1985) *Issues in Cognitive Modeling*, Lawrence Erlbaum Associates, London.

Anderson, R. C., Spiro, R. J. and Montague, W. E. (1977) *Schooling and the Acquisition of Knowledge*, Lawrence Erlbaum Associates, Hillsdale, NJ.

Anno, M. (1981) *The King's Flower*, the Bodley Head, London.

Arnheim, R. (1972) *Art and Visual Perception*, Faber & Faber, London.

Athey, C. (1977) Humour in children related to Piaget's theory of intellectual development, in A. J. Chapman and H. C. Foot (eds.) op. cit., pp. 215-18.

Bailey, R. A. and Burton, E. C. (1982) *The Dynamic Self*, C. V. Mosby, London.

Bainbridge, J. W., Stockdale, R. W. and Wastnedge, E. R. (1970) *Junior Science Source Book*, Collins, London.

Baldwin, A. L., Kalhorn, J. and Breese, F. H. (1945) Patterns of parent behaviour (*Psychological Monograph*, Vol. 58, no. 268), in M. V. Hunt (1961) op. cit., p. 279.

Barrett, H. E. and Koch, H. L. (1930) The effect of nursery-school training upon the mental test performance of a group of orphanage children, *Journal of Genetic Psychology*, Vol. 37, pp. 102-22.

Bartlett, F. C. (1932) *Remembering: A Study in Experimental and Social Psychology*, Cambridge University Press.

Bayley, N. and Jones, H. E. (1937) Environmental correlates of mental and motor development: a cumulative study from infancy to six years, *Child Development*, Vol. 8, pp. 329-41.

Beadle, M. (1971) *A Child's Mind: How Children Learn During the Critical Years from Birth to Age Five*, MacGibbon & Kee, London.

Beilin, H. (1972) The status and future of preschool compensatory education, in J. C. Stanley (ed.) op.cit., pp. 165-81.

Bereiter, C. and Engelmann, S. (1966) The Bereiter and Engelmann Language Development Programme, in *Deprivation and Disadvantage*, (*Educational Studies*, E.262, block 8) The Open University Press, Milton Keynes.

Berman, P. W., Cunningham, J. G. and Harkulich, J. (1974) Construction of the horizontal, vertical and oblique by young children: failure to find the oblique effect, *Child Development*, Vol. 45, pp. 474-8.

Bernstein, B. (1974a) *Class, Codes and Control* (Vol. 3), Routledge & Kegan Paul, London.

Bernstein, B. (1974b) Class and pedagogy: visible and invisible, in W. B. Dockrell and D. Hamilton (eds.) op. cit., pp. 115–139.

Blackstone, T. (1971) *A Fair Start: The Provision of Pre-school Education*, Allen Lane, London.

Blenkin, G. M. and Kelly, A. V. (eds.) (1988) *Early Childhood Education: A Developmental Curriculum*, Paul Chapman Publishing, London.

Blenkin, G. M. and Whitehead, M. (1988) Education as development, in G. M. Blenkin and A. V. Kelly (eds.) op. cit., pp. 32–60.

Blomberg, I. (1982) Swedish Orienteering Association (can be obtained from J. R. Martland, School of Education, Liverpool University, 19 Abercromby Square, PO Box 147, Liverpool, L69 3BX).

Bloom, B. S. (1964) *Stability and Change in Human Characteristics*, Wiley, New York, NY.

Bloom, B. S., Krathwohl, D. R. and Masia, B. B. (1956) *Taxonomy of Educational Objectives: The Classification of Educational Goals. The Cognitive Domain*, Longman, London.

Bloom, B. S., Krathwohl, D. R. and Masia, B. B. (1964) *Taxonomy of Educational Objectives: The Classification of Educational Goals. The Affective Domain*, Longman, London.

Bond, M. (1976) *Paddington Decorator*, Fontana, London.

Bone, M. (1977) *Pre-school Children and the Need for Day Care*, HMSO, London.

Bower, T. G. R. (1974) *Development in Infancy*, W. H. Freeman, San Francisco, Calif.

Bower, T. G. R. (1977a) *A Primer of Infant Development*, W. H. Freeman, San Francisco, Calif.

Bower, T. G. R. (1977b) *The Perceptual World of the Child*, in J. Bruner, M. Cole and B. Lloyd (eds.) Fontana, Glasgow.

Bowlby, J. (1953) *Child Care and the Growth of Love*, Pelican Books, Harmondsworth.

Brearley, M. and Hitchfield, E. (1966) *A Teacher's Guide to Reading Piaget*, Routledge & Kegan Paul, London.

Brierley, J. K. (1987) *Give me a Child until he is Seven: Brain Studies and Early Childhood Education*, Falmer Press, Basingstoke.

Brimer, M. A. and Dunn. L. M. (1962) *English Picture Vocabulary Test (EPVT)*, Educational Evaluation Enterprises, Marsh St, Bristol 1.

Britton, J. (1970) *Language and Learning*, Penguin Books, Harmondsworth.

Brown, B. (1978) *Found: Long Term Gains from Early Intervention* (*Selected Symposia Series*), Westview Press, Boulder, Colo.

Brown, R. (1973) *A First Language: The Early Stages*, Allen & Unwin, London.

Bruce, T. (1987) *Early Childhood Education*, Hodder & Stoughton, Sevenoaks.

Bruner, J. S. (1971) The growth and structure of skill, in J. S. Bruner (1974) op. cit., pp. 245–69.

Bruner, J. S. (1974) *Beyond The Information Given*, Allen & Unwin, London.

Bruner, J. S. (1980) *Under Five in Britain* (Oxford Pre-School Research Project – OPRP), Grant McIntyre, London.

Bruner, J. S., Olver, R. R. and Greenfield, P. M. *et al.* (1966) *Studies in Cognitive Growth*, Wiley, New York, NY.

Burningham, J. (1975) *The Cupboard*, Jonathan Cape, London.

Butterworth, G. and Jarret, N. (1982) Piaget's stage 4 error: background to the problem, *British Journal of Educational Psychology*, Vol. 73, pp. 175–85.

Cane, B. and Schroeder, C. (1970) *The Teacher and Research*, NFER/Nelson, Windsor.

Carle, E. (1969) *The Very Hungry Caterpillar*, Puffin Books, Harmondsworth.

Central Advisory Council for Education (1967) *Children and their Primary Schools* (the Plowden Report), HMSO, London.

Chalmers, N., Crawley, R. and Rose, P. R. S. (1971) *The Biological Bases of Behaviour*, Harper & Row, London.

Chapman, A. J. and Foot, H. C. (eds.) (1977) *It's a Funny Thing Humour*, Pergamon Press, Oxford.

Chazan, M., Laing, A., and Jackson, S. (1971) *Just Before School* (Schools Council Research and Development Project in Compensatory Education), Blackwell, Oxford.

Chomsky, N. (1980) On cognitive structures and their development: a reply to Piaget, in M. Piattelli-Palmarini (ed.) op. cit., pp. 35-54.

Chukovsky, K. (1966) *From Two to Five*, University of California Press, Berkeley, Calif. (first published in the Soviet Union in 1925).

Clay, M. (1975) *What Did I Write?*, Heinemann Educational, London.

Cohen M. (1985) *The Nature of Children's Scientific Misconceptions* (lecture given at the Froebel Institute, 29 January 1985).

Connolly, K. J. (ed.) (1971) *Motor Skills in Infancy*, Academic Press, London.

Cratty, B. (1973) *Intelligence in Action*, Prentice-Hall, Englewood Cliffs, NJ.

Cromer, R. F. (1974) The development of language and cognition: the cognition hypothesis, in B. Foss (ed.) op. cit., pp. 184-252.

Cromer, R. (1979) The strengths of the weak form of the cognition hypothesis for language acquisition, in V. Lee (ed.) op. cit., pp. 63-102.

Curtis, A. (1986) *A Curriculum for the Pre-School Child*, NFER/Nelson, Windsor.

Curtis, A. (1987) The education of four year olds in school, *Update: Current Issues in Early Education, Organisation Mondiate pour Education Prescolaire. UK Nat. Committee*. no. 16, February.

Dally, A. (1982) *Inventing Motherhood*, Burnett Books, London.

Day, M. D. and Parker, R. K. (eds.) (1977) *The Pre-School in Action: Exploring Early Childhood Programs*, Allyn & Bacon, Newton, Mass.

Dearden, R. F. (1984) *Theory and Practice in Education*, Routledge & Kegan Paul, London.

Denenberg, V. H. (ed.) (1970) *Education of the Infant and Young Child*, Academic Press, New York, NY.

DES (1972) *Education: A Framework for Expansion*, HMSO, London.

DES (1975) *A Language for Life* (the Bullock Report), HMSO, London.

DES (1983) *Teaching in Schools: The Content of Initial Training* (HMI discussion paper) HMSO, London.

DES (1985) *The Curriculum from 5 to 16* (*Curriculum Matters 2*), HMSO, London.

DES (1987a) *National Curriculum: Science Working Group. Interim Report*, DES and Welsh Office, HMSO, London.

DES (1987b) *The Task Group on Assessment and Testing: A Report*, DES and Welsh Office, HMSO, London.

DES (1989a) *Aspects of Primary Education: the Education of Children under Five*, HMSO, London.

DES (1989b) *National Curriculum: From Policy to Practice*, Publications Despatch Centre, DES, Honeypot Lane, Canons Park, Stanmore.

DES (1989c) *Statistics Bulletin No.7. Pupils Under Five Years in each Local Authority in England, January 1988*, Publications Despatch Centre, DES, Honeypot Lane, Canons Park, Stanmore.

Derrick, J. (1977) *The Child's Acquisition of Language*, NFER Publishing, Slough.

Dienes, Z. P. and Holt, M. (1972) *Zoo, Teacher's Book*, Longman, London.

Dockrell, W. B. and Hamilton, D. (eds.) (1980) *Rethinking Educational Research*, Hodder & Stoughton, Sevenoaks.

Dodd, B. (1972) Effects of social and vocal stimulation on infant babbling, *Developmental Psychology*, Vol. 7, pp. 80-3.

Donaldson, M. (1978) *Children's Minds*, Fontana, Glasgow.

Duckworth, E. (1974) The having of wonderful ideas, in M. Schwebel and J. Raph (eds.)

op. cit., Chapter 12.

Earwaker, J. (1973) R. S. Peters and the concept of education, *Proceedings of the Philosophy of Education Society of Great Britain*, Vol. 7, no. 2, pp. 239-59.

Elkind, D. (1969) Piagetian and psychometric conceptions of intelligence, *Harvard Education Review*, Vol. 39, no. 2, pp. 319-37.

Elkind, D. and Flavell, J. H. (eds.) (1969) *Studies in Cognitive Development: Essays in Honor of Jean Piaget*, Oxford University Press.

Eng, H. (1959) *The Psychology of Children's Drawings*, Routledge & Kegan Paul, London (first published in 1931).

Fantz, R. L. (1961) The origin of form perception, *Scientific American*, Vol. 204, pp. 66-72.

Ferguson, C. A. and Slobin, D. I. (eds.) (1972) *Studies in Child Development*, Holt, Rinehart & Winston, New York, NY.

Ferreiro, E. and Teberosky, A. (1982) *Literacy Before Schooling*, Heinemann Educational, London.

Fodor, J. (1980) On the impossibility of acquiring 'more powerful' structures, in M. Piattelli-Palmarini (ed.) op. cit., Chap. 6, pp. 142-62.

Forman, G. E. (ed.) (1982a) *Action and Thought: From Sensorimotor Schemes to Symbolic Operations*, Academic Press, New York, NY.

Forman, G. E. and Fosnot, C. T. (1982) The use of Piaget's constructivism in early childhood education programs, in B. Spodek (ed.) op. cit., Chap. 9, pp. 185-211.

Foss, B. (ed.) (1974) *New Perspectives in Child Development*, Penguin Books, Harmondsworth.

Furth, H. G. (1969) *Piaget and Knowledge: Theoretical Foundations*, Pentice-Hall, Englewood Cliffs, NJ.

Galton, F. (1869) *Hereditary Genius: An Inquiry into its Laws and Consequences*, Macmillan, London.

Gerhardt, L. (1973) *Moving and Knowing: The Young Child Orients Himself in Space*, Prentice-Hall, Englewood Cliffs, NJ.

Gesell, A. (1971) *The First Five Years of Life*, Methuen, London.

Gopnic, A. (1984) Words and plans: early language and the development of intelligent action, in A. Lock and E. Fisher (eds.) op. cit., pp. 83-101.

Gordon, I. J. (1971) Early child stimulation through parent education, in I. J. Gordon (ed.) op. cit., pp. 146-54.

Gordon, I. J. (ed.) (1971) *Readings in Research in Developmental Psychology*, Scott, Foresman, Glenview, Ill.

Gray, S. W. and Klaus, R. A. (1970) The early training project: a seventh year report, *Child Development*, Vol. 41, pp. 909-24.

Greene, M. (1971) *Curriculum and Consciousness* (reprinted in G. Esland *et al.* (1977) *Schooling and Pedagogy*, Unit 6, The Open University Press, Milton Keynes).

Hamilton, D. (1980) Educational research and the shadows of Francis Galton and Ronald Fisher, in W. B. Dockrell and D. Hamilton (eds.) op.cit., Chap. 1.

Hamilton, D., Jenkins, D., King, C., MacDonald, B. and Parlett, M. (eds.) (1977) *Beyond the Numbers Game*, Macmillan Education, Basingstoke.

Harlen, W., Darwin, Sr. A. and Murphy, M. (1977) *Match and Mismatch: Finding Answers*, Oliver & Boyd for the Schools Council, Edinburgh.

Harris, D. B. (1963) *Children's Drawings as Measures of Intellectual Maturity, A Revision and Extension of the Goodenough Draw-a-Man Test*, Harcourt, Brace & World, New York, NY.

Harris, P. L. (1975) Development of search and object permanence during infancy, *Psychological Bulletin*, Vol. 3, no. 82, pp. 332-44.

Hayes, P. J. (1979) The naive physics manifesto, in D. Michie (ed.) op. cit,, pp. 242-70.

Held, R. and Hein, A. (1963) Movement-produced stimulation in the development of visually guided behaviour, *Journal of Comparative Physiology and Psychology*, Vol.

37, pp. 87-95.

Hellmuth, J. (ed.) (1969) *The Disadvantaged Child*, (Vol. 2) Special Child Publications, Seattle, Wash.

Hewison, J. (1982) Parental involvement in the teaching of reading, *Remedial Education*, Vol. 17, pp. 156-62.

Hindley, C. B. (1965) Stability and change in abilities up to five years: group trends, *Journal of Child Psychology and Psychiatry*, Vol. 6, pp. 85-99.

Hirst, P. H. and Peters, R. S. (1970) *The Logic of Education*, Routledge & Kegan Paul, London.

HMI (1984) *English From 5 to 16*, HMSO, London.

HMI (1987) *Primary School: Some Aspects of Good Practice*, HMSO, London.

Hohmann, M., Banet, B. and Weikart, D. (1979) *Young Children in Action*, High/Scope Educational Research Foundation, Ypsilanti, Mich.

Hubel, D. H. (1963) The visual cortex of the brain, in N. Chalmers, R. Crawley and P. R. S. Rose (eds.) op. cit., pp. 122-32.

Hubel, D. H. and Wiesel, T. N. (1962) Receptive fields, binocular interaction and functional architecture in the cat's visual cortex, *Journal of Physiology*, Vol. 160, pp. 106-56.

Hubel, D. H. and Wiesel, T. N. (1965) Receptive field and functional architecture in two non-striate visual areas (18 and 19) of the cat, *Journal of Neurophysiology*, Vol. 28, pp. 229-89.

Huizinga, J. (1949) *Homo Ludens: A Study of the Play Elements in Culture*, Routledge & Kegan Paul, London.

Hunt, J. McV. (1961) *Intelligence and Experience*, The Ronald Press, New York, NY.

Hutchinson, T. (1969) *Wordsworth Poetical Works*, Oxford University Press.

Huxley, R. and Ingram, E. (eds) (1971) *Language Acquisition, Models and Methods*, Academic Press, London.

Inhelder, B. (1969) Memory and intelligence in the child, in D. Elkind and J. A. Flavell (eds.) op. cit., pp. 337-64.

Inhelder, B. (1980) Language and knowledge in a constructivist framework, in M. Piattelli-Palmarini (ed.) op. cit., pp. 131-41.

Inhelder, B. and Piaget, J. (1964) *The Early Growth of Logic in the Child: Classification and Seriation*, Routledge & Kegan Paul, London.

Inhelder, B., Sinclair, H. and Bovet, M. (1974) *Learning and the Development of Cognition*, Routledge & Kegan Paul, London.

ILEA (1981) *The Study of Places in the Primary School: Curriculum Guidelines*, Publishing Centre, Highbury Station Rd, London N1 1SB.

Isaacs, S. (1960) *Intellectual Growth in Young Children*, Routledge & Kegan Paul, London (first published in 1930).

Jensen, A. R. (1969) How much can we boost IQ and scholastic achievement?, *Harvard Education Review*, Vol. 39, no. 1, pp. 1-123

Johnson, R. (1989) Personal correspondence.

Jones, H. E. (1954) The environment and mental development, in L. Carmichael (ed.) *Handbook of Child Psychology*, Wiley, New York, NY.

Jones, M. R. (ed.) (1970) *Miami Symposium on the Prediction of Behaviour, 1968: Effect of Early Experience*, University of Miami Press, Miami, Fla.

Judd, J. (1988) Britain's educational underclass, *The Observer*, 10 April.

Kamii, C. and De Vries, R. (1977) Piaget for early education, in M. D. Day and R. K. Parker (eds.) (1977) op. cit., pp. 363-420.

Kamii, C. and De Vries, R. (1978) *Physical Knowledge in Pre-school Education: Implications of Piaget's Theory*, Prentice-Hall, Englewood Cliffs, NJ.

Katz, L. (1984) Lecture given at the National Children's Bureau, London, 10 May.

Katz, D. and Katz, R. (1936) *Conversations with Children*, Routledge & Kegan Paul, London.

Kay, K. (1974) I.Q. tests fiddled to get stable scores, *The Times Educational Supplement*, 25 January.

Kellmer-Pringle, M. L., Butler, N. R. and Davie, R. (1966) *11,000 Seven Year Olds* (first report of the National Child Development Study, 1958 cohort), Longmans, London.

Kellogg, R. (1968) The biology of aesthetics, in *Anthology of Impulse. Annual Contemporary Dance 1951-1966* Dance Horizons, Brooklyn, NY.

Kellogg, R. (1969) *Analyzing Children's Art*, National Books, Palo Alto, Calif.

Kelso, J. and Clark, J. (eds.) (1982) *The Development of Movement Control and Co-ordination*, Wiley, New York, NY.

Klaus, R. and Gray, S. W. (1968) *The Early Training Project for Disadvantaged Children: A Report after Five Years* (*Monographs of the Society for Research in Child Development*) Vol. 33, serial no. 120, p. 4.

Kohlberg, L. (1968) Early education: a cognitive-developmental view, *Child Development*, Vol. 39, pp. 1014-62.

Kohlberg, L. and Mayer, R. (1972) Development as the aim of education, *Harvard Educational Review*, Vol. 42, pp. 449-96.

Land, F. (1960) *The Language of Mathematics*, John Murray, London.

Lawton, D. (1975) *Class, Culture and the Curriculum*, Routledge & Kegan Paul, London.

Lazar, I. and Darlington, R. (1979) *Lasting Effects after Preschool. Consortium for Longitudinal Studies (US Department of Health Education and Welfare Office of Human Development Series)*, Department of Health, Education and Welfare, OHDS 73-30179.

Lee, V. (ed.) (1979) *Language Development*, Croom Helm, Beckenham.

Leehey, S. C., Moskowitz-Cook, A., Brill, S. and Held, R. (1975) Orientational anistropy in infant vision, *Science*, Vol. 190, no. 4217, pp. 900-2.

Lesgold, A. M., Pellegrino, J. W., Fokkema, S. D. and Glaser, J. (eds.) (1981) *Cognitive Psychology and Instruction*, Plenum Press, New York, NY.

Light, P. (1979) *The Development of Social Sensitivity*, Cambridge University Press.

Ling, B. C. (1941) Form discrimination as a learning cue in infants, *Comparative Psychology Monographs*, Vol. 17, pp. 1-66.

Lock, A. and Fisher, E. (eds.) (1984) *Language Development*, Croom Helm in association with the Open University, London.

Lovell, K. (1959) A follow-up study of some aspects of the work of Piaget and Inhelder on the child's conception of space, *British Journal of Educational Psychology*, Vol. 29, pp. 104-17.

Lowenfeld, V. (1957) *Creative and Mental Growth*, Macmillan, New York, NY.

Makins, V. (1987) High/Scope in Britain, *The Times Educational Supplement*, 2 October.

Mann, M. and Taylor, A. (1973) The effects of multi-sensory learning systems on the concept formation of young children, *Journal of Research and Development in Education*, Vol. 6, no. 3, pp. 35-43.

Matthews, J. (1984) Children drawing: are young children really scribbling?, *Early Child Development and Care*, Vol. 18, pp. 1-39.

Matthews, J. (1987) The young child's early representation and drawing, in G. M. Blenkin and A. V. Kelly (eds.) op. cit., pp. 162-183.

McCandless, B. R. (1970) *Children, Behaviour and Development*, Holt, Rinehart & Winston, London.

Medawar, P. B. (1967) Scientific method, *The Listener*, 12 October.

Michie, D. (1979) *Expert Systems in the Micro-Electronic Age*, Edinburgh University Press.

Modgil, S. and Modgil, C. (eds.) (1982) *Piaget: Controversy and Consensus*, Holt, Rinehart & Winston, London.

Moore, T. W. (1982) *Educational Theory: an Introduction*, Routledge, London.

Morsbach, G. (1982) *Attitudes Towards Nursery School Education held by Parents, Nursery School Staff and Infant School Staff* (pre-publication draft), Department of

Psychology, Adam Smith Building, University of Glasgow, Glasgow G12 8RT.

Mortimore, P., Sammons, L. S., Lewis, D. and Ecob, R. (1988) *School Matters*, Open Books, Wells.

Mussen, P. H., Conger, J. J. and Kagan, J. (1969) *Child Development and Personality*, Harper & Row, New York.

Neale, M. D. (1966) *Neale Analysis of Reading Ability*, Macmillan Education, London.

Neary, J. (1970) Jensenism: variations on a racial theme, *Life Magazine*, 12 June.

Neisser, U. (1976) *Cognition and Reality*, W. H. Freeman, San Francisco, Calif.

Newell, K. and Barclay, C. (1982) Developing knowledge about action, in J. Kelso and J. Clark (eds.) op. cit.

Nicholls, R. (ed.) with Sedgewick, J., Duncan, J., Curwin, L. and McDougall, B. (1986) *Rumpus Schema Extra*, Teachers in Education, Cleveland, LEA, Cleveland.

Norman, D. A. (1985) Twelve Issues for Cognitive Science, in A. M. Aitkenhead and J. M. Slack (eds.) op. cit., pp. 309-36.

Nutbrown, C. (1988) *The Role of a Teacher in the Development of Early Writing Skills and Understanding of a Group of Three and Four-Year-Old Children* (unpublished paper for an in-service M Ed), Sheffield Polytechnic.

Oates, J. (ed.) (1979) *Early Cognitive Development*, Croom Helm in association with the Open University Press, London.

O'Connor, D. J. (1972) The nature of educational theory, in *Proceedings of Philosophy of Education Society of Great Britain, 6*, Blackwell, Oxford.

Oldfield, R. C. (1954) Memory mechanisms and the theory of schemata, *British Journal of Psychology*, Vol. 45, pp. 14-23.

Oldfield, R. C. and Zangwill, O. L. (1942) Head's concept of the schema and its application in contemporary British psychology, *British Journal of Psychology*, Vol. 32, pp. 267-86 (part 1); Vol. 33, pp. 58-64 (part 2); Vol. 34, pp. 113-29 (part 3).

Olson, D. R. (1970) *Cognitive Development: The Child's Acquisition of Diagonality*, Academic Press, London.

Open University Course Book (1973) E262, block 8, Open University Press, Milton Keynes.

Opie, I. and Opie, P. (1959) *The Lore and Language of Schoolchildren*, Clarendon Press, Oxford.

Osborn, A. F. and Milbank, J. E. (1987) *The Effects of Early Education*, Clarendon Press, Oxford.

Payton, S. (1984) *Developing Awareness of Print: A Young Child's First Steps Towards Literacy*, *Educational Review* (off-set publication no. 2), University of Birmingham.

Peters, R. (1966) *Ethics and Education*, Allen & Unwin, London.

Piaget, J. (1951) *Judgement and Reasoning in the Child*, Routledge & Kegan Paul, London.

Piaget, J. (1953) *The Origin of Intelligence in the Child*, Routledge & Kegan Paul, London.

Piaget, J. (1959) *The Construction of Reality in the Child*, Basic Books, New York, NY.

Piaget, J. (1962) *Play, Dreams and Imitation in Childhood*, Routledge & Kegan Paul, London.

Piaget, J. (1965) *The Child's Conception of Number*, Routledge & Kegan Paul, London.

Piaget, J. (1968a) Quantification, conservation and nativism, *Science*, Vol. 162, pp. 976-9.

Piaget, J. (1968b) *Six Psychological Studies*, University of London Press.

Piaget, J. (1969) *The Mechanisms of Perception*, Routledge & Kegan Paul, London.

Piaget, J. (1970) *The Child's Conception of Movement and Speed*, Routledge & Kegan Paul, London.

Piaget, J. (1971a) *Biology and Knowledge*, Edinburgh University Press.

Piaget, J. (1971b) *Science of Education and the Psychology of the Child*, Longman, London.

Piaget, J. (1972a) *Psychology and Epistemology: Towards a Theory of Knowledge*,

Penguin Books, Harmondsworth.

Piaget, J. (1972b) *The Child and Reality: Problems of Genetic Psychology*, Viking Press, London.

Piaget, J. (1972c) *The Principles of Genetic Epistemology*, Routledge & Kegan Paul, London.

Piaget, J. (1973) *Main Trends in Psychology*, Allen & Unwin, London.

Piaget, J. (1974a) *The Child and Reality*, Frederick Muller, London.

Piaget, J. (1974b) *Understanding Causality*, Norton, New York, NY.

Piaget, J. (1976) *To Understand is to Invent*, Penguin Books, Harmondsworth.

Piaget, J. (1977) *The Grasp of Consciousness: Action and Concept in the Young Child*, Routledge & Kegan Paul, London.

Piaget, J., Apostel, L. and Mandelbrot, B. (1977) *Logique et Equilibre (Etude D'Epistemologie Genetique)* ii, Press Universitaires de France, Paris.

Piaget, J. and Inhelder, B. (1956) *The Child's Conception of Space*, Routledge & Kegan Paul, London.

Piaget, J. and Inhelder, B. (1969) *The Psychology of the Child*, Routledge & Kegan Paul, London.

Piaget, J. and Inhelder, B. (1971) *Mental Imagery in the Child*, Routledge & Kegan Paul, London.

Piaget, J. and Inhelder, B. (1973) *Memory and Intelligence*, Routledge & Kegan Paul, London.

Piaget, J., Grize, J. B., Szeminska, A. and Vinh-Bang (1968) *Epistémologie et Psychologie de la Fonction, (Etudes D'Epistemologie Genetique, xxiii)*, Press Universitaires de France, Paris.

Piattelli-Palmarini, M. (ed.) (1980) *Language and Learning: The Debate between Jean Piaget and Noam Chomsky*, Routledge & Kegan Paul, London.

Plowden Report (1967) See Central Advisory Council for Education (1967).

Pugh, G. and De'Ath, E. (1984) *The Needs of Parents: Practice and Policy in Parent Education (National Children's Bureau Series)* Macmillan Education, Basingstoke.

Reynell, J. (1969) *Reynell Developmental Language Scales*, NFER, Windsor.

Rice, E. (1977) *Sam Who Never Forgets*, Puffin Books, Harmondsworth.

Ripin, R. (1933) A comparative study of the development of infants in an institution with those in homes of low socio-economic status, *Psychological Bulletin*, Vol. 30, pp. 680-1.

Roberts, M. and Tamburrini, J. (1981) *Child Development: 0 to 5*, Holmes McDougall, Edinburgh.

Rose, S. (1978) Molecular neurobiology: an examination of growing points in a new science, *New Scientist*, 6 July, pp. 31-3.

Rose, S. P. R. and Chalmers, N. (1971) The environmental determinants of brain function, in N. Chalmers, R. Crawley and S. Rose (eds.) op. cit. pp. 246-7.

Rudel, R. G. and Teuber, H. L. (1963) Discrimination of the direction of line by young children, *Journal of Comparative and Physiological Psychology*, Vol. 56, pp. 892-8.

Ruff, H. A. (1978) Infant recognition of the invariant form of objects, *Child Development*, Vol. 49, no. 2, pp. 294.

Rumelhart, D. E. and Norman, D. A. (1985) Representation of knowledge, in A. M. Aitkenhead and J. M. Slack (eds.) op. cit., pp. 15-62.

Sanderson, A. (1987) *The Early Years: How Children Develop as Writers*, Language Development Centre, Sheffield Polytechnic.

Sauvy, J. and Sauvy, S. (1974) *The Child's Discovery of Space*, Penguin Books, Harmondsworth.

Schaefer, E. S. (1970) Need for early and continuing education, in V. H. Denenberg (ed.) op. cit., pp. 61-82.

Schools Council (1972) *A Study of Nursery Education*, Working Paper 41, Methuen, London.

Schools Council (1974) *Early Mathematical Experiences* (EME), Schools Council, London.

Schwebel, M. and Raph, J. (eds.) (1974) *Piaget in the Classroom*, Routledge & Kegan Paul, London.

Schweinhart, L. J. and Weikart, D. P. (1980) *Young Children Grow Up: The Effects of the Perry Preschool Program on Youths Through Age 15* (Monograph no. 7) The High/Scope Educational Research Foundation, Ypsilanti, Mich.

Schweinhart, L. J. and Weikart, D. (1981) *High-Quality Early Childhood Programs for Low-Income Families Pay For Themselves* (research report) High/Scope Educational Research Foundation, Ypsilanti, Mich.

Shapiro, E. and Biber, B. (1972) The education of young children, *A Developmental Interaction Record*, Vol. 74, no. 1, pp. 55–79.

Sharp, A. (1987) *The Learning and Development of Three to Five Year Olds: Schema*, City of Sheffield Education Department.

Sharp, C. (1988) Voluntary Organisations Liaison Council for Under-Fives, Co-ordinate, no. 11.

Sheridan, M. D. (1975) *Children's Developmental Progress from Birth to Five Years: The Stycar Sequences*, NFER Publishing, Slough.

Shipman, M. D. (1972) *Exploring Education: Childhood, A Sociological Perspective*, NFER, Slough.

Sigel, I. E. (1970) The distancing hypothesis: a causal hypothesis for the acquisition of representational thought, in M. R. Jones (ed.) op. cit.

Sinclair, H. (1971) Sensorimotor action patterns as a condition for the acquisition of syntax, in R. Huxley and E. Ingram (eds.) op. cit.

Sinclair, H. (1974) From pre-operational to concrete thinking and parallel development of symbolization, in M. Schwebel and J. Raph (eds.) (1974b) op. cit., pp. 35–40.

Sinclair-De-Zwart, H. (1969) Developmental psycholinguistics, in D. Elkind and J. H. Flavell (eds.) op. cit., pp. 315–36.

Skeels, H. M. Updegraff, R., Wellman, B. and Williams, H. M. (1938) A study of environmental stimulation: an orphanage pre-school project, *University of Iowa Studies in Child Welfare*, Vol. 15, no. 4.

Skemp, R. R. (1962) The need for a schematic learning theory, *British Journal of Educational Psychology*, Vol. 32, pp. 133–42.

Skemp, R. R. (1971) *The Psychology of Learning Mathematics*, Penguin Books, Harmondsworth.

Slobin, D. (1973) Cognitive prerequisites for the development of grammar, in C. A. Ferguson and D. I. Slobin (eds.) op. cit. pp. 155–208.

Smith, T. (1980) *Parents and Preschool* (Oxford Preschool Research Project) Grant McIntyre, London.

Smith, L. A. H. (1985) *To Understand and to Help: The Life and Works of Susan Isaacs: 1885–1948*, Associated University Presses, London and Toronto.

Smith, N. R. and Franklin, M. B. (eds.) (1979) *Symbolic Functioning in Childhood*, Lawrence Erlbaum Associates, Hillsdale, NJ.

Spodek, B. (1982) *Handbook of Research in Early Childhood Education*, The Free Press, London.

Stanford–Binet Intelligence Scale (1976) See L. M. Terman and M. A. Merrill (1976).

Stanley, J. C. (ed.) (1972) *Preschool Programs for the Disadvantaged* Johns Hopkins University Press, Baltimore, Md and London.

Starters Science (1974) *Coverings*, Macdonald Educational Science 5/13 Project, Macdonald, London.

Statistical Package for the Social Scientist version 6.52 (1977) Vogelback Computing Centre, North Western University, USA.

Stern, W. (1924) *Psychology of Early Childhood up to the Sixth Year of Age*, Holt, Rinehart & Winston, New York, NY.

Stevenson, C. (1987) *Four Year Olds in School. Policy and Practice*, DES Statistics Bulletin, NFER/SCDC, London.

Stukat, K. G. (1976) *Current Trends in European Pre-School Research (European Trend Reports on Educational Research)*, NFER, Windsor.

Sundberg, N. and Ballinger, T. (1968) Nepalese children's cognitive development as revealed by drawings of man, woman and self, *Child Development*, Vol. 39, pp. 969–85.

Sutton-Smith, B. (1970) The psychology of childlore: the triviality barrier, *Western Folklore*, Vol. 29, pp. 1–8.

Sylva, K., Roy, C. and Painter, M. (1980) *Childwatching at Playgroup and Nursery School* (Oxford Preschool Research Project) Grant McIntyre, London.

Sylva, K., Smith, T. and Moore, E. (1986) *Monitoring the High/Scope Training Program, 1984–5* (final report), Department of Social and Administrative Studies, University of Oxford.

Tamburrini, J. (1982) Some educational implications of Piaget's theory, in C. Modgil and S. Modgil (eds.) op. cit., pp. 309–24.

Taylor, A. (1951) *English Riddles from Oral Tradition*, University of California Press, Berkeley, Calif.

Temple, C. A., Nathan, R. G. and Burris, N. A. (1982) *The Beginnings of Writing*, Allyn & Bacon, London.

Terman, L. M. and Merrill, M. A. (1976) *Manual for the Third Revision, Form L–M. Stanford–Binet Intelligence Scale*, Harrap, London (first published in France, 1916).

The Times Educational Supplement (1987) Leader, 28 August.

Tizard, B., Mortimore, J. and Burchell, B. (1981) *Involving Parents in Nursery and Infant Schools*, Grant McIntyre, London.

Uzgiris, I. C. and Hunt, J. McV, (1975) *Assessment in Infancy*, University of Illinois Press, Urbana–Champaign, Ill.

Van der Eyken, W. (1981) The ethos of the nursery school, in M. Roberts and J. Tamburrini (eds.) op, cit., pp. 228–35.

Vernon, M. D. (1955) The functions of schemata in perceiving, *Psychological Review*, Vol. 62, pp. 180–92.

Volpe, R. (1981) Knowledge from theory and practice, *Oxford Review of Education*, Vol. 7, no. 1, pp. 41–57.

Vygotsky, L. S. (1962) *Thought and Language*, Wiley & Sons, New York and London.

Weikart, D. P. (1972) Relationship of curriculum, teaching and learning in preschool education, in J. C. Stanley (ed.) op. cit, pp. 22–67.

Weikart, D. (1983) Serving children: the High Scope Foundation, *Concern* (National Children's Bureau), issue no. 49, autumn pp. 23–31.

Weikart, D. P., and Lambie, D. Z. et al. (1969) Preschool intervention through a home tutoring program, in J. Hellmuth (ed.) op. cit.

Werner, H. (1948) *Comparative Psychology of Mental Development*, Follett, Chicago, Ill.

Werner, H. and Kaplin, B. (1967) *Symbol Formation*, Wiley, New York, NY.

Westinghouse Learning Corporation (1969) The impact of Headstart: an evaluation of the effects of Headstart experience on children's cognitive and affective development, Westinghouse Learning Corporation, Ohio University, cited in J. C. Stanley (ed.) op. cit., pp. 29.

Whitbread, N. (1975) *The Evolution of the Nursery-Infant School: A History of Infant and Nursery Education in Britain 1800–1970*, Routledge & Kegan Paul, London.

White, B. L. (1969) The initial co-ordination of sensorimotor schemas in human infants, Piaget's idea of the role of experience, in D. Elkind and J. H. Flavell (eds.) op. cit; pp. 237–56.

Wilson, P. S. (1969) *Child-Centred Education (Proceedings of the Annual Conference of the Philosophy of Education Society of Great Britain)* January, pp. 105–26.

Williams, E. M. and Shuard, H. (1980) *Primary Mathematics Today*, Longman, London.

Williams, P. and Jinks, D. (1985) *Design and Technology 5–12*, Falmer Press, Lewes.

Wolde, G. (1975) *The Vacuum Cleaner*, Hodder & Stoughton, Sevenoaks.

Wood, D., McMahon, L. and Cranstoun, Y. (1980) *Working with Under-Fives*, Grant McIntyre, London.

Wooley, H. T. (1925) The validity of standards of mental measurement in young childhood, *School and Society*, Vol. 21, pp. 476–82.

Young, J. Z. (1978) *Programs of the Brain*, Oxford University Press.

Subject Index

acceleration 30, 42, 76, 82
accommodation 32, 35, 37, 38, 41, 60,
   76, 175, 183
accountability 19
action 14, 31–3
   effects of 29, 89, 178, 194
   as signifiers 40, 58, 88, 90, 108, 131
   to thought 14, 31, 45, n.9, 49, 62,
      68–78, 82, 128–170, 180
addition 41
affect 75–6
   categories of 75–6
   and cognitive structure 77, 162, 196
angles, triangles and quadrilaterals
      107–110
arcs (see semi-circle)
area 32
   conservation of 32, 146
articulate professional knowledge 19, 31,
   50, 61
assimilation 14, 27, 32–3, 37–8, 41, 58,
   79, 130, 175, 183, 204
   distorting 180
associative thinking 42

brain functioning 14
   'hard and soft-wire' mechanisms 205
   structure 205

capacity 138, 197
cardination 134
child-centred pedagogy 25
   defined 25, 30
   Weikart's evaluation of 26
circles and enclosed curves 65–6, 79, 83,
   97–99
   extension of 195
circular direction and rotation 92,
   139–143
classification 32, 41–2, 75, 98, 134, 138
cognition xii, 17, 82
   and affect 75, 77, 97, 162
   critical periods 14
   deficit description of xii, 17, 29, 87
cognition hypothesis of language
      acquisition 73, 179
   definition 179–181
   Froebel project findings on 181
cognitive constants 43, 49, 50, 83

search for 61, 128
cognitive;
   competence 17, 38
   content 10, 14, 42–3, 130
   forms of thought xi, xii, 16–7, 28,
      42–3, 58, 130, 187
   functioning 14, 32, 187
   structure 28, 32, 37, 44, 51
   improvement 10, 13, 20, 205
comparative terms 179–80
comparison group 49, 54
compensatory education 14–16
   Plowden recommendations on 14
configuration 29, 37, 84, 87–8, 155,
      186–188
concepts xi, 14
   clusters of 193
   of education 9–10
conceptual; knowledge 11, 32
   diagnosing 11
concrete-operations 17–18, 28, 30, 33,
      107, 146
constructivist
   pedagogy 23–4
   research in language and thought
      175–8 teacher 31–2
Constructivism 23, 29, 43–4, 62
   and child-centredness 30–31
   defined 25–6, 31–2
   development of 30
   and research 16, 32
   Weikart's evaluation of 25–8, 30
conservation 32
   defined 21n.6, 34, 41–2, 146, 194
   and speech 179
containing and contained 64, 72, 75,
      130, 136, 149–156
   and functional dependencies 151
content of thinking 42, 58
   and cultural specifics 204
continuity xii, 14, 44, 59
   in the curriculum 173–8
   and discontinuity 174
   in language and thought 175–8
   between stages 183, 69, 128
   between dynamic schemas and early
      writing 183–5
co-ordination
   of concepts 196, 199
   of fixed positions and action
      displacements 187–8
   of marks 99–100, 183
   of marks for letter formations 188
   of schemas 37–8, 51, 110, 129, 184,

190 of trajectories 138
core and radial 78, 82, 94, 99–102, 107,
 131, 183
and functional dependency 101
correspondence
 between action and effect 34
 figural 90, 100
coverings 195–8
curriculum 12, 16, 19, 43–4
 content xi, xii, 16–17, 25
 development 174
 extension of schemas 28–9, 186–201,
  193–4
 offered 8–9, 14, 19–20, 43, 173, 204
 received 8–9, 20, 43, 204, 207
 display and delivery 19, 173
curves
 categories of 80
custodial care 7
 defined 24

decalage 186–187
deferred imitation 179
Department of Education and Science
  (DES) 3, 4, 9, 27, 173–4, 189, 219
design, technology and schemas 191
development in thinking xi
 prospective and retrospective view of
  16
developmental sequence of schemas 49
direction 193
displacements 62, 74, 134, 136, 152, 155
 and additive partitioning 190
 and intelligence tests 189–90
 as precursors of mapping 129, 188
 in literature 192–3
 group of 37, 89, 129, 161, 186
distance 75, 91, 138, 193
division 41, 104, 109, 152, 155, 197
Draw-a-Man Test 84, 88
drawing
 action and 89
 content and form in 82–3
 development of 81
 normative studies of 81–2

early education
 aims of 12
 efficacy of xi, 6, 8, 13, 16, 18, 205
 investment in 6
 quality of xii, 8
education
 and schooling 10
 concept of 9–10

defined 9
and evaluation 10
Educational Priority Area (EPA) xii
Education Reform Act (ERA) 14, 19,
 173
educational theory 19–20
 denigration of 8–10, 31–2
enactive schemas 64, 66
enclosure 63, 65, 83, 87, 91, 107
 in one, two and three dimensions 146
enrichment programme 54
enveloping space 72, 104, 149, 188
 extending 192, 197
 and functional dependency 154
environment xii, 12, 15–16
 changes in 13
 quality of 15
 stability of 54
 symbolic aspects of 13
environmentalists 22n.19
equality of opportunity 4
equivalence 35, 37
 of configuration between perception
  and representation 73
 of distance 129, 131, 136
 of length 136, 191
 of speed 136
 of topological notions 187
 of weight 95, 191
ethnic differences 31, 52, 143
Euclidean space 131
experience xii, 7, 9, 14, 28, 36, 37, 43–4,
 57–8, 73
 and educational visits xi, 202–5
 defined 58, 204
 and speech 187
extending throught (cognition) 4, 17, 28,
 37, 44, 75–6, 82, 92

figurative (figural) aspects of
 representation 35, 78, 129
figurative effects of action 108
figurative images 40
figurative 'knowing' 189
fitting or flitting 83, 107
five (concept of) 63
flexibility principle 183
'food' for thought 176
formative evaluation 11, 13, 16, 19, 50,
 57
forms of thought xi, xii
four (concept of) 63, 100
four-year-olds in primary school 3, 6, 7,
 174

Author Index